The FIGHT for
LEGITIMACY

Sir,

To my first mentor in
the Army. Thank you for
your inspiring leadership,
mentorship, and example.

Sincerely,

Cindy

The FIGHT for LEGITIMACY

Democracy vs. Terrorism

CINDY R. JEBB, P. H. LIOTTA,
THOMAS SHERLOCK, AND
RUTH MARGOLIES BEITLER

Foreword by Kori Schake

PRAEGER SECURITY INTERNATIONAL
Westport, Connecticut • London

Library of Congress Cataloging-in-Publication Data

The fight for legitimacy : democracy vs. terrorism / Cindy R. Jebb ... [et al.].
    p.   cm.
Includes bibliographical references and index.
ISBN 0–275–99189–X (alk. paper)
1. Terrorism—Prevention.   2. Democratization.   3. Legitimacy of governments.
4. Political stability.   5. Separatist movements—Case studies.   6. National liberation
movements—Case studies.   I. Jebb, Cindy R., 1960–
    HV6431.F53   2006
    363.325′16–dc22   2006015197

British Library Cataloguing in Publication Data is available

Library of Congress Catalog Card Number: 2006015197
ISBN: 0–275–99189–X

First published in 2006

Praeger Security International, 88 Post Road West, Westport, CT 06881
An imprint of Greenwood Publishing Group, Inc.
www.praeger.com

Printed in the United States of America

The paper used in this book complies with the
Permanent Paper Standard issued by the National
Information Standards Organization (Z39.48–1984).

10 9 8 7 6 5 4 3 2 1

for our children's future
Ben, Alex, Olivia, Gaia, Andrew, Hannah, and Eliyana

I have walked that long road to freedom. I have tried not to falter; I have made missteps along the way. But I have discovered the secret that after climbing a great hill, one only finds that there are many more hills to climb. I have taken a moment to rest, to steal a view of the glorious vista that surrounds me, to look back on the distance I have come. But I can rest only for a moment, for with freedom come responsibilities, and I dare not linger, for my long walk has not yet ended.

Nelson Mandela

CONTENTS

FOREWORD

This superb book confirms the fundamental truth too little recognized in combating terrorism: that social acceptance of indiscriminate violence has roots in political grievances that must be addressed if we are to delegitimize terrorism. It would seem an obvious point except that it is so infrequently reflected in either studies of countering terrorism or government policies designed to foster democracy and create international opprobrium for terrorism.

We Americans have a tendency to think about terrorism as a problem that occurs only elsewhere, neglecting to remember that within living memory there was a serious debate in our own country about the acceptability of resorting to violence when the majority was complacent about state-sanctioned racism. Had Malcolm X won the argument on means to ensure black Americans received their inalienable rights and constitutional protections, we would be a very different country. In retrospect it seems obvious that Martin Luther King's nonviolent approach would better serve to legitimize the cause and turn the hearts of the white majority, but this is to ignore the justifiable bitterness and longstanding indifference that prompted calls for violence. The experience of Spain, Macedonia, Turkey, Russia, and Palestine chronicled in this book are not so far removed in either time or content from our own circumstances.

Democracy versus Terrorism reviews a series of pivotal case studies in which transitional democracies are simultaneously facing terrorism. Interestingly, the authors not only chose cases in which the state is struggling for legitimacy against an internal terrorist threat, but also the case of Palestine, in which a government comes to power that gains domestic legitimacy from support for external terrorism. With a spare five cases, they have managed to draw out the full range of difficulties, draw interesting parallels, and reach conclusions that illuminate paths for scholarship and provide helpful advice to policymakers.

In reading this book, I was struck at how rare are the "optimal conditions" for democratization. Few established democracies meet the standard outlined here—which is not to argue the standard or excuse failures of engaging in the hard work of building democracy, but to point out the difficulty in achieving it. Tolstoy opens Anna Karenina with the observation that every happy family is alike, but unhappy families are all unhappy in their own way. Just as every transitional democracy is transitional in its own way, understanding the nature of its fragility or incompleteness is essential to improving the ability of the government to redress grievances that gain terrorists acceptance in the broader society. Of necessity, shoring up societies against this recourse to violence against noncombatants must rest on the legitimacy of local solutions. This book is an important contribution to understanding several important cases in their regional and historical contexts.

The central thesis of this book is that combating terrorism and promoting democracy are mutually supporting objectives. It is an argument often dismissed as naïve liberalism by those who believe transitional states are too fragile to tackle hard problems of reconciliation. These authors argue persuasively that giving transitional democracies a pass on addressing violent extremism, or accommodating undemocratic practices by governments that are fighting terrorism, are counterproductive. The great challenge for societies faced with terrorism in their midst is to delegitimize the use of indiscriminate violence as a means of achieving political goals. By working concurrently the problems of democratization and fighting terrorism, states maximize the space for political agreement and provide opportunities for making advocates of violence responsible for broadly acceptable outcomes. Democratic inclusion requires those who accept participation to take responsibility for elements of governance. As a result, publics can judge, as in the case of Hamas in Palestine, what the cost of their ideology will be in the practical facts of their daily lives. By setting up a competition for legitimacy on terms favorable to good governance, advancing on both democratization and combating terrorism can "reduce the *prevalence* as well as the *political success* of terrorism."

As these authors acknowledge, the main elements of successful democratization are internal to a country: political culture, government legitimacy, and political community. However, we can and do affect choices internal to other countries by state and nonstate means. Aid, trade, political attention, NGO involvement, and numerous other tools are available to leverage our interests and have worked to some success. In many of the case studies, the authors are suggesting means with the prospect for fostering positive change, but those changes have not occurred. The one criticism I would make of this book is that it deals principally with the optimistic scenarios of how to succeed. It assumes the goal is the classic liberal firmament in which good things—democracy and safety—go together. For many unsuccessful societies, I doubt this paradigm is how they view their choices. With the good fortune of living in a successful and optimistic political culture, we Americans tend to underestimate the extent to which unsuccessful societies will absorb bad outcomes in order to prevent others from succeeding.

This book tells us how to persuade violent extremists that acceptable political resolution is possible. It shows the reason and self-interest for governments to adopt these approaches. And yet, as the stubborn persistence of these conflicts demonstrates, many will remain. I hope this same talented team will now turn their attention to educating us on the unpleasant question of how to treat states and terrorist movements that cannot be coopted into our liberal paradigm by the prospect of inclusion in governance.

Kori Schake, Ph.D.
Distinguished Professor of International Security Studies
Department of Social Sciences
United States Military Academy
Director for Defense Strategy and Requirements on the
National Security Council (2000–2004)

PREFACE

This project began before September 11, 2001. Since 9/11, we have both relooked and reevaluated our initial findings. Interestingly, this valuable reflection largely confirmed much of our initial intuitions and analyses. Terrorism cannot be treated as a monolithic threat. Moreover, as much as we may wish to focus on the terror tactics and terrorist means, we cannot overlook the ends. In fact, good policy can only be crafted with an understanding of the terrorist strategy; that is, how terrorists integrate their means to secure their goals, given their perception of the security environment.

The groups covered in this book change and evolve. While governments must take aggressive actions to secure their populations against attacks, those governments that recognize real grievances can simultaneously take action that address those grievances. This two-pronged approach simultaneously bolsters state legitimacy across the ethnic minority and majority populations, while demonstrating state effectiveness regarding security. Thus, governments that effectively use reconciliation to address real grievances, while cooperating with other states to effectively attack the terrorists mitigate the appeal of these groups. Subsequently, states that effectively integrate their elements of power in cooperation with other states and international organizations ultimately win the struggle for legitimacy.

This study uses an interdisciplinary approach to address the challenge of transnational threats, namely terrorism, to transitional democracies. Terrorism poses unique challenges to the transitional democratic state, and the transnational nature of terrorism necessitates cooperation between and among states. However, terrorism must be analyzed in a political and strategic context. The forces of globalization and fragmentation and the increasing claims of irredentism and secession, as well as the rise of political ideology rooted in religion, require a reexamination of the state legitimacy formula. The best way for states to win legitimacy vis-à-vis terrorists is by adhering to liberal democratic values, cooperating with other states, and applying prudent counterterrorist tactics. Interstate cooperation, which affects domestic and foreign policies, requires some convergence of political cultures among those cooperating states. This study begins by analyzing five transitional democracies in the context of their regions: the Basques in Spain; the ethnic Albanians in Macedonia; the Kurds in Turkey; the Chechens in Russia; and the Palestinians, Israelis, and a future Palestinian state. These regional contexts further illustrate the importance of understanding the regional implications when dealing with transnational threats, namely terrorism. The Spanish case serves as a model for other transitional states; however, as we move away from the European region, the question of how much Spain serves as a model becomes more significant.

It is for this reason that we included the Russian and Palestinian cases, both very complex studies. Additionally, Turkey straddles a variety of geographic regions and has particular elements that impact upon its democratizaton process. As the United States builds policy based on democracy and nation building, it is critical that we take a more nuanced approach to such studies. Indeed, there is cause for extending Kenneth Waltz's levels of analysis to the regional level.[1] In truth, regional dynamics, whether they be culture, environment, geography, or history all influence the security environment, which includes state stability and extremist groups. Understanding these complex interconnections will help shed some light on their influence concerning the success or failure of transitional democracies facing terrorist threats.

ACKNOWLEDGMENTS

Sections of this manuscript previously appeared in the following journals: *Parameters, Problems of Post-Communism, Mediterranean Quarterly, Security Dialogue, Journal of Conflict Studies*, and *European Security*. Part of the chapter on Russia draws on Cynthia Roberts and Thomas Sherlock, "Bringing the Russian State Back In," *Comparative Politics*, July 1999.

Sections have also appeared in P. H. Liotta and Cindy R. Jebb's book, *Mapping Macedonia: Idea and Identity*. We would like to thank the Department of Social Sciences at West Point, the National Security Decision Making Department at the Naval War College, Salve Regina University, and the Pell Center for International Relations and Public Policy. Most of all, we are so grateful to our families without whose support, love, and kindness, this project would not have been possible.

The views expressed here are those of the authors and do not purport to reflect the position of the United States Military Academy, the Naval War College, the Department of the Army, the Department of the Navy, or the Department of Defense.

INTRODUCTION

This study is motivated by several questions that have immediate relevance to the U.S. security environment in the twenty-first century. Democratic Peace Theory posits that democracies share essential values and, therefore, do not fight one another. The Bush Doctrine embraces and extends this logic, maintaining that democracy is the best antidote to the virus of terrorism. According to this argument, terrorism is nurtured by the toxic environment of dictatorship and repression, and forms one variant of political extremism, directed at either the host country or foreign targets. Democracy, by contrast, holds the possibility that political, social, and economic grievances may be redressed, and in so doing isolate or convert the supporters of terrorism.

This book examines the logic that democracy can be a powerful tool against terrorism by presenting several case studies of transitional polities that face the twin challenges of democratization and terrorism. The central questions of this study are: How does terrorism threaten the transitional process in democratizing states, and how have new democracies attempted to cope with terrorism? Which states have been most successful in combating terrorism, while still remaining committed to democratization? Why?

A core assumption of this study is that combating terrorism and promoting democracy are not mutually exclusive goals, even in unstable transitional polities, but can and must be pursued simultaneously. In other words, security and liberty need not be locked in a zero-sum struggle for control of the political agenda of a transitional regime. We argue that young democracies must deepen their commitment to democratic values and institutions, while at the same time confronting terrorism with efficient force. This two-sided approach is the most powerful weapon in the arsenal of the regime against extremism.

We also recognize that advancing on these two fronts is not easy. The ideal conditions for successful democratization and effective counterterrorism are a web of mutually supportive political, social, economic, and cultural conditions. Political culture and political institutions are key variables. Elites and publics must be willing to play by new democratic rules of the game, and authoritative institutions must exist—or be quickly built—that channel the political energy and demands of newly enfranchised publics.

The state provides the essential framework for the democratic process. Effective and efficient state institutions are the load-bearing walls of democratization. In optimal conditions, the state comprises professional bureaucracies that deliver essential public goods with the potential to lessen the social and economic strains of democratization. For example, a strong state trains and equips law enforcement agencies that effectively hunt terrorists without brutalizing the society in which the terrorists operate and live. For democratization to be successful the state must support the rule of law and provide public goods that satisfy the demands of newly empowered publics, including good schools; fair taxes; honest police who exercise restraint; effective supports for job creation and investment; and so on. It is important that such public goods be provided in sufficient measure to social groups who are economically and political marginalized and who serve as recruiting grounds for terrorist organizations.

The ultimate determinant of the struggle between nascent democracy and violent extremism is how successful either side is in generating political legitimacy, or power transformed into authority. The democratizing regime must foster policies that generate legitimacy among disaffected groups within the population, while maintaining the support of other elites and publics who favor repression of the disaffected population, or a return to authoritarian rule, or both.

Our case studies focus on the winners, the losers, and those regimes still running in the vital race to create and sustain a democratic political system that addresses political grievances, augments the legitimacy of the new regime, and undermines the political strength of the terrorist movement. The countries that comprise our cases did not start this race with the same assets or disadvantages. The quintessential success story is Spain in the 1970s, which contained separatist terrorism, while establishing an institutionalized democracy. When Spain began the process of democratization, it possessed a stable state as well as political, economic, and civil societies that were either relatively developed or readily revived—important foundations for successful democratization. Transitional politics in Spain was guided by liberal elites (above all King Juan Carlos), who enjoyed significant legitimacy and who were firmly committed to democratization. Finally, Spain was located in a supportive international environment, close to mature democratic states, which were willing and able to cooperate with Spain on counterterrorism and support its efforts to democratize. Although Basque terrorism increased under Spanish democratization, Spain was able to contain the threat by addressing Basque grievances, while attacking the terrorist organization.

The success of the Spanish case should not blind us to the fact that other fledgling democracies are not so favorably blessed at their inception and that reaching the goal of institutionalized democracy may be considerably more difficult. Nevertheless, the Spanish case holds important lessons for any transitional regime facing the dual challenges of fostering democracy and combating terrorism. We will later turn to these lessons and how they should help shape a realistic American strategy of democracy promotion.

This chapter first addresses the question of how best to define the phenomenon of terrorism. It then enters the debate over whether democratization has the capacity to reduce the threat of terrorism, and if so, under what conditions. The chapter then turns to an examination of the importance of developing a democratic political culture in transitional regimes, and concludes with a brief description of the case studies.

DEFINING TERRORISM

Before we begin a critical analysis of terrorism in the context described above, it is important to consider the myriad definitions, categories, and perceptions of the term, terrorism. Alex Schmid cautions that it is imperative to recognize the source—governmental or otherwise—of a particular definition.[1] Similarly, Boaz Ganor explains the functional necessity of developing a definition because without an understanding of what terrorism encompasses, it will be impossible to combat.[2]

According to Donald Hanle, "Terrorism is called terrorism because it violates the normative values of the target entity regarding the employment of lethal force."[3] Philip B. Heymann illustrates the subjectivity of the term by reviewing several countries' definitions. According to the Office for the Protection of the Constitution, Germany's internal security agency, terrorism is the "enduringly conducted struggle for political goals, which are intended to be achieved by means of assaults on the life and property of other persons, especially by means of severe crimes [such as murder, kidnapping, arson]." Britain's "Prevention of Terrorism Act" of 1974 defines terrorism as "the use of violence for political ends, and includes any use of violence for the purpose of putting the public or any section of the public in fear." The U.S. State Department views terrorism as any violent act conducted for political purposes by sub-state actors or "secret state agents" against normally noncombatants with the goal of influencing an audience. U.S. laws (18 U.S.C. 3077) define a terrorist act as criminal violence that "appears to be intended (i) to intimidate or coerce a civilian population; (ii) to influence the policy of a government by intimidation or coercion; or (iii) to affect the conduct of a government by assassination or kidnapping." And according to a group of

European Interior Ministers coordinating their efforts concerning the challenges of terrorism, they state: "Terrorism is ... the use, or the threatened use, by a cohesive group of persons of violence (short of warfare) to affect political aims."[4]

Interestingly, the United Nations expressed its frustration with the lack of an unambiguous definition. Without clarity and precision, the UN is prevented "from sending an unequivocal message that terrorism is never an acceptable tactic, even for the most defensible of causes."[5] This inability for actors to agree on a definition of terrorism raises some important questions. Does terrorism differ from criminal activity? In other words, do motivations or consequences matter? Is terrorism warfare or something other than war? Heymann concludes that "terrorism is an illegal form of clandestine warfare that is carried out by a sub-state group to change the policies, personnel, structure, or ideology of a government, or to influence the actions of another part of the population—one with enough self-identity to respond to selective violence."[6]

Paul Wilkinson also views terrorism as a means to a political end, while Peter Chalk contends that terrorism endeavors to upset the societal status quo.[7] Its destructive acts are designed to attain "... the long-term objective of gradually removing the structural supports which ultimately give society its strength."[8] Cindy Combs describes terrorism as a "synthesis of war and theatre, a dramatization of the most proscribed kind of violence—that which is perpetrated on innocent victims—played before an audience in the hope of creating a mood of fear, for political purposes."[9] Bruce Hoffman agrees, defining terrorism "as the deliberate creation and exploitation of fear through violence in the pursuit of political change." Moreover, it "is designed to create power where there is none or to consolidate power where there is very little ... and to obtain the leverage, influence and power they otherwise lack to effect political change on either a local or an international scale."[10]

The majority of definitions of terrorism suggest that terrorist acts have political goals, are conducted outside normal political bounds, and involve symbolic violence usually perpetrated against innocent victims. These definitions compel academics and policymakers to consider terrorism in a historical, social, and political context.[11] Terrorism is not only linked to globalization but also to the fragmentation or breakdown of local, national, and regional politics. These seemingly opposite forces actually complement and reinforce each other in deepening the problem of terrorism. They have increased the accessibility of weapons of mass destruction (WMD) and have promoted the rise of religious fundamentalism. Globalization has revolutionized information technology and greatly increased the accessibility of information. Technology has reduced the power of the nation-state, introduced the Internet as a tool for terrorist tactics, and enhanced networking and communications for terrorist strategies.[12] John Arquilla and David

Ronfeldt explain that networks favor autonomy, flexibility, and adaptability, and challenge traditional jurisdictional lines of responsibility. These networks will eventually be comprised of actors that are primarily sub-state and transnational in nature and who will develop novel doctrines and strategies to exploit these technologies.[13] As one journalist discovered while reporting on events in Afghanistan, Al-Qaida innovatively leveraged computers for recruiting, communicating, and other managerial-type tasks.[14]

While use of the Internet for communication and propaganda is not revolutionary, its "global immediacy" is significant. Lorenzo Valeri and Michael Knights categorize the convergence of terrorism and the Internet as Offensive Information Warfare, defined as a "set of activities carried out by individuals and/or groups with specific political and strategic objectives, aimed at the integrity, availability, and confidentiality of the data collected, stored, and transferred inside information systems connected to the Internet."[15] Clearly, states that rely heavily on information technology are extremely vulnerable to this terrorist method of attack. Moreover, the transnational nature of these activities complicates identification and apprehension of the perpetrators necessitating international cooperation.[16]

Jessica Stern argues that terrorists may increasingly look to WMD to achieve their ends. Russian scientists, facilitated by diminished safeguards on nuclear material, are selling their knowledge to interested groups.[17] Robert Bunker introduces the idea of weapons of "mass disruption," which not only aim to demolish people and things, but also to destroy societal and political bonds by precipitating a decrease in public confidence in the government's ability to protect them, thereby increasing insecurity.[18] President Bush warns that:

> The gravest danger to freedom lies at the crossroads of radicalism and technology. When the spread of chemical and biological and nuclear weapons, along with ballistic missile technology—when that occurs, even weak states and small groups could attain a catastrophic power to strike great nations.[19]

The rise of radicalization, especially with religion serving as a political ideology, was a response to the end of the ideological competition between democracy and communism. With the rise of illegitimate regimes, stemming from secular ideologies, people needed to embrace an alternative view of the world. Unfortunately, many illegitimate regimes in the developing world have resulted from problematic experiments of democracy.[20] Subsequently, radical and extremist views have potential under such conditions to appear attractive. Combining this radicalization of religion as a political ideology with increased accessibility of weapons of mass destruction creates an urgent security situation that cannot be ignored.

TERRORISM AND DEMOCRACY

Although Washington has turned increasingly, since the events of 9/11, to the promotion of democracy as an important weapon in the fight against terrorism, most studies have found that democracy actually encourages terrorism.[21] Gregory Gause, in a widely discussed article, takes an unequivocal stand, arguing that democracy cannot eliminate the threat of terrorism. He notes that even institutionalized democracies fall victim to terrorist attacks, thus calling into question the utility of democracy as a means to undermine terrorism.[22] However, the question should not be simply whether "more democracy leads to less terrorism." Instead, it is more useful to ask whether democracy is able to reduce the *prevalence* as well as the *political success* of terrorism. The answer is "yes," at least in terms of stable democracy. For example, it is true that the Red Brigades in Italy, the Red Army Faction in West Germany (or the Baader-Meinfof Gang), and other terrorist groups were able to emerge in Western democracies in the 1960s and 1970s and create considerable havoc in their efforts to destabilize the political system. Nevertheless, in each of these European cases a legitimate democratic regime and a strong state held terrorism at bay and ultimately destroyed it. The political system of each of these polities retained the overwhelming support of its citizenry, demonstrating the legitimacy of the regime, or the belief of most citizens in its right to rule the country.

The legitimacy of each of these regimes was supported by a strong, effective state, whose institutions—particularly its military and law enforcement arms—eventually defeated terrorism on the urban battlefield. The state also bolstered the authority of the democratic system by providing important public goods apart from security, including economic stability and social welfare. Absent political legitimacy and effective institutions, these democratic regimes would doubtless have faced a greater incidence of terror attacks as well as deepening fissures in the polity that would have threatened to tear apart the political community.

When dealing with terrorism, mature democracies confront challenges similar to those faced by transitioning democracies. In both cases, political culture emerges as an important variable in how the political system manages the problem of terrorism. While definitions of terrorism may differ, consensus exists concerning the importance of society's support for the state's counterterrorist policies. Society's consent is important in this regard because of the danger that even mature, liberal democracies might undermine their own values by imposing police-state tactics as a means to defeat terrorism. Grant Wardlaw warns, "The danger lies in the possibility of doing the terrorists' job for them by taking unnecessary steps in an attempt to counter the perceived threat and thereby fundamentally altering the nature of democracy."[23] In this sense, both state and society must remain committed to the core political values of liberal democracy even when under attack.

In essence, a democracy's response to terrorism must be framed initially within the context of its dominant political culture.[24]

POLITICAL CULTURE, POLITICAL COMMUNITY, AND LEGITIMACY

Undeniably, political culture is at the crux of this study. Terrorists target political culture precisely because it represents a society's support for its leaders and their policies, while it is the deficient element of many so-called democracies. Inherent in the concept of political culture is the notion of a political community that indicates the level of a society's loyalty toward its political system. These concepts—political culture, legitimacy, and political community—are intricately interwoven and provide keen insights into state behavior. As mentioned previously, terrorists target a state's political culture and legitimacy to destroy its political community and make the state ineffective.

Ralf Dahrendorf explains legitimacy and effectiveness as two keys to a state's stability.[25] Interestingly, these two concepts are asymmetrically related. Governments, such as totalitarian regimes, may be effective without being legitimate, but "over time, ineffectiveness will probably erode legitimacy."[26] Dahrendorf is most concerned about the erosion of legitimacy because for democracies "there is a great danger that the response to a crisis of legitimacy will be authoritarianism and illiberty."[27] Augustus Richard Norton believes that state survival depends upon legitimacy defined as "that authority which rests on the shared cultural identity of ruler and ruled."[28] When legitimacy dissolves, the regime is vulnerable to change.[29]

Connected with the concept of legitimacy is the idea of a political community or a core political identity.[30] David Easton refers to a political community as a "domain of support" for the political system.[31] Michael C. Hudson links the concepts of political community with legitimacy by further explaining that a society divided along ethnic or class cleavages exacerbates attempts at fostering legitimacy.[32]

These ideas of a political community and attitudes toward the political system describe the concept of political culture. In fact, Robert Dahl's work on political opposition groups helped reveal political culture based on a society's attitudinal orientations toward problem solving, the political system, cooperation and individuality, and people. Interestingly, even among democracies, political cultures differ. For example, citizens of Italy and France have been described as having alienated or apathetic attitudes toward their political systems; West German citizens exhibited detached attitudes; and citizens of the United States and Great Britain tended to have an allegiant orientation toward their political systems.[33]

According to Gabriel Almond and Sidney Verba, a civic or democratic political culture describes a society in which people feel that they make a difference politically; they tolerate others; they trust their fellow citizens and political elites; and they are loyal to the political system.[34] Therefore, this study incorporates concepts of civic culture, criteria for liberalism, and the idea of political community to assess the impact of terrorism on transitional states. Specifically, this study examines shifts in attitudes at the elite level toward liberal, democratic values; shifts in societal attitudes toward its members and groups, and societal attitudes concerning the political system. A liberal, democratic culture is not only the essence of democracy, but also a clear target for terrorists. As such, the adherence to democratic values constitutes a fight for legitimacy.

Although it is clear that a mature democracy supported by an effective state represents a powerful bulwark against the spread of internal terrorist organizations, it is also true that democratization—the process of reaching this positive end-state—can be exceedingly dangerous. For democratization to ultimately succeed, dominant political actors and publics must have a democratic state of mind.[35] Francis Fukuyama claims that it is not the mere existence of democratic institutions that will secure the fate of transitioning democracies; rather, it will be in the critical realm of civil society and culture that will determine successful transitions.[36]

The importance of political culture is supported by studies pointing to the increase in the number of electoral democracies worldwide but also to the decline in actual political freedoms. The connection between democracy and liberty is not linear, and culture seems to be the intervening variable.[37] According to Larry Diamond, "elections are only one dimension of democracy. The quality of democracy also depends on its levels of freedom, pluralism, justice and accountability." He continues to explain liberal democracy as having the following conditions:

> Freedom of belief, expression, organization, demonstration, and other civil liberties, including protection from political terror and unjustified imprisonment; a rule of law under which all citizens are treated equally and due process is secure; political independence and neutrality of the judiciary and other institutions of "horizontal accountability" that check the abuse of power, such as electoral administration, audits, and a central bank; an open and pluralistic civil society, including not only associational life but the mass media as well; and civilian control of the military.[38]

A democratic political culture is the foundation of the core traits of liberal democracy: civil liberties, rule of law, civil society, and civilian control of the military.

As we have argued, transitional polities—or polities on the verge of transition—are not created equal. Some, like Spain, Poland, or Hungary, had significant initial advantages, such as a burgeoning middle class with a developing civic culture. Building a relatively effective state and a legitimate democratic regime was within their reach after only 10 years following the fall of communism. Other states, including many of those in the Middle East, have yet to attempt significant democratization, and it is uncertain what the results will be even if they do so. Indeed, Gause and others suggest that the cure of democratization proposed by the Bush administration will actually prolong and deepen the disease of terrorism due to a host of unfavorable socioeconomic, political, and cultural conditions in the region, including radical Islamism and opposition to the United States.

Gause observes that groups such as Al Qaida have no interest in participating in democratic institutions, which its members vilify as corrupt cultural grafts imposed by the West. He argues that Al Qaida "certainly would not close up shop if every Muslim country in the world were to become a democracy." Although Gause is probably correct about Al Qaida remaining true to its Manichean worldview and extremist tactics, it is still useful to remember that extremist movements historically have often undergone deradicalization over time. Western Europe's Marxist parties in the nineteenth century come immediately to mind but so do other, much smaller, radical movements. More recently, many Chechen separatists who were avowed Jihadists opted to accept the Russian government's offer of amnesty and participate in a renewed political process in Chechnya, thereby abandoning terrorism as a political tool.

But the larger point is that if "every Muslim country" did indeed become a relatively stable democracy supported by a reasonably effective state, the strength and appeal of die-hard Al Qaida loyalists would certainly diminish among their natural constituencies, in part because the very large numbers of citizens who are politically and economically alienated and who supply Al Qaida with recruits and passive support would now calculate that their grievances might best be addressed through the ballot box.

THE POLITICS OF DEMOCRATIC TRANSITION AND THE SPECTRUM OF CONDITIONS

The question remains: What are the requirements of a successful transition to a stable democracy? Democratization encounters far fewer difficulties if supportive conditions exist in the dimensions of economic society, civil society, and political society when the transition begins. Simply put, polities with relatively high per capita incomes, dense civil society networks, and liberal political cultures have built-in shock absorbers that help smooth regime change.[39] Polities that score well in each of these categories at the start of the transition have an important store of human capital. Citizens are better educated and have higher expectations of government performance and of their role in the political process. Furthermore, they tend to be more tolerant of debate, and more confident of their political capabilities. Ideally, political institutions should have developed, prior to democratization, safeguards that protect human and civil rights, and ensure the rule of law.

Successful democratization also relies heavily on the existence of a state with the capacity to govern effectively. State capacity depends on a number of factors. A strong state possesses national political institutions that formulate and enforce fundamental political and economic rules. Most important is the legitimacy of these rules, particularly among political elites.[40] An effective democracy also enjoys a sufficient degree of autonomy from pressure groups.

A state's effectiveness also depends on cooperative links with society and on the capacities of society itself. Following Robert Putnam, we argue that strong societies are vital supports for state capacity in democratic polities.[41] Here, we are speaking primarily about the willingness and ability of society to support and monitor the activities of the state, and the willingness and ability of the state to identify and address social, economic, and political problems in society.

The administrative dimension is the last indicator of state capacity and measures the ability of the state to provide essential public goods, including law and order, education, and the infrastructure of market economies. In an era of increased globalization, even advanced industrialized states must continuously modernize capacity or suffer the consequences. This task depends on the fiscal resources and extractive capabilities of the state, and the professional competencies of the state's bureaucracies. The organizational coherence of these bureaucracies and their compliance to the directives of central authorities also determines the provision of essential public goods. States that suffer from the extreme weakness of institutional and administrative supports are particularly vulnerable to exogenous or domestic shocks, from currency crises to mass worker strikes over low wages and poor living conditions.

Regardless of regime type, states that exhibit very low capacity across these various dimensions of state strength may be classified as weak or failed (or collapsed). Such states are a breeding ground for terrorist groups who thrive in political vacuums. Erica Chenoweth persuasively makes this point in her analysis of Afghanistan. Although Al Qaida may have been drawn to Afghanistan by the radical ideology of the Taliban regime, the terrorist group placed even greater value on the inability of the Taliban regime to control Al Qaida's actions. Similarly, Arab terrorists flocked to Chechnya because the Russian state was too weak to control its borders or police effectively in its territory located in the northern Caucasus.

Following the conditions described above, transitional polities may be placed on a spectrum from "extremely favorable" to "extremely unfavorable." Those transitional polities that suffer from a weak state, and from a shallow civil society, divided elites, a poor economy, and tenuous rule of law, are risky candidates for surviving the rigors of democratization. In such an environment, it is unlikely that electoral contestation will remain peaceful or that existing levels of human security will be maintained, let alone improve. By producing anarchic conditions, a derailed democratic transition may itself create a supportive environment for terrorist activities, thereby mocking Washington's justification for advocating democracy.

POLICY RESPONSES

The inherent difficulties of democratization as well as the diversity of countries that may begin—or have already begun—a political transition underlines the importance of carefully examining "facts on the ground" in order to craft an appropriate strategy for democracy promotion. For example, strong U.S. support for Ukrainian civic groups pressing for political reform played an important part in mobilizing civil society in 2004 for a peaceful—and successful—confrontation with the Ukrainian government over the issue of electoral fraud.[42]

At the same time, and in keeping with careful attention to "facts on the ground," the democratization strategy that worked in Ukraine is unlikely to yield similar results next door in Russia, where the popular President, Vladimir Putin, pushed through legislation in early 2006 that gives him significant power to regulate the activities of foreign and domestic NGOs. In stark contrast to its robust Ukrainian counterpart, Russia's anemic civil society was unable to mount any significant opposition to this measure. Judging by the success of Putin's assault on Russian civil society and other political and social supports for democratization, including the media, it is unlikely that transnational pressure can play a significant role by itself in reversing Russia's slide into authoritarianism.

In those regions of the world where the conditions supporting democratization may be even weaker than in Russia—such as the Middle East—the United States must be particularly careful to choose strategies that limit risks and promise gains. An initial approach to this problem should be to assume that the further a country is from the favorable conditions that Spain enjoyed when it began its own transition, the more "fast-track" democratization—particularly in the form of free and fair elections—should be reconsidered and other strategies emphasized. This is so because rapid democratization in the absence of supportive conditions—such as a strong civic culture or the presence of effective and legitimate institutions that can peacefully organize the participation of newly empowered citizens—may lead to political and social chaos. The electoral victory in early 2006 of Hamas in Palestine seems to confirm the wisdom of this approach.

Careful strategies that press authoritarian regimes to build within themselves the prerequisites of successful democratization would seem to hold out more promise. Such efforts would include extending financial support and training to advocacy groups that seek reform in a number of important arenas, including gender equality in employment, the provision of the rule of law, and freedom of the press. United States Agency for International Development, as well as other organs of the U.S. government, has a significant amount of experience in crafting democratization programs for crucial regions of the world, particularly the Middle East.

Yet it should also be recognized that such incremental efforts by their very nature are often painfully slow in yielding results, and require a degree of patience and commitment that has often been difficult for Washington to maintain, particularly across administrations. Perhaps more important, the evidence increasingly suggests that autocratic governments have become more adept at promoting limited forms of liberalization, such as controlled elections and closely supervised domestic and transnational NGOs, which are effectively contained by the regime.[43] These liberalized autocracies are unlikely to preside willingly over the growth of an autonomous political society with political parties able to participate in authentic and stable political contestation.

An additional disability of the incremental approach to supporting democratization is that most of the population in most of these autocracies, particularly in the Middle East, is deeply alienated from the existing regime, and would welcome its demise. Although Western advocates of gradual reform in the Middle East point to the danger of radical Islamists coming to power in free and fair elections, and therefore emphasize not only moderate change but also the need to support secular forces of liberalism in the Middle East, it seems clear that most groups pressing for change in the Islamic world will continue to link their political identities closely to Islam due in part to its cultural power and mobilizing potential.

Despite the risks of democratization, U.S. foreign policy toward individual countries should not rely on weighing the virtues of stability (and support for American security interests) against those of liberty. Rather, the issue should be how forcefully the United States promotes democracy in particular countries, and with what instruments. For those countries that fall short of the favorable preconditions for democracy possessed by Spain in 1975, it seems clear that the United States must craft strategies that do not threaten destabilization but nonetheless push for authentic liberalization. The United States must be particularly steadfast in applying pressure to those autocracies that have learned to co-opt and tame domestic manifestation of political pluralism. The United States should also come to grips with the inevitable presence of Islam in the politics of the states of the Middle East, and in the politics of many states in Asia. The forces of secularism in the Middle East are likely to remain weak, despite the best efforts of the United States to strengthen them. The United States should instead identify and seek to support Islamic groups that are moderate within the context of Middle Eastern politics. The rise of "Muslim Democracy" in Indonesia, Bangladesh, and Turkey should help assure Washington that pluralism within the Islamic tradition is a very real possibility, given the proper conditions. The United States should also discard preconceptions of what the political beliefs and platforms of "moderates" should look like. The task should be to nurture moderate Islamic organizations and help them mobilize democratic opinion.

Unfortunately, the United States is not viewed as a positive force for change by such groups and their existing or prospective constituencies. In the present climate of anti-Americanism in the Middle East, it is virtually impossible for any mass Islamic group to publicly support the United States, and it would be unreasonable to expect them to do so. These attitudes are due in large measure to America's previous, and sometimes ongoing, support for autocracy in the region. Anti-Americanism has also been effectively cultivated by regional autocrats seeking to deflect popular anger outward and away from the regime. Nevertheless, public opinion polls consistently find that majorities in Middle East countries favor democracy, even as anti-Americanism is on the rise.[44]

Here the United States would do well to cooperate more closely with Europe. Despite the contentious nature of its relationship with several European states since the invasion of Iraq, the United States remains the close friend and ally of Europe in the fight against global terrorism. Happily, the members of the European Union enjoy considerably more legitimacy among Middle East publics, including those who are deeply alienated from politics and often provide passive and active support for national and transnational terrorism emanating from the region. The EU is therefore much better placed to support regional moderates who favor "Islamic Democracy" but are unwilling to work with the United States. For its part, Washington should step up its pressure on regional autocrats to deliver on, until now, empty promises of democratization.

We should not forget that the West is already directly involved in promoting democratization in the Middle East through its leadership of multilateral efforts in rebuilding the Afghan state and political community. It is difficult to overstate the practical and symbolic importance of this task. If democratization is successful in Afghanistan, it will not only have powerful demonstration effects on its immediate neighbors, including Iran, Pakistan, Uzbekistan, and Turkmenistan, but also on the region as a whole. The West, particularly the United States, has established a legitimate presence in Afghanistan, and possesses sufficient support from the Afghan people—unlike conditions in Iraq—to focus its attention on state building and democratization for the mid- to long-term. Yet the West has faltered in this mission. According to one knowledgeable observer, the international community's failure to "provide sufficient economic and security support ... over the past four years [has] created a power vacuum that was filled by warlords, criminals, and the drug trade."[45] The most ominous indicator of the tenuous nature of the Afghan state is the increasing number of attacks by a resurgent Taliban against government troops and installations. It is in the obvious interest of the United States and its allies that Afghanistan not be forgotten, but be given the long-term assistance required for it to serve eventually as a regional model of the good intentions of the West and its authentic commitment to democratization.

The Middle East is not the only region where effective multilateralism may promote democracy and weaken terrorism. Just as the European Community provided strong inducements for Spain to democratize and to fight terrorism effectively, the European Union has fostered similar political impulses in Turkey. Ironically, the fear of importing political and economic instability, but also terrorism, has recently led many Europeans to oppose the entry of Turkey into the ranks of the European Union.

NATO, as a transnational organization with an overwhelmingly democratic membership, has also played an important role in promoting democracy throughout Europe, most recently in the Balkans. Although the supports for democratization are weaker as one moves east, the prospect of NATO membership for Ukraine and Georgia is likely to strengthen democratization in both of those countries. As we have noted, the supports for democracy in Russia are still relatively weak. It should also be noted that Russia, unlike Spain, has suffered because of its distance from the core of liberal democracy in Western Europe. But if NATO continues its peaceful march to Russia's borderlands, and if those borderlands continue to democratize, democratic Europe will have finally come to Russia. It is to be hoped that such external demonstration effects, coupled with other Western policies to advance democracy in Russia, will reverse its slide into authoritarianism.

The shared burden of the liberal international community in confronting terrorism, while supporting democracy, was dramatically illustrated at a conference held in Madrid in March 2005 to mark the first anniversary of the deadly terrorist attacks that occurred on March 11, 2004 against four commuter trains during the height of the rush hour in the Spanish capital. Almost 200 innocent civilians lost their lives as a result of the explosions. Speaking at the conference, Mary Kaldor and Miguel Darcy de Oliveira observed that the attacks of September 11 and March 11 have become symbols of "an all-pervasive sense of global insecurity."[46] Strong Western states remain vulnerable to attacks that originate outside their borders, to international terrorism that is rooted in political alienation and can only be countered by a combination of military and political measures. According to Kaldor and Dardy de Oliveira, terrorism "breeds in situations where there is no legitimate political authority, in war zones, or in authoritarian states. The key to dealing with political violence is . . . the establishment of legitimate political authority."[47] It is the purpose of this book to help advance the discussion on the relationship between democracy and terrorism, and on how best to support the spread of legitimate political authority through democratization.

CASE STUDIES

To explore whether or not transitioning democracies can combat terrorism, in part, through encouraging and implementing liberal democratic values and institutions, this book presents several case studies including the Basques in Spain, ethnic Albanians in Macedonia, Kurds in Turkey, Chechens in Russia, and a future Palestinian state. The first case assesses the Spanish government's successful democratic transition during the period of 1975–1992, while battling Basque separatists. This case provides a foundation for the book by demonstrating how a transitioning democracy overcame terrorist challenges, especially from a group claiming legitimacy based on ethnic roots. In the late 1970s, Spain addressed valid grievances in the Basque community, while effectively combating Euskadi Ta Askatasuna (ETA). As a base case, Spain provides lessons that have applicability to the subsequent cases, although clearly each case carries its own specific internal and external dynamics.

Although the Basque terrorist group, ETA, was not eradicated during Spain's democratic transition, the state fostered legitimacy in major segments of the Basque community by building representative institutions and encouraging democratic values. Regional support from France and the European Community aided Spain in both building democracy and combating terrorism. The fact that Spain's neighbors were mature and consolidated democracies sustained Spain in its democratic transition and mitigation of ETA, while also strengthening France's liberal democratic principles by forcing that country to reassess its own policies. Through collaboration, both countries addressed the transnational terrorist problem as they secured the legitimacy of their liberal democratic orders. In fact, Europe as a whole benefited from Spain's handling of the Basque issue as it paved the way for increased regional cooperation regarding transnational threats. Moreover, Spain's persistent adherence to liberal democratic principles, even in the midst of its democratic transition and increased violence from ETA, bolstered its legitimacy among the Spanish and Basque population.

The next case explores Macedonia's attempts to democratize despite the violent regional conflict on its border throughout the 1990s. Macedonia frequently appeared on the verge of civil war, but through courageous internal political actions and support from the European Union and the international community, Macedonia managed to successfully thwart attempts by terrorist organizations to derail the government's quest for legitimacy by inciting the ethnic Albanian population. As such, the implications of the events in Macedonia are intertwined with events in both Kosovo and Serbia.

The third case discusses the effect that Turkey's military dominance of the state has on Turkey's democratic transition and consequently on how it contends with the terrorist activities of the Kurdish Workers Party (PKK). Turkey's unwillingness to recognize Kurdish cultural rights and implement substantive changes in policy has exacerbated tensions within the Kurdish community. Nonetheless, Turkey has been vying for membership in the European Union and as such, is pressured to modify its policies to meet the requirements of good governance to gain access to the Union. Recognizing minority cultural rights has the potential to decrease the appeal of terrorist groups operating within Turkey.

The case of Russia and the Chechens stands in stark contrast to the case of Spain, and underlines the importance of objective and subjective factors in determining how a transitional polity copes with the threat of secession and terrorism. In contrast to Spain, Russia did not begin its transition with a strong middle class supportive of democratization. Also unlike Spain, Russia did not have the advantage of close proximity to institutionalized liberal democracies that might support internal reform as well as reconciliation with alienated minorities. These negative objective factors were reinforced by the presence of weak, tentative reformers on both the Russian and Chechen sides. Vladimir Putin's understanding of Russian modernization—his central priority—emphasizes the role of the Russian state, placing considerable power in the hands of "power" ministries like the Army and the secret police that have little interest in democratization or negotiation with aggrieved and hostile minorities like the Chechens. Matters are made worse by Putin's willingness to legitimate his authority by equating Chechen resistance to Russian rule with "terrorism." Although the conflict has been characterized by missed opportunities for a resolution favorable to both sides, the external environment, particularly in the form of pressure from the West, may still determine a positive outcome through properly crafted policies that induce both Russians and Chechens to negotiate in good faith.

The final case analyzes state formation in the Palestinian territories where a nation is transitioning to democracy, while simultaneously continuing its struggle for national liberation to determine the final boundaries of a Palestinian state. The chapter explores whether or not the Palestinian Authority, led by the Islamic militant group Hamas, has the capability to address genuine Palestinian grievances and continue the democratic transition. Additionally, the Palestinian Authority's ability and willingness to combat terrorism emanating from its territory during the unstable and volatile period of democratic transition remains questionable because Hamas does not recognize Israel's right to exist. Although this case diverges significantly from that of Spain's as it does not deal with an ethnic minority or a state that has determined boundaries, there are still lessons to be gleaned from Spain's successful transition to democracy. Since 1967, when Israel occupied the West Bank and Gaza Strip, the Palestinians have witnessed democracy firsthand as they served as laborers in Israel. Yet how the Palestinian leadership approaches building democratic institutions will determine its future and whether or not terrorist activity will decrease. The United States and its

European allies should support the Palestinian transition, while simultane-ously taking an active role to restart the Palestinian–Israeli peace process.

Although it is impossible to transplant the conditions for Spain's demo-cratic transformation to other states, crucial insights from successful cases provide a more nuanced understanding of democratic transitioning states experiencing terrorist threats that challenge legitimacy.[48] The urgency for discerning the implication of these events is apparent. The wider war on global terror necessitates a comprehensive grasp of regional conditions that cultivate real societal grievances. Clearly, illegitimate regimes combined with societal despair have the potential to make terrorism an attractive political option. As Secretary of State Colin Powell stated, "[A] shortage of economic opportunities is a ticket to despair. Combined with rigid political systems, it is a dangerous brew indeed."[49]

CHAPTER 1

THE BASQUES IN SPAIN AND REPERCUSSIONS IN FRANCE: CASE I

INTRODUCTION

To help determine whether or not transitioning democracies can combat terrorism, in part, through encouraging and implementing liberal democratic values and institutions, this case investigates the Spanish government's successful democratic transition from the period 1975 to 1992, while battling Basque separatists. Although the Basque terrorist group, Euskadi Ta Askatasuna (ETA), was not eradicated, the state fostered legitimacy in major segments of the Basque community by building representative institutions and encouraging democratic values. This case provides a foundation for our study by demonstrating how a transitioning democracy overcame terrorist challenges, especially from a group claiming legitimacy based on ethnic roots. In the late 1970s, Spain addressed real grievances in the Basque community, while effectively combating ETA.

Regional support from France and the European Community aided Spain in both building democracy and combating terrorism. Cooperation between Spain and France facilitated Spain's democratic consolidation by weakening ETA in the field and by strengthening the commitment of both countries to liberal democratic principles. Over time, Spain's improved relationship with democratic Europe as a whole paved the way for increased regional cooperation on the Basque problem and other transnational threats. Spain's persistent adherence to liberal democratic principles, even in the midst of its democratic transition and increased violence from ETA, bolstered its legitimacy among the Spanish and Basque population and weakened the appeal of ETA.

Samuel Huntington discusses Spain's political transformation as part of the "third wave" of democratization.[1] Spain's transition was "regime-initiated;" the authoritarian regime did not collapse, but rather began the process of democratization itself. The Spanish transition was particularly complex because it occurred in the context of a multilingual and multi-national state possessing a deeply conservative political culture.[2] Howard Wiarda points to the significant changes in Spain's political culture during the period we are examining:

> Perhaps in no other country in the world has . . . the political culture, changed as dramatically in so short a time—during the 1960s and 1970s—as in Spain. In that period Spain went from being a funda-mentally conservative, traditional, and exceedingly Catholic society to being liberal, radical, innovative, and secular . . .[3]

The fact that Spain was able to transform its political culture in a relatively short period of time should be kept in mind as we examine other transitional countries that seek to legitimize the values and institutions of democracy. The chapter therefore discusses how Spain successfully confronted Basque terrorism within the larger framework of Spain's struggle for the legitimacy of democracy.

BACKGROUND

The history of the Basques and the Spanish state has been a long, con-tentious one. The Basque region, according to Basque nationalists, includes the northeastern portion of Spain and southern France: four provinces in Spain (Alava, Vizcaya, Guipuzcoa, and Navarra) and three provinces in France (Labourd, Basse Navarre, and Soule).[4] The most distinguishing fea-ture of Basques is the language called *euskara*. In fact, a Basque person is referred to as an *euskaldun*, meaning "possessor of the Basque language" although there is much disagreement concerning the origins of both the Basques as well as their language.[5] The beginnings of Basque national-ism, however, appears to have emerged in the late 1800s with the rise of industrialization and accompanying social developments. Industrializa-tion in the Basque provinces created social tensions based in large part on conflict between emerging Basque industrialists and rural, traditional, and Catholic Basques. The latter group developed strong sentiments of Basque nationalism.[6]

In the modern era, three themes are particularly important in Spain's po-litical development. First, Spain has had to deal with the tension between the central authority and regional areas. Geography reinforced regional and tribal isolation, and the authority of the local caudillos or military strong-men, vis-à-vis the state. Secondly, conflict was common between the state and various components of the corporate sphere, including the military, religious fraternities, guilds, and towns. Finally, Spain has confronted an ideological split between advocates of tradition and faith against those of liberalism.

The tensions that arose from these conflicts over the fundamental political identity of Spain and the distribution of power within the state were exacerbated in the early twentieth century by industrialization and the rule of a reactionary Spanish monarchy. Under the First Republic (1931–1936), Spain experienced significant political liberalization. The government also awarded autonomy to the Basque provinces, positioning the Basques against Franco, who ultimately won the Civil War. Franco's rule after the Spanish Civil War rolled back many of the advances made under the Republic; however, during the 1960s and 1970s, Franco did allow for some opening in the economic, political, and social realms. This liberalization characterized the change of his regime from a "dictadure" (hard dictatorship) to a "dictablanda" (soft dictatorship).[7]

Franco's goal was to restore what he viewed as Spanish authenticity. He sought to instill values that reflected conservatism, tradition, Catholicism, anticommunism, and hierarchy. Public opinion polls in the 1960s reflected these values, suggesting that Franco was somewhat successful.[8] Franco was also determined to create "a single personality, Spanish." In pursuit of this goal, Franco's regime dealt with the Basques in a repressive manner, forbidding any outward expression of Basque culture and political identity. In response, the Basques formed a "we–they" identity between themselves and Madrid, viewing the Spanish as an occupying foreign force.[9] The inability to express cultural or political aspirations through legitimate means created a growing sense of discontent and disenfranchisement among the younger Basque nationalists. From 1956 to 1975, Franco declared twelve *states of exception* due to political unrest in which five were directed against all of Spain and six were directed only against the Basque region. Approximately 8,500 Basques were directly affected by arrests, imprisonment, torture, or flight from Spain out of fear of repression.[10]

Tensions between the Spanish center and the Basque periphery deepened as Franco launched a drive to modernize the country by increasing industrial production in the economically developed Basque and Catalan regions. This strategy had devastating effects on the Basques. With the lure of greater industrialization in the Basque region, non-Basques flooded the area in search of jobs, competing sharply with the indigenous population for employment, housing, and social services. The failure of the regime to alleviate the social costs of this economic growth was yet another source of political alienation among the Basques.[11]

ETA (*Euzkadi ta Askatasuna* or Basque Homeland and Freedom) was founded in 1959 as a response to these conditions. ETA sought to secure

Basque cultural integrity and ultimately, to achieve political independence.[12] The unique regional dialect, *euskera*, provided a source of identity for ETA's nationalist aspirations. Many of the rural areas spoke the dialect by the end of the nineteenth century, but Basques embraced it as a means to preserve cultural identity. General Franco forbade the dialect because it detracted from centralism and unity, the basis of his Fascist Falange goal. Initially, ETA did not call for a terrorist strategy or violent insurgency, although it did not share the PNV's (Partido de Arana—the recognized nationalist party) goals at the time. However, provoked by Franco's continued brutalization of their homeland, and encouraged by successful anticolonial struggles in the third world, ETA opened its terrorist campaign in 1968.[13] Although ETA violence did not directly cause Spain's democratic transition, it did play an important role in weakening the political supports of the Franco regime. By attempting to stamp out ETA through severe repression, Franco's regime inadvertently alienated not only the Basques, but also much of the larger population in Spain.[14]

DEMOCRATIC TRANSITION AND CONSOLIDATION

On the eve of its transition, which began in November 1975 with the death of Franco and the designation of Juan Carlos as King according to the Francoite law of succession, Spain possessed significant facilitating conditions that supported democratization. Spain's economy was doing well, and ranked tenth among capitalist countries worldwide. Although its economy dipped during the subsequent transition, it did not adversely affect the people's support of the new political regime. Spanish civil society was relatively developed as was the rule of law.

The international environment also played an important role in supporting Spain's democratic transition. Although Spain did not become a member of the EEC until 1986, the prospect of future membership, on the condition of successful democratization, was a powerful incentive for Spain's political elites to work together to craft a post-Franco political settlement. Prime Minister Adolfo Suarez submitted Spain's request for EEC membership in 1977, and he received full backing from the Spanish Parliament. In the run up to Spain's admission, the EEC lent credibility to democracy, and its members were very supportive of Spain's democratization.[15]

However, ETA activities threatened to upend Spain's democratic transition. ETA goals in the post-Franco period remained the same as in the past: delegitimize the Spanish regime, mobilize public support, and achieve Basque independence. ETA targeted six audiences: the Spanish public at large, with the aim of deepening political polarization; the Basque public, with the goal of eliciting nationalist sentiment; the Spanish military, which ETA wanted to put at odds with the state; the Spanish state, which ETA wanted to delegitimize by provoking repressive reactions; ETA members, with the aim of sustaining solidarity; and the Basque regional government and its political parties, which ETA viewed as traitors to the Basque cause, but nevertheless sought their support.[16]

The main challenge posed by ETA was the possibility that its terror tactics might provoke harsh police state-like responses by the new Spanish government constituted under the leadership of Juan Carlos and Adolfo Suarez. Although critics of Spain's fledgling democracy point to its alleged torture of ETA members and the regime's support of right-wing counterterrorist groups, such harsh responses occurred only infrequently, and did not represent the mainstream policy of the transitional regime.[17] Also, the Spanish state did not officially sanction any counterterrorist activities.

During the Spanish transition, elite and popular opinions about the identity and structure of the state wavered. On the issue of the political status of the Basque region, Spanish public opinion changed in significant ways over time: in 1977 approximately 45 percent of Spaniards in national surveys supporting regional autonomy for the Basques, but in 1979 the number had risen to 56 percent in favor of autonomy. As for Basque public opinion, in 1977 63 percent of respondents in opinion surveys supported autonomy and 16 percent supported independence, but in 1979 (with the ratification of the new Spanish constitution), 20 percent supported independence and 54 percent favored autonomy. Interestingly, the Spanish population's support for regional autonomy increased, while Basque opinion became somewhat more polarized. Although the Basque population had not yet reached a consensus as to its political aspirations in the early stage of the Spanish transition, the important development was the rejection by most of the Spanish population of state repression in the Basque region. The Spanish people wanted rule of law and they supported negotiation. In the face of a conciliatory Spanish state and population, Basque public opinion had less incentive to unite around the banner of independence. The diversity of Basque public opinion was naturally reflected in several Basque parties, including, Partido Nacionalista Vasco (PNV) and Euskadiko Ezkerra (EE), which represented the Basque region.[18]

Internal divisions over political goals were particularly strong in the leading party, the PNV. In order to balance its internal factions, but also to attract support from as many opinions groupings in Basque society as possible, the PNV crafted an ambiguous political platform whose goals seemed to encompass both autonomy within the Spanish state *and* independence from Spain. One PNV leader remarked that the party's goal was "to reunify the Basque provinces so that we can [eventually] join our brothers in France."[19] One Basque Socialist leader, explained PNV's situation:

[The PNV] cannot dare to condemn the convent [ETA] because they are orthodox; it cannot renounce *posibilismo* because that is salvation. As a consequence, its ambiguity persists; ambiguity in its behavior, ambiguity in its words, and in its strategy . . . It wants at one and the same time to be with the constitution and with ETA.[20]

Given its attempts to embrace both autonomy and independence, the PNV-led Basque government did not publicly condemn ETA violence until 1985, which followed ETA attacks against PNV officials.[21] Goldie Shabad and Francisco Ramo make an insightful observation that moderate parties may manipulate extremist or violent terrorist groups to strengthen their own bargaining power with the state.[22] The Basque province itself was wracked with ambiguity and polarization. In 1983, one former Socialist leader remarked:

Something paradoxical has occurred in the Basque Country. In these moments, it is the corner of Spain that is most remote from democratic principles practiced in Europe . . . It is the corner in which intolerance, fanaticism, and violence are most entrenched. They are the ones who represent the old Spaniard . . . the intolerant Spaniard, the fanatic.[23]

Despite this context of intolerance, the Spanish government remained conciliatory and committed to pluralism. Juan Linz and Alfred Stepan credit the leadership of Adolfo Suarez as a critical factor in Spain's democratization. Suarez convinced the Cortes (legislature) to sanction new elections, which ultimately meant that its members would be voted out of office. Consequently, the Cortes passed the Law for Political Reform and the people, through a referendum, approved it on December 15, 1978. Suarez exploited this opportunity to make inroads with opposition party members, and he began the process of creating an inclusive political regime. Political reform was the first step; economic reform would follow. According to Suarez, "As long as political unknowns [incognitas] hang over the country, there cannot be either economic reactivation or stability."[24]

Robert Hislope aptly identifies the reasons why Suarez's inclusive steps were so important to the Spanish transition:

When minority elites are invited into the political process and regularly interact with elites from the dominant group, common norms and values can be discovered, friendships forged, and hostile stereotypes dispelled . . . Inclusion, voice, and routinized patterns of interaction give minority groups a sense of having a stake in the system.[25]

The political leadership was determined to undo Franco's harsh cultural hegemonic policies. To reflect this goal, it invited moderate Basque and Catalan representatives to serve on the initial committee that guided the transition immediately following Franco's death. Thus, the 1978 constitution recognized Spain as a multicultural entity and authorized the devolution of power to regional governments. Suarez, however, excluded the Basque representatives from the constitutional negotiations, and the Basques nationalists called for "no" votes or abstentions during the ratification process. Suarez did not make the same mistake in 1979; he wanted consensus on the autonomy statute. He gained support from the head of the PNV through private meetings. By 1985, electoral imperatives led to a coalition between the PNV and the PSOE (Spanish Socialist Party). The PNV, as a result of this coalition, publicly strongly supported the constitution and denounced terrorism. The Basque Left (EE) also publicly supported the state and renounced terrorism. Only the Herri Batasuna (HB) remained steadfast in its commitment to Basque independence and support of terrorism. As a result, the PNV and EE elites have been integrated into the political system, while HB and ETA have been increasingly isolated.[26]

This policy of inclusion, while ultimately successful, extended over several years and was initially vulnerable to instability and ETA took advantage of this opportunity by launching terror attacks and paramilitary operations. Between 1960 and 1975, the year of Franco's death, the ETA was responsible for forty-three deaths. In 1978, the year in which the new Spanish constitution was approved, ETA caused sixty-five deaths; in 1979, the total number rose to seventy-eight, and in 1980, the year, of the first regional elections, the total reached ninety-six. This period also saw the first killings of military officers due to Basque terrorist activities.[27] Significantly, the Spanish population did not blame the transitional regime for these atrocities, in part because Suarez had skillfully built political bridges joining the Spanish and Basque communities. Elections played an important role in this process of conciliation. National parties campaigned in the Basque and Catalan regions and four of them captured 51.4 percent of the Basque vote. Linz and Stepan convincingly argue that by holding statewide elections before regional elections, Spain defused Basque nationalist fervor. Regional politicians had political incentives to build coalitions with national politicians and organizations and hammer out long-term relationships. This political process fostered overlapping regional and national identities that were supportive of democracy.[28]

Although the Spanish government has yet to eradicate ETA terrorism, it has been able to significantly reduce the level of support enjoyed by ETA. Simply put, Spanish democracy has outpaced ETA in the race for political legitimacy. In 1979, 5 percent of Basques viewed the members of ETA as criminals and 17.1 percent viewed them as patriots; in 1989, 16 percent considered them criminals, and 5 percent saw them as patriots. Other surveys indicate that 8 percent of the Basque population fully supported ETA in 1981, but in 1989 that figure dropped to 3 percent. Finally, in 1981, 23 percent totally rejected ETA and 48 percent responded with "don't know" or "no answer" and in 1989, 45 percent totally rejected ETA, while 16 percent responded with either "don't know," or "no answer." Even among ETA-affiliated respondents, opinion surveys reveal diminished support for the organization. Responses identifying ETA members as patriots by those who voted for the main nationalist party, the PVN, dropped from 40 percent in 1981 to 16 percent in 1989. A similar decline occurred among those who voted for the Herra Batasuna party.[29]

A 1986 survey asked respondents to agree or disagree with the following statement: "That violence is not necessary to achieve political goals..." Only supporters of the radical Basque Party disagreed in significant numbers. The other Basque political parties, including the PNV, overwhelmingly agreed in part or completely with the statement. Even the response, "somewhat disagree" never rose above single digit percentages, except in the case of voters for the HB, 28 percent of whom disagreed "somewhat" with the statement.[30] In another survey in 1986, eight out of ten Basques rejected violence and expressed positive sentiment for Spain's democratic system.[31] Barely 10 years after the beginning of the Spanish transition, ETA's violent activities no longer enjoyed significant political support: it had failed politically.

In line with this crucial change in political attitudes at the regional level, the Spanish public as a whole also responded positively to the new democratic regime. By 1986, 76 percent of the population expressed pride in the regime, and only 9 percent responded negatively. Public opinion remained strongly supportive of the regime throughout the 1980s. By 1988, 81 percent agreed with the following statement: "Democracy is the best political system for a country like ours."[32] Howard Wiarda concludes that during this period Spain became more "Europeanized." He argues that attitudes reflecting less affiliation with the Catholic Church; strong support for democracy; more emphasis on merit than family or personal ties as a means of social mobility; consumerism and materialism; changes in traditional gender roles; and political moderation and even apathy mark an important shift toward a civic culture. Although Wiarda believes that Spain is not yet fully Europeanized, he also recognizes that its movement in that political and sociocultural direction has been remarkable.[33]

COOPERATION: FRANCE AND SPAIN

Although Spain was able to politically marginalize ETA, it still needed to provide physical protection to Spanish society from ETA's terror campaigns. Spain needed the help of France, but French cooperation did not come easily. Since 1927, French law had protected asylum seekers. While this law favored human rights, it was vulnerable to exploitation by extremist groups who lived peacefully in France but carried out violent operations across the border. It was a law that was also abused by the French government, which used it for political effect, and as a means to register opposition to a particular government or to its policies. Legitimate extradition requests were often denied by the French government for political reasons. It is useful to note that the history of French politics has influenced the way the French view political violence, including terrorism. The French Revolution was born from it, and through the years French leaders, citizens, and institutions have engaged in terrorism. There is an ambivalence in French counterterrorist policies that reflect the French experience. President Giscard D'Estaing's statement in 1980 reflects this ambivalence: "France must and will remain a land of the asylum," and "France will not allow its soil to become a base for foreigners seeking to organize violent actions here."[34]

The most serious case of French leniency toward terrorist groups was its relationship with ETA. Opposing the Franco regime, France allowed ETA freedom of movement within its borders.[35] ETA was a transnational terrorist organization; Basques lived on both sides of the French–Spanish border, which was difficult terrain to monitor and control. France helped legitimize ETA's activities by offering sanctuary.[36] Additionally, ETA coordinated such activities as training and arms supplies with other terrorist organizations in Europe and the third world, and it adopted foreign frameworks to assist with legitimizing its activities and developing strategies. Specifically, ETA members have received training in Yemen, Libya, and Algeria, with the Middle East supplying arms and Libya providing funds. Other European terrorist groups have coordinated the purchase of weapons from Communist Czechoslovakia and the former Soviet Union, and close ties were established with the IRA. Finally, ETA adopted anticolonial ideological views and insurgent strategies from many terrorist groups from the third world.[37]

Two events in 1973 were noteworthy in terms of France's relationship with ETA. The first event was the emergence of ETA's French counterpart, Iparretarak, and the second event was ETA's assassination of the Spanish prime minister. The French counterpart of ETA was Iparretarak, which formed in 1973. Its goal was also Basque independence. Violence erupted between ETA and Iparretarak when the two groups clashed over ideology and interests, leading ETA to strike a deal with the French police in 1981. In return for French toleration, ETA promised not to commit violence on French soil. As a result, Iparretarak lost legitimacy in its struggle for Basque independence, and by 1988, Iparretarak was defunct.[38] In the case of the assassination of the Spanish prime minister, the perpetrators fled to France and held a press conference claiming responsibility. France arrested the assassins in 1974, denounced ETA as a terrorist organization and banned separatist groups. However, it was not until Franco's death in 1975 that France made more concerted efforts against ETA activity on its soil.[39]

In 1976, France placed harsher restrictions on attaining work and residential status and work permits. France conducted searches without warrants, surveillance, and harassment of ETA members, and in 1977, France began a policy of preventive detention. In January of that year, France sent seven Spanish Basques to Spain. Still France refused extradition of any ETA members. By the end of the decade, however, France was experiencing its own Basque separatist problem with unofficial Spanish anti-Basque activities causing much violence in France. France learned that providing sanctuary to terrorists was dangerous.[40]

However, France still embraced the view that ETA terrorists were freedom fighters. In 1981, a French court ruled in favor of the extradition of Tomas Linanza. Linaza was wanted in Spain for murdering six civil guards; however, the French political authorities nullified the court's ruling. Gaston Defferre, the interior minister, ruled against extradition of ETA members, comparing their activities to the French resistance.[41] However, French public opinion was becoming less and less tolerant of political violence in the 1980s. The election of a Socialist president for the first time in the Fifth Republic in 1981 and again, in 1988, with a socialist majority in parliament from 1981 to 1986 reflected an important shift in political power. However, the French government elected in 1981 still firmly rejected Spanish requests for extradition of members of ETA living in France. For its part, Spain continued to insist that France change its asylum and extradition policies.[42]

In 1982, the French government reviewed its extradition and asylum policies, and by 1984, reversed course. The leadership of the French government realized that it could be held responsible if Spain's transitional democracy weakened or failed due to terrorism and unrest in the Basque region. France was also favorably influenced by Spain's emerging policy of reconciliation, not retribution, toward ETA members living in France. France and Spain signed an antiterrorist cooperation agreement, after which Gaston Defferre declared, against his earlier statements, that "A terrorist is not a political refugee."[43] This agreement, which led to France's cooperation with Spain on Spanish requests for extradition and also France's denial of ETA requests for asylum, had far-reaching consequences. France was no longer the guarantor of sanctuary. It agreed to ratify the European Convention on Suppression of Terrorism, and it broadened its cooperative efforts with other European countries. In May 1987, France hosted an EC/Summit Seven conference of interior and justice ministers, at which France's Interior Minister declared "a willingness to take all the measures necessary" to strengthen international cooperation against terrorism.[44]

IMPLICATIONS

An analysis of the Basque case underlines the challenge terrorism poses to transitioning democracies. ETA increased its violent activities during the Spanish transition, seeking political advantage against a vulnerable, fledgling regime. One lesson of the Spanish transition is that the quality of political leadership is a crucial variable in determining the outcome of efforts at democratization. In the Spanish case, significant and timely political reforms bolstered the regime's legitimacy vis-à-vis ETA. Even as ETA stepped up its

campaign of violence, Prime Minister Suarez pushed ahead with an inclusive regime-building strategy and the creation of a multiparty structure that
allowed for multivocal political discourse. Basque leaders, parties, and mass
publics developed a stake in the new democratic system. The autonomy
statute sent a strong signal that cultural diversity and political pluralism
was valued by the state. Regional governments derived legitimacy not only
from the regional, political community, but also from the state through
the autonomy statute. In another example of intelligent political leadership,
the Spanish government held national elections prior to regional elections,
which delegitimized ETA and fostered Basque acceptance of dual and com-
plementary Basque and Spanish identities.[45] The national referendum on the
constitution also demonstrated the pluralist quality of the post-Franco government. By crafting effective and legitimate institutions, Spain's democratic
leadership was able to mobilize loyalties at the national and regional levels, creating new political communities with a shared interest in democratic
government.

The political culture of the broader elite and mass publics was also an
important variable in supporting the Spanish transition. The Spanish population as a whole did not support repressive measures against the Basques,
even during the most tense periods of the transition. Such attitudes reinforced
the willingness of the regime to demonstrate restraint on the Basque issue,
and this stance of the government in turn bolstered its legitimacy in Spanish society. As the transition continued through the consolidation phase,
regional and national support for ETA and its violent tactics dwindled still
further, reflecting the strengthening of tolerance, trust, and consensus as
core values of Spanish political culture.

What does the Spanish case reveal about the relationship between terrorism and democratization? Terrorism clearly poses serious threats to democratization and may even derail the process. In the case of Spain, the political
threat of Basque terrorism was effectively contained by the positive interaction of objective conditions—including the pluralist political culture of much
of the Spanish population and the supportive international environment—
and subjective conditions—above all the effective leadership and policies
of Spain's national political leaders. Simply put, the new regime was able
to isolate ETA and delegitimize its cause in Spain's newly opened political
space. Democratic values and institutions won the battle for political legitimacy. Although domestic factors were decisive in determining the success
of the Spanish transition, external factors were also clearly important. Larry
Diamond logically argues that institutionalized liberal democracies must be
able to protect their societies from political terror. This simple but important
point became politically relevant during the early period of the Spanish transition when France itself became the target of Basque terrorism. Realizing
that Spain and France required each other's cooperation in the fight against
violent politics, the French leadership revised its long-standing official

assessment of the Basque cause in Spain and adopted the new asylum and extradition laws that Spain had requested. This altered French perspective was not based solely on the grounds of national security. France had long been divided over the legitimacy of political violence, including Basque terrorism. Perhaps the most important factor that pushed France to cooperate with Spain against Basque terrorism was the clear evidence that Spain was on the path of authentic democratization.

Shabad and Ramo convincingly argue that the passage of the liberal Spanish constitution, the statutory recognition of Basque autonomy, and Spain's entry into the EC, led France to enact stricter policies against the ETA.[46] Spain's adoption of a conciliatory policy toward ETA members left France unable and unwilling to maintain its policies of nonextradition and its lenient asylum laws.

While Spain's political culture made much greater shifts toward the establishment of a civic culture, France as a mature democracy also experienced shifts in attitudes. French political culture is difficult to assess because it lacks consensus and many issues as reflected by its numerous regime changes. Consequently, its counterterrorist policies appear ambivalent. However, increased cooperation with Spain and other countries, especially with fellow EU members who increasingly coordinate their efforts through such organizations as EUROPOL, may serve to further influence France's political culture and vice versa. As countries increasingly face transnational threats, domestic and foreign policies will necessarily blur. Cooperation among states will be an imperative for security, and values such as justice and civil liberties may collectively be examined, as each state must strike the right balance between securing its population, while maintaining freedoms.

The case underscores the importance of analyzing terrorism in a strategic and political context. Spain was able to address the concerns of the Basques politically through its inclusive democratization efforts. Additionally, the regime built the foundations for a civic culture as described by Diamond, Almond, and Verba. As a result of its legitimacy, Spain was able to marginalize ETA and approach it more as a criminal adversary than a wartime one. And with France's cooperation, Spain effectively protected its society. For its part, France bolstered its liberal democracy by more effectively protecting its society through cooperation, while modifying its views on justice, concerning terrorism. Furthermore, how EUROPOL affects Europe remains to be seen, but the case of the Basques reveals convergence of political cultures. A concluding point is that liberal democracies must recognize the dynamic nature of terrorism and its shifting contexts. The March 2004 bombings in Madrid, executed by Al Qaeda, underlined again for liberal democracies the requirement for understanding the altered nature of the transnational security environment. Not only must we understand the evolving nature and strategy of terrorist groups; but we must also evaluate events in light of the changing nature of the national, regional, and global environments.

The larger lesson from Spain's recent history, particularly its successful democratization, is that effective cooperation among liberal democracies must be coupled with steadfast adherence to democratic principle. This course of action will help ensure that governments under attack by terrorists do not adopt repressive policies that may generate legitimacy for those very terrorists both within the target country and in the external environment.

CHAPTER 2

THE KURDS IN TURKEY: CASE II

INTRODUCTION

The analysis of Turkey, a country on the periphery of Europe, reveals additional insights on the relationship between the democratization process, legitimacy, religion, and terrorism. Turkey holds a unique position at the crossroads of three continents and remains the only declared secular state within the Islamic world. Although Turkey maintains a tenuous association with the European Union (EU), the relationship profoundly affects the internal politics of the Turkish state.[1] Turkey's global role is as yet undefined, but has clearly broadened since the end of the cold war. Although often described by some as the only democracy in the Middle East with the exception of Israel, most scholars agree that Turkey is in the midst of a democratic transition.

According to Svante Cornell, the link between Turkey's handling of the Kurdish issue has both significant domestic and global consequences. "The Kurdish question is arguably the most serious internal problem in the Turkish Republic's 77-year history and certainly the main obstacle to its aspirations to full integration with European institutions."[2] As the case of Spain indicated, there is an increased possibility of political culture shifts as state interests converge. As Turkey sits at the crossroads of the Middle East, Europe, and the Caucuses, its future has the potential for far-reaching consequences on a regional and global scale.

A key difference between Turkey's challenges and those faced by Spain is that the Turkish government has been reluctant to acknowledge its Kurdish issue. Although the Turkish government has taken steps to reform some of its most blatant anti-Kurdish polices, it has not implemented sufficient reform to manage its terrorist challenge, as did Spain. Moreover, the military's dominance in government violates Larry Diamond's democratic criteria of civilian control of the military and the implementation of basic freedoms. Turkey's desire to build a Turkish political community in support of the state has been at the expense of civil liberties. This chapter explores Turkey's battle with the Partiya Karkaren Kurdistan or Kurdistan Workers Party (PKK), which began in earnest in 1984, and the effect that struggle has had on Turkey's transition to democracy. Moreover, regional dynamics in the post-September 11 context necessitates a discussion of the external factors influencing Turkey's democratization process and its continued fight with terrorism. Turkey has been vying for membership in the EU and as such, is pressured to modify its policies to meet the requirements of good governance to gain access to the EU. Recognizing minority cultural rights has the potential to decrease the appeal of terrorist groups operating within Turkey.

BACKGROUND

Turkey's Kurds comprise from 15 to 17 percent of its population with about half living in the southeast part of the country. The Turkish–Kurdish tensions can be traced to the period of Ottoman control, but took a more ominous and violent turn in 1984 with emergence of the PKK led by Abdullah Öcalan. Within the Ottoman Empire, the Kurds were one of many ethnic groups located within the boundaries of the empire. Although the Ottomans recognized religious minorities, such as Jews and Christians, and bestowed them special privileges, they did not define minority status in terms of ethnicity.[3] As such, the Kurdish population was expected to forgo their cultural identity and define themselves as part of the "Muslim nation."[4]

The Ottoman focus on religion resulted from the foundations of Ottoman rule, which granted the sultan legitimacy as the caliph or the spiritual leader of the world's Muslims.[5] Due to its vast size, the Empire became home to many non-Muslim ethnic groups and consequently, many Jews and Christians became subjects of the Empire.[6] The Ottomans organized the non-Muslim groups, specifically Armenians, Greek Orthodox Christians, and Jews, into self-governing entities called *millets*. The leader of each community reported to the Sultan and was responsible for community actions. Due to linguistic skills and experience as traders, these communities provided useful services for the Empire. Nonetheless, the Empire's rich multiculturalism declined with the birth of Turkey's statehood. During World War I, most Armenians were deported, and in accordance with the 1923 Treaty of Lausanne, the Greeks of Anatolia were exchanged for the Muslims of Greece.[7] The Turkish state declared its independence in 1923.

In 1925, the Kurds rebelled against the Turkish government during Turkey's struggle with Britain over the oil-rich areas of present-day northern

Iraq. Some Turks claim that the British encouraged the rebellion; however, the uprising was also a response to the Turkish government's intrusion on Kurdish autonomy and the call for a "Turkey for the Turks."[8] Kurdish unrest continued throughout the 1930s, resulting in increased governmental repression. For the Kurds, new policies intended to culturally assimilate them were ineffective due to Kurdish regional isolation, tribalism, and economic dependency on "landed elites."[9] In the name of security, the Turkish government withheld foundational freedoms that scholars claim are essential for liberal democracy including the rule of law, social justice, pluralism, and accountability.

Modern Turkey's founder, Mustafa Kemal Atatürk, emulated France's route to nationalism and designated six principles as the basis for Turkey's political development: republicanism, nationalism, secularism, popularism, etatism, and reformism. Although Atatürk flirted briefly with a multiparty system, he did not establish a democracy, but instead broke from the traditional precepts of monarchical rule. Atatürk's principles of secularism and nationalism had a significant impact on the Kurdish population. Under the Ottoman Empire, the key to Ottomanism was Islam. Under Atatürk, the emphasis on Turkish identity and secularism delegitimized and offended Kurdish rulers who derived their authority from Islam. All groups within the former multiethnic Ottoman Empire had to assume the Turkish identity at the expense of their ethnic one.[10]

Atatürk's civic conception of the Turkish state was expressed by his maxim, "Happy is he who says he is a Turk." For Atatürk, citizenship corresponded to a national community that included all ethnic communities who were expected to shed their primordial roots and assume the Turkish identity. Interestingly, Atatürk's use of the term "Turk," reversed the previously derogatory connotation of the expression under the Ottomans, which had referred to the peasants of Anatolia. The imposition of the Latin alphabet and the Turkish language served to reinforce the new nature and construct of the nation.[11] Thus, the foundation of the Turkish state encompassed an inherently nontolerant, antipluralist society in the name of assimilation. Atatürk's creation of a Turkish political community was devoid of liberal democratic values. Doğu Ergil remarks, "The Turkish mentality invariably confuses unity with uniformity."[12] Clearly, if there is unity only with uniformity, then the ideas of tolerance, diversity, freedom of expression, and other basic freedoms do not exist.

The Turkish government's Kurdish policy reflected the philosophy of Kemalism and its conception of political community. For years, the Turkish government avoided counting minorities in a census because such a tally would acknowledge their existence. In 1980, the government banned the use of Kurdish in public and changed the names of Kurdish towns to Turkish ones. For the most part, Kurds who have succeeded in Turkish society are those who have not politicized ethnicity.[13]

As a reaction to Turkish policy, in 1978, Abdullah Öcalan established the Kurdish Workers' Party (PKK) to revive Kurdish nationalism. Many members fled to Syria and Lebanon following the military coup in 1980, including Öcalan.[14] By 1984, the PKK revived its violent attacks in the southeast region of Turkey with the goal of polarizing Kurdish and Turkish populations by targeting military and economic centers along with civilians. The PKK sought to weaken the state by denying it the ability to protect its citizens and provide public services. Consequently, the PKK focused its efforts on disrupting infrastructure and tourism. According to the U.S. State Department, in 1993, the PKK kidnapped thirteen tourists and bombed hotels, restaurants, and tourist sites. The PKK's military targets included ambushing patrols and targeting gendarmerie stations, thereby demonstrating that in southeastern Turkey, the PKK, not the Turkish government, was in control. Additionally, the PKK targeted civilians, not to gain support, but to frighten them into submission. From 1987 to 1990, PKK strategy included burning villages, although Öcalan eventually halted these extremist and unpopular practices. Nonetheless, violence increased from May 1993 to October 1994 resulting in 1,600 deaths.[15]

The PKK also targeted schools in the southeast region, which the organization perceived as a mechanism through which to assimilate the Kurdish population. Between 1984 and 1994, a Turkish Human Rights Foundation report claimed that 128 teachers had been killed, mostly at the hands of the PKK. According to the Turkish Minister of the Interior 5,210 schools closed (the PKK burned 192 of these schools) in the eastern and southeastern sections of Turkey between 1992 and 1994 due to security problems. After the murder of ten teachers in 1994, the PKK announced that only those teachers sanctioned by the PKK could teach.[16]

The state gave the Turkish military *carte blanche* to eliminate terrorism, and by the spring of 1994, the PKK was effectively weakened.[17] But in February 1999, Turkey's Kurdish issue was reinvigorated on both a domestic and international level with Öcalan's seizure in Italy. Öcalan, who had established a base in Syria, was forced to flee that country after Turkey threatened to invade Syria to curtail PKK attacks into its territory. Öcalan was denied asylum in Russia, Belgium, and the Netherlands. Finally, he went to Italy, but was pressured by the Italians to leave. Finally, the Turks apprehended Öcalan on February 16, 1999 in Nairobi, Kenya, under the auspices of the Greek Embassy.[18]

DEMOCRATIZATION

After Atatürk's death in November 1938, the cult of his personality grew. In fact, the Republican People's Party (RPP)[19] declared him the "eternal party chairman."[20] His legacy continued, notably his paradoxical authoritarianism that included his vision of a modern, secular, and democratic Turkey.

During the elections of 1950, the prospects for democracy broadened when Atatürk's successor, Ismet Inönü, stepped aside after the Democratic Party (DP) took 408 seats in the national assembly compared to the RPP's sixty-nine. Unfortunately, the DP, charged with repression of the opposition and economic mismanagement, was removed as the ruling party by a military coup in 1960.[21]

As such, to understand Turkish politics, it is crucial to grasp the pervasiveness of the military in politics and society. For Atatürk, the military was to serve as the "guardian of the reforming ideals of his regime."[22] The military is a body autonomous from politics and has, following several coups, strengthened its role in the political system. Turkey has had its democratic process interrupted three times by military coups in 1960, from 1971 to1973, and from 1980 to 1983.[23] Additionally, the military interfered with the political process in 1997 causing the government's collapse in what scholar Cengiz Çandar refers to as a "postmodern coup" and what many Turks refer to as the "February 28 Process."[24]

The results of the 1960 and 1980 coups produced both new constitutions and institutions. Although the military greatly influenced the new constitutions, its intention was not to create a military regime, but rather to restore democracy, albeit with a stronger role for the military in politics. For instance, the military was rewarded for its role in the restoration of democracy with a guarantee of "exit rewards" consisting of immunity from investigation and manipulation of the electoral system.[25]

After democracy was restored in 1961, the new Justice Party won the elections, but did not maintain a clear majority. Instability and ineffective control ensued precipitating the 1971 military intervention. Although the military did not dissolve the Grand National Assembly, it ruled from behind the scenes. During the March 12, 1970 coup, the military forced the government to resign in order to replace the prime minister with one that met their approval.[26] The following statement was issued by memorandum by the military:

> The Parliament and the Government, through their sustained policies, views and actions, have driven our country into anarchy, fratricidal strife, and social and economic unrest. They have caused the public to lose all hope of rising to the level of contemporary civilization, which was set for us by Atatürk.[27]

As a result, the government led by Suleyman Demirel resigned, and Nihat Erim formed a new government. From 1971 to 1973, the military revised the constitution prescribing more executive authority and fewer civil liberties.[28]

After almost a decade of continuous parliamentary rule, in 1980, the military intervened due to continued ineffective governance and anarchy. There were significant political struggles between Demirel's Justice Party and Bulent Ecevit's RPP, stifling the political process. Furthermore, left and right extremist groups conducted large-scale political violence, and the major political parties were accusing each other of not equitably applying rule of law to these groups. General Kenan Evren, the chief planner of the 1980 intervention, wanted a more permanent role for the military in politics.

The nature of civil-military relations transformed significantly following the 1980 coup solidifying a major role for the military in politics and granting the executive enhanced veto power on constitutional amendments proposed by the parliament.[29] The National Security Council (NSC) was established and dominated by five high-ranking military generals. Among its powers to oversee the political process, this council had the authority to screen candidates for office. According to Cengiz Çandar, the NSC "is the most important institutional channel through which the military can exert its political authority."[30] The military's institutional restructuring reflected a distrust of the "national will" in the form of elected assemblies, political parties, and other civil society institutions. Clearly after the 1980 military coup, the executive role was strengthened with General Evren serving as President for the next 7 years.[31]

Moreover, the NSC remained the most significant institution in Turkish politics. Robert Kaplan recounts a discussion with a foreign diplomat who revealed that the Turkish General Staff developed foreign policy, not the Foreign Ministry.[32] Examination of the NSC reveals the pervasive influence of the military on the political process. The NSC is comprised of the president, who serves as Chair, and council members including the chief of staff, commanders of the Army, Air Force, Navy, and Gendarmerie, the prime minister; the ministers of foreign affairs, interior, and defense, the director of National Intelligence, and, the secretary general of the Council, who is a military general.

The power of the NSC continued to grow after its establishment in 1980 and it effectively ousted the Erbakan government on February 28, 1997. In fact, the military formed the Western Study Group (WSG), charged with investigating "public enemies" and conducting campaigns to discredit people or organizations distasteful to the military.[33] Mesut Yilmaz, who came to power after Erbakan's removal, attempted to disband the WSG, but was unable to combat the political clout of the military.[34]

The military's ouster of the Necmettin Erbakan government is instructive of the military's role as "guardian of the state." The Refah (Welfare) party was, in a sense, a vestige of the Pro-Islamic National Salvation party of the 1970s. Erbakan had led that party, but was banned from government subsequent to the 1980 military coup. In 1987, Erbakan reentered politics to head the Refah party, which has been described as "a party of Muslim values rather than an 'Islamic' party."[35] The party's critics claimed its goals as the implementation of Sharia or Islamic law on the country. By 1994,

Refah had begun to make real gains during municipal elections and had captured 22 percent of the votes in the general elections.

To prevent Refah from gaining real power, the True Path Party formed a shaky coalition with the center-right Motherland Party. Yet, when this government collapsed in 1996, the True Path Party invited Refah to form a government leading to Erbakan's eventual prime ministerial position. Erbakan's initial policies reflected his desire to strengthen the country's Muslim values. He visited numerous Muslim countries including Iran and Libya causing speculation about his true intentions. At the time, the United States was debating the Iran–Libya Sanctions Act, which recommended trade restrictions on investments in Iran or Libya's energy sector. Despite U.S. pressure on Turkey to resist buying natural gas from Iran, Erbakan finalized a deal worth billions of dollars with Iran. The Welfare Party's appeal stemmed from the changing dynamics within Turkish society. Globalization and the resultant culture, coupled with economic dislocations that it engendered, broadened Refah's allure. With increased urbanization and the prior government's inability to effectively address labor and social issues, Refah's platforms gained momentum.[36]

The military quickly unleashed a propaganda war discrediting Refah and Erbakan and associating the party with "fundamentalism." Through the West Working Group, established to monitor religious extremist activity, the military exerted intense pressure on Erbakan who resigned on June 18, 1997.[37] Additionally, the war against Rafah's credibility as a legitimate party in the Turkish system continued. On January 16, 1998, the party was banned for breaching Articles 68 and 69 of the Turkish constitution, which require parties to uphold secularism.[38] Erbakan was barred from politics for 5 years along with other members of the party.

Outside observers were unmistakably concerned about the future of Turkish pluralist politics. The military reintroduced a period of "radical secularism" that had been muted following the coup in 1980.[39] Although still a strong, centralized state steeped in Kemalist ideology, the period from 1980 to 1997, "allowed for negotiation, compromise, and reconciliation between Turkey's political Islamists and the establishment."[40] This was exhibited by the emergence of the Refah Party and the popularity of its platform espousing a just social and economic order.[41] Clearly, by 1997, the military was alarmed by the expansion of the "Muslim environment" and set out to reinvigorate and highlight the prevalence of a strong, centralized, and highly secular state. The religious schools training prayer leaders were eliminated and schools instituted expanded programs emphasizing secularism.[42]

The elites fostered a clear nexus between what they deemed Islamic fundamentalism and terrorism. Similar to the principles guiding policymaking with regards to Islamists, Turkish Kurdish policy has been produced by an elite committed to a unitary state with a single national identity. For the most part, the Turkish elite discounts diversity and alternative identities. The interventionist military bolstered by a constrained media has muted intellectuals, the growth of civil society, and had thus fostered the "Kemalist consensus."[43]

Interestingly, this consensus had been perpetuated throughout the Turkish public. Even within mainstream Turkish public opinion, the Kurdish issue was obfuscated. For many years, the state denied the idea of a distinct Kurdish identity as Kurds were referred to as "mountain Turks" and their language as a Turkish dialect. In fact, the state ridiculed Kurdish demands for linguistic rights because it deemed the Kurdish language as an inferior vehicle for communication. Even those Kurds who peacefully sought language rights or state recognition of their identity were labeled as traitors, separatists, or terrorists. Barkey and Fuller claim that "the state has created for itself one of the single biggest obstacles to future dialogue: the formation of public opinion that finds the concept of 'Kurdish identity' absurd, unnecessary, and subversive, and that all who talk about Kurdish rights are terrorists and enemies of the nation."[44] By classifying all political activity as terrorism, opportunities for political dialogue were stifled and real grievances disregarded. In Spain, the government did not associate terrorist activities with the entire ethnic population and instead addressed genuine grievances within the political system. ETA was politically marginalized with the government deliberately and clearly differentiating between the terrorist organization and the Basque ethnic community.

Furthermore, a Turkish ban on ethnically based parties muffled Kurdish voices and offered few avenues to air discontent. From the 1950 multiparty elections, all parties espousing a Kurdish agenda were closed, usually with their leaders facing prosecution. By not offering the Kurds an opportunity in the political process to propel their issues to the forefront, the Kurds saw only assimilation or extrapolitical activities as options for political gain.

As such, the PKK emerged to give Kurds an avenue for political, yet violent expression. Though on close inspection, PKK goals were complex espousing alternatively Marxism, nationalism, or both.[45] Abdullah Öcalan adopted a Maoist strategy, and the idea of a Kurdistan was a means to an end, that being a base from which to promote socialism regionally and globally. This agenda did not truly represent the majority of the Kurdish people. Initially, the PKK included non-Kurds and had difficulty recruiting Kurds. Öcalan's message fluctuated between the promotion of socialism and the promotion of nationalism. When nationalism spurred on the cause, then Öcalan incorporated it into his message. In 1977, Öcalan connected the PKK's goals and those of other Kurdish movements such as Masoud Barzani's Kurdistan Democratic Party (KDP), one of two main Kurdish parties in Iraq.[46] They formed an alliance that crumbled when the PKK adopted its violent tactics in 1984. In 1989, the PKK began to incorporate Islamic phrases in the PKK literature.[47]

For many reasons, Öcalan never seemed to truly represent the interests of a majority of Turkish Kurds. For starters, PKK leftist ideology lost its popularity after the fall of the Soviet Union communist regime. Moreover, the Kurds became increasingly more geographically dispersed disrupting the PKK's ability to concentrate its efforts. The PKK discovered that to control particular areas in the southeast, it had to co-opt tribal leaders, which gave the PKK a stake in tribal society. Paramount, however, was the fact that many Kurds did not support the separatist concept.[48] Öcalan himself recanted the PKK's program after his incarceration recognizing that the organization "should have taken into account the development the country had undergone both when it was founded and in the 1990s."[49]

The lack of Turkish Kurdish support for the PKK seems well substantiated. A leading Kurd in exile, Kerim Yildiz of the Kurdish Human Rights Project, stated that Kurdish desires are unclear because free speech is squelched. According to Yildiz, Kurds reject the creation of a separate state due to historical links to the country. Additionally, Yildiz advocated some form of federation or autonomy in the southeast province.[50] As recently as March 2001, a *New York Times* article confirmed that "most Kurds say they want nothing more than the right to observe their Kurdish heritage within Turkey."[51] Nevertheless, four provinces within southeastern Turkey remained under emergency rule even after PKK laid down its arms.[52] The emergency regulations were eventually lifted, although problems remained with the return migration of villagers who had been forced to leave.[53]

In a 1993 poll conducted in Istanbul, among those who self-identified as Kurds, almost half felt that the PKK was a "terrorist organization" and 17 percent said that it was possible that the PKK was a "terrorist organization." Of the 13.3 percent who identified themselves as having Kurdish roots, 3.7 percent considered themselves Turks and only 3.9 percent considered themselves Kurds. Seventy-eight percent did not want a separate state; instead, they wanted to live with Turks. Interestingly, those Kurds who self-identified as Turks were economically better off than those who considered themselves Kurds.[54]

Although the PKK did not elicit potent internal support, it appealed to the international community. The PKK depended on the Kurdish Diaspora in Western Europe as well as on the cooperation of other states in the region. According to Kemal Kirişci and Gareth Winrow, "The PKK leadership was correct to remark that violence made 'the world accept the existence of a Kurdish question.'"[55] President Mitterand's wife even addressed him as "Dear President Öcalan" in a 1998 letter. She ended it with: "[R]est assured, Abdullah, that I am committed to be beside you in the bid for peace. Sincerely yours, Danielle Mitterand."[56] Estimates indicate that the PKK received from $200 million to $500 million annually from Kurds living in Western European and from crime networks in Germany, Switzerland,

France, Scandinavia, and the Benelux countries. Paradoxically, this leftist and global support highlights the PKK's weakness; the organization never really represented the Kurds in Turkey.[57] Clearly, while the Turkish government took drastic means to wipe out the PKK, it neglected the Kurdish issue because it erroneously linked PKK goals with the plight of the Kurds. The Turkish approach contrasts significantly with the Spanish government's perception of ETA and the Basque community, in which the government used restraint and differentiated between the ethnic community and the terrorist organization.

In 1987, Turkey deployed its forces in southeastern Turkey, declaring a state of emergency, a move that would be repeated twenty-six times by March 1996. The state of emergency allows civilian governors to exercise "certain quasi-martial law powers, including restrictions on the press and removal from the area of persons whose activities are believed inimical to public order."[58] These actions suspended the application of the European Convention on Human Rights (ECHR) in those regions of Turkey and "curbed the application of Turkey's emerging political liberalization process in the region."[59]

The Anti-Terror Law of April 1991, targeted domestic security challenges, specifically PKK terrorism including "actions involving repression, violence and force, or the threat to use force, by one or several persons belonging to an organization with the aim of changing the characteristics of the Turkish Republic including its political, legal, social, secular and economic system."[60] Although this law was passed in 1991 to curb PKK activity, it fostered an environment marked by human rights abuses. By the end of 1994, violations of the Anti-Terror Law resulted in detention for ninety-five intellectuals, politicians, and academics.[61] In 1998, a Turkish journalist, Ragip Duran, was imprisoned for publishing an article that was sympathetic to Abdullah Öcalan. According to Duran, there are several subjects that are considered unmentionables in the Turkish press including the notion that Kurds are a distinct ethnic group and that Islam continues to play a role in Turkish society. Moreover, the discussion of the military's role in Turkish society is off-limit for open debate.[62] In July 2005, Turkey began proceedings to amend the antiterror law in the face of increased PKK attacks. Additionally, local groups with professed links to Al-Qaida have executed suicide bombings in Istanbul in 2003 where sixty-three people were killed.[63] Turkish officials are exploring the antiterror laws of other European countries such as Spain and France to modify their existing one.

Despite many setbacks for the Kurdish population, in 1991, President Turget Özal rescinded a law that prohibited the use of the Kurdish language. In 1992, Turkey passed a law, known as the Code of Criminal Trial Procedures (CMUK), which attempted to conform to international standards regarding arrests, detention periods, and interrogations.[64] A U.S. State Department Human Rights Report in 1996 noted that the human rights situation in Turkey improved in some regions, but significant problems remained. Although CMUK provided a foundation for important political changes, it did "not apply equally to the State Security Courts, to so-called 'terrorist' crimes, or to the state of emergency area of the Southeast."[65]

President Özal, who claimed Kurdish roots, took the first steps to acknowledge and address the Kurdish issue. Unfortunately, he died in 1993, and his successor, Süleyman Demirel reversed Özal's reforms. President Demirel viewed the Kurdish issue solely through the terrorist prism. In 1996, when Prime Minister Erbakan tried to establish an indirect dialogue with the PKK to convince the organization to cease violent attacks, Demirel blocked his efforts. Prime Minister Çiller also embraced hard-line policies, and she too equated the Kurdish issue with terrorism. Kurdish policy was reduced to PKK elimination, body counts, and cross-border raids. Çiller implemented sufficient cosmetic reforms, however, to appease the EU and the United States to ensure Turkey's accession to the European Customs Union. By 1995, the party apparatus was defunct, and Çiller replaced many party members with her loyalists. Because these loyalists lacked constituencies, they were beholden to her. Consequently many politicians perceived the state as more powerful than the elected government.[66]

Çiller's True Path Party's (DYP) coalition with the Refah Party in 1996 resulting in Erbakan's rise to prime minister haunted her in the 1999 elections. Unmistakably distrusted by the virulently secular elite, the DYP, which continued its association as an electoral partner of one of the Islamist parties in 1999, was not permitted to form a government. The April 1999 elections produced a coalition of the Democratic Left Party (DSP) and the right-wing Nationalist Action Party (MHP), with Bülent Ecevit from the DSP emerging as the prime minister. The Virtue Party (successor of the Refah Party), Motherland Party (center-right) and the True Path Party suffered defeat and garnered fewer votes than the previous election. Both the Republicans People's Party (Atatürk's party) and the People's Democracy Party (HADEP) failed to meet the 10 percent threshold nationwide.[67] Consequently, a coalition government was formed by the DSP, MHP, and Motherland parties, shifting politics from the center.[68]

During the 1999 elections, voters registered their dissatisfaction with the status quo and government corruption. Yet even after the elections, continued economic difficulties challenged Ecevit's credibility.[69] According to a 2001 poll, six in ten Turks blamed Ecevit (21 percent) or the government (42 percent) for Turkey's problematic economic conditions. Seventy-three percent of people surveyed had little or no confidence in the government's ability to address the problems. Even more sobering, 87 percent were dissatisfied with how the coalition was governing and 87 percent were dissatisfied with Ecevit. Furthermore, the polls indicated that 53 percent opposed any military intervention to change the government even if the politicians could not effectively solve Turkey's economic problems.[70]

During the November 2002 elections, the Justice and Development Party (AKP), an Islamic party, was elected with 34.3 percent of the national vote, although the party gained 359 seats in the 555-member parliament, an overwhelming majority. The only other party to clear the 10 percent minimum proportion in the national vote to gain parliamentary seats was the Republicans People's Party with 19 percent of the vote. Despite its Islamic proclivities, the AKP was able to play upon the social and economic grievances of a variety of groups and meld both religious and secular business associations to obtain electoral support.[71] The new ruling party desired to strengthen its strategic partnership with the United States and facilitate Turkey's EU membership. Initially, AKP party leader and former mayor of Istanbul, Recep Tayyip Erdogan, was barred from assuming the prime ministerial position due to a previous conviction for "inciting hatred based on religion."[72] Yet in 2003, Turkey's Constitutional Court lifted the ban on Erbakan's participation in politics and after Abdullah Gül, the acting prime minister stepped down, Erdogan assumed that key position.

Erdogan's party has implemented a "silent revolution" against what scholar Ahmet Insel calls the September 12 regime.[73] The constitutional changes following the 1980 coup empowered the military rulers and excluded voices from the parliament by implementing a 10 percent minimum threshold for representation in parliament. The military regime was obsessed with the maintenance of stability, referring "to a state of immobility in which the institutions of the September 12 regime and the hierarchy among them would not be upset."[74] Since political and cultural channels were ostensibly shut to society following the 1980 coup, the state allowed economic liberalization, which fostered the emergence of a new middle class whose support fell behind the AKP in 2002.[75]

Under Erdogan, significant changes have been implemented with the potential to transform the quality of Turkish democracy by enhancing individual rights vis-à-vis a potent state. In 2003, the Right to Information Law was passed allowing access to government documents, a new penal code was enacted modifying laws pertaining to women and children, and power was granted to the Court of Auditors to investigate the military.[76]

With regard to the Kurdish issue, as recently as 1998, the Constitutional Court banned the Democratic Mass Party, which represented the Kurdish cause, rejected violence and sought a peaceful and democratic process to address the Kurdish problem.[77] When Öcalan was captured in 1999, he renounced separatism and eventually threw his support behind the pro-Kurdish Democratic People's Party (DEHAP), which was established in 1998.[78] By 2002, DEHAP was able to run and campaign freely for election.[79] Many Kurds have modified their earlier views that Kurdish autonomy would best serve their interests and have worked toward a more inclusive, multicultural, state.[80]

In August 2005, Prime Minister Erdogan visited portions of Southeast Turkey when PKK violence reemerged. Although there had been a sharp decrease in violence following Öcalan's arrest in 1999, the southeast region was reeling from high unemployment, poverty, and the ruinous vestiges of 15 years of violence. Kurdish frustration ran high directed specifically at what they viewed as the government's disinterest in the region. Erdogan's visit raised hope that the government would focus on the economic and political plight of the Kurds. During the visit, the prime minister said that the government would need to solve the Kurdish issues through democratization.[81] Subsequent to the visit, the PKK issued an order to the rebels to implement a ceasefire as they viewed the prime minister's remarks as "conciliatory."[82] The reemergence of PKK violence will test the AKP government and its commitment to the implementation of liberal democratic values within its society.[83]

COOPERATION

Undoubtedly for Turkey, an important element in combating terrorism is to strengthen liberal democratic values to gain legitimacy with the disaffected groups within its population. Assessing the influence of cooperation on political culture shifts is complex. The effect of the December 1999 EU decision at the Helsinki summit approving Turkey's candidacy for EU membership has clearly effected domestic politics in Turkey. The EU requires states to meet specific internal criteria before negotiations can occur. As such, pressure to reform and create a convergence of political culture is high on the EU agenda.

Turkey has sought to be part of the European organization since 1959 when it applied for membership in the European Economic Community. In 1963, Turkey signed an associate agreement that granted it special connections to the organization, but the question of whether or not it would become a full member was always dubious. Turkey's invasion of Cyprus in 1974, coupled with its inability to settle the dispute politically, was a setback for Turkey's inclusion into the European club.[84] A series of other important events during the 1980s hampered Turkey's integration process. When, in 1981, Greece was admitted to the EC, Turkey's relations with Europe became even more strained. This increased tension was due to both Greece's accession to the EEC along with Turkey's domestic strife in the form of a military coup in 1980. By 1984, the PKK had been increasing its violent attack precipitating harsh military reprisals by the Turks. Europe viewed these events as a retreat from European values.[85]

Although Turkey was a member of NATO, "all were members of a 'security community', they were not all members of the same 'value community'. Turkish political culture did not share the norms of its alliance partners."[86] Additionally, Turkey witnessed the acceptance of post-communist states into

the EU, due partially to the factor of geography. For the EU, the incorporation of Turkey requires a reassessment of the boundaries of Europe.[87] Furthermore, the EU's stress on the quality of democracy has placed Turkey's
domestic political system under harsh scrutiny and has forced some tangible changes. The Helsinki summit hastened significant political changes
within the Turkish domestic sphere. Additionally, Turkish antireformists
reassessed their objection to Turkey's entrance into the EU due to severe
economic hardships during the period from 2000 to 2001. Many argued
that membership in the EU would increase economic and material profits
for Turkey.[88]

Several Turkish governments put EU membership as a clear priority. Prime
Minister Çiller implemented liberalizing measures to assure Turkey's entry
into the European Customs Union. Indeed, with the arrest and conviction
of Öcalan in 1999, Turkey has delayed his death sentence based on the
European Court of Human Rights' stance on capital punishment. Turkey's
future EU membership rests on Turkey's overall record of human rights, and
the Öcalan case serves as a key measuring stick for that record.[89]

Turkey's death penalty hindered cooperation among states as some European states refuse to extradite criminals to Turkey.[90] Yet by 2003, Turkey
implemented significant domestic policy modification including increased
cultural rights for minorities and the elimination of the death penalty.[91] As
the Spanish case revealed, common extradition and asylum policies among
states are key to combating transnational terrorist activity. The price for cooperation seems to be a consensus on basic values and a common perspective
on what constitutes terrorism. The EU's "post-Westphalian" nature is the
price for membership.[92] In other words, the EU greatly influences and, at
times, directs domestic policies of its members. As Buzan and Dietz explains,
"Part of the price to be paid even for partial association with an international organization such as the EU is tolerance of a high level of mutual
interference in domestic affairs, aimed at harmonizing a wide range of legal,
moral, and institutional practices."[93] The high value that the EU places on
the convergence of values has pressured Turkey to reconsider some of its
key policies.

This harmonization of practices and values is an arduous task. Subsequent
to the EU announcement of Turkey's candidacy, Foreign Minister Ismail
Cem of the Democratic Left Party claimed that "each Turkish citizen should
be able to speak his or her mother tongue on television."[94] His statement
evoked visceral and harsh responses from some critics. Enis Oksuz of the
Nationalist Movement Party shot back that "One nation can have only one
official language."[95] Although President Demirel argued that Turkey must
respect individual rights, the granting of collective rights would "encourage
tribalism and open the way for separatist violence and terrorism."[96] Despite
continued internal debate over the issue of cultural rights, Turkey's bid for
EU membership has appealed to Turkish Kurds, Islamists, democrats, and

human rights activists who posit that membership will lead to increased democratization, and economic prosperity.[97]

Turkey has made some modest changes with regard to the use of the Kurdish language and its dialects. Under EU pressure to reform, Turkey modified its law in 2002 to allow limited Kurdish language education. Yet Kurdish is taught only in private schools, most of which are too expensive for the majority of Kurds to afford. In 2005, eight private schools teaching the Kurdish languages were closed. Critics of the government's cosmetic reform have argued that the Kurdish language should be taught in state schools with Turkish.[98] Additionally, in 2002, parliament approved the use of Kurdish on state-run television for a half hour a week. Despite the law's limitations, the acceptance by the Grand National Assembly to allow the broadcast of languages other than Turkish is a positive move.[99] The gradual removal of emergency law in thirteen Kurdish-populated provinces reflected Turkey's acquiescence to EU demands for reform.[100]

The most tangible change signaling a significant political culture shift in Turkey was its compliance with the ECHR's ban on capital punishment concerning Öcalan. Interestingly, the Öcalan incident indirectly impacted Greece as well. Since Öcalan's arrest, although initially strained because of the incident, relations between Turkey and Greece improved. Greece's initial noncooperation with Turkey's pursuit of Öcalan and actual complicity with Öcalan's escape resulted in the resignation of some of Greece's hard-line ministers. More liberal politicians replaced them, including Foreign Minister George Papandreou, who played a pivotal role in reversing Greece's objection to Turkey's future membership in the EU. The year 2000 marked the first time in 40 years that the Foreign ministers of both countries visited each other's state.[101]

Papandreou linked Greece's long-term interests with Turkish democracy and prosperity via the EU. Greece's stance influenced other leaders' stances concerning Turkey's EU membership. Prior to Greece's reversal, many European states were adamant about blocking Turkey's membership in the EU. Premier Jean-Claude Junker, the host at the 1997 EU summit in Luxembourg, said that he would not "sit at the same table with a bunch of torturers."[102] Helmut Kohl once declared the EU as "a Christian club."[103] Valery Giscard d'Estaing, Chairman of the EU's federal constitution project and former president of France, remarked that Turkey had no place in the EU because of its different culture, its "way of life."[104] Despite these views, Cengiz Çandar and Graham Fuller believe that "Turkey's Islamic identity will not, in the long run, hinder Turkey's entry into the EU, for it will be the very presence of Turkey that will demonstrate that Europe truly embraces universal values above narrow Christian or European ones."[105]

A key query emerges from the debate on whether or not Turkey should be admitted into the EU. How will Turkey challenge the idea that a European identity is necessary to be part of the EU? Barry Buzan and

Thomas Dietz pose a similar question: "If Turkey meets the criteria, then why not North Africa, Russia, or Central Asia?"[106] In 1986, Morocco's application to the EU was denied clearly because it was a non-European nation. Several European leaders anticipate membership for Turkey in the organization. British Prime Minister Tony Blair viewed the December 1999 decision as "important for Europe, for Turkey, and the stability and security for our part of the world."[107] German Chancellor, Gerhard Schroeder and U.S. President Bill Clinton held that Turkey's membership would benefit both Turkey and the EU and therefore should not be excluded from the organization.[108]

Although there may be movement in terms of political culture shifts for Turkey, it has been at best incremental and insufficiently institutionalized with the presence of the NSC. Likewise, although EU members are beginning to see Turkey within the European prism, without genuine political reform, these views may be ephemeral. Turkey was a crucial U.S. strategic ally throughout the cold war and although its significance to the United States waned after the demise of the Soviet Union, it has reemerged as an important partner in the war against terror since the catastrophic events of September 11. As such, the United States has continued to pressure Europe into accepting Turkey as a member of the EU.

From the U.S. perspective, the admittance of a Muslim country would have profound ramifications on regional and security interests.[109] For many years, the United States was interested in anchoring "Turkey firmly to the West by integrating it into its institutional settings." NATO was one of the key institutions; the EC/EU was another.[110] Turkey represents a pro-Western, predominantly Muslim state in an unstable region with the potential to transition into a strong and consolidated democracy.

U.S. pressure, however, has limited effectiveness on whether or not Europe will acknowledge Turkey as a member. Constraints on American influence regarding the EU stem from an American perspective more concerned with security benefits attained by Turkey's membership in the EU rather than Turkey's "democratic deficits."[111] The contrasting EU and U.S. perspectives on the Middle East in general emanate from differing geographical prisms coupled with alternative concerns and interests. According to Volker Perthes, "divergent priorities and different perceptions of threats distinguish policymaking on either side of the Atlantic."[112] For the United States, maintaining the security of Israel and unfettered access to oil have remained key interests in the Middle East and although these objectives do not necessarily conflict with Europe's goal of regional stability, pursuit of them has led to dissimilar approaches to policy. The EU's *raison d'être* is the rule of law and a commitment to common institutions, in conjunction with the establishment of interdependencies. Unmistakably, and clearly evident with the U.S. invasion of Iraq in March 2003, a more idealistic European perspective counters the *realpolitik* guiding U.S. policy in the Middle East. Viewing the issue through the European lens, Turkey must undertake profound and significant political reform to acquire the key to the EU door.

An example of the limits of U.S. power was the 2002 Copenhagen summit where a date was set for December 2004 to decide when negotiations would begin for Turkish accession to the Union. Clearly, both Turkey and the United States desired an expedited process and were dissatisfied with the distant date. This frustration manifested itself with the AKP government's weakened determination to counter its anti-EU coalition, which viewed EU demands as infringing upon Turkey's sovereignty.[113]

Interestingly, the U.S. invasion of Iraq in March 2003 to overthrow Saddam Hussein's regime, exacerbated tensions and rifts between the United States and Europe and within the EU itself. But the invasion also impacted upon Turkish membership in the EU. In the months before the invasion, the United States in its quest to secure support and bases in Turkey intensified U.S. lobbying for Turkish membership to the EU.[114] Therefore, when the Turkish parliament denied the United States access to bases on its territory from which to launch the war, the Bush administration was stunned.

Although Turkey recognized the importance of cooperating with the United States in the war on terror, it was reluctant to support the American invasion of Iraq, a conflict that had the potential to destabilize its own country. During the first Gulf War in 1991, Turkey suffered economic and political dislocations due to its compliance with a U.S. request to prevent Iraqi oil flowing through its pipelines and due to migrations from Iraq's Northern region. As such, the war was highly unpopular with the Turkish population. Nevertheless, Prime Minister Erdogan signaled the United States that the Grand National Assembly would pass a resolution allowing the United States use of Turkish bases and air space.[115]

However, Turkish support for the American invasion was unpopular in Turkey because of some anticipated a resurgence of PKK terrorist activities as a result of U.S. activities and the potential creation of an independent Kurdistan in Northern Iraq. Following the Gulf War in 1991, the creation of a semiautonomous Kurdistan complicated matters for the Turks. Over 5000 PKK fighters found refuge in the mountainous region over the Iraqi–Turkish border and attacked Turkish targets from their sanctuary, inviting cross-border retaliation from the Turkish military. For years, the PKK had been operating out of Iraqi Kurdish territory, despite the protests of several Iraqi Kurdish factions. In 1995, Öcalan attacked the Iraqi Kurdish Democratic Party led by Massoud Barzani for supporting Turkey against the PKK.[116] Turkey continued reprisal operations in Iraqi Kurdish territory and prior to the U.S. invasion of Iraq in 2003, Europe and the United States warned an anxious Turkey to refrain from its cross-border operations in Iraq. Under intensive pressure, Turkey has restrained its activities in northern Iraq.

Despite the reemergence of PKK violence in June 2004, the PKK lacks support from the Kurdish population in Turkey who are indisposed to return to the violent days of the 1980s and 1990s.[117] Apparently, the PKK's motive for its renewed violence is to convince the Turkish government to grant amnesty to PKK fighters who are operating out of Iraq.[118] Prime Minister Erdogan has refused this request; however, the Turkish government, eager to gain EU membership, has continued political reform to grant the Kurds cultural rights.[119]

IMPLICATIONS

Although some scholars and policymakers may refer to Turkey as a democracy, this study demonstrates that it has not yet met the criteria to be labeled a liberal democracy. According to Samuel Huntington, a country is considered as having a consolidated democracy after two consecutive transformations in government through fair elections.[120] Although this has occurred in Turkey, the role of the military in politics, the sketchy record on minority rights, and the focus on statist policies are factors that affect the quality of Turkey's democracy and consequently its ability to combat terrorism effectively by garnering legitimacy from its minority ethnic group. Furthermore, the pervasiveness of the Kemalist ideology, although altered over time, still informs the political culture of many in Turkish society. The Kemalist tendencies reflect "an ambivalent attitude toward the notion of popular legitimacy."[121] Clearly, this influences the quality of Turkish democracy.

In contrast to Spain's approach to democratization, Turkey's political development has not replicated similar inclusive political measures. Elements in Turkey's political culture, including the Kemalist tradition, have led to political intransigence on the part of the elite. According to some scholars, "Turkish identity has become more homogenous; as such it carries the risk of growing less civic and more ethnic in nature."[122] Paradoxically, the state's deliberate assimilation policies that squelched diversity to create a civic political community have inadvertently fostered a backlash. Forced homogenization of a diverse populace, has come at a "steep cultural cost."[123] Turkey runs the risk of experiencing the same fate as many of its Balkan neighbors.

Whereas Spain's policies acknowledged, to some degree, overlapping political communities on a domestic and European level, Turkey has viewed similar acceptance of these intertwined identities as threatening. Spain institutionalized its recognition by sanctioning ethnically based political parties with the ability to influence the governing coalition by articulating interests of their constituents. Consequently, Spaniards perceived participation to be significant and altering. Unfortunately for Kurds, for many years, Turkey banned ethnically based political parties and prohibited public discourse concerning Kurdish issues. Even though a transformation appears underway, not all in the Turkish government have embraced the concept of expanded cultural rights.

Several factors posit well for the Turkish state's ability to garner legitimacy from most elements of its population, strengthen its democracy, and decrease the appeal of terrorist groups. First, PKK violence frustrated a majority of Turkish Kurds who suffered at the hands of both the Turkish military and the PKK. The violent tactics by the PKK and the Turkish state cost both groups internal legitimacy. Insufficient state restraint, as evidenced by harsh military operations, fostered international sympathy for the PKK and elevated the Kurdish plight to international attention. Turkey's initial reluctance to recognize the cultural rights of minority groups served as a significant source of tension in Turkey's bid for EU membership and underscores the potential for global influence on a state's domestic politics. Turkey retains an opportunity to gain support from the Turkish Kurds by implementing genuine political reform and executing a proportionate response to PKK terrorism. Furthermore, most Kurds reject separatism and desire full incorporation in Turkish political and cultural society. Looking to Spain for an example, combined restraint and reconciliation with its ethnic minority allowed Spain to lessen support for ETA.

With the disappearance of the cold war framework, which included alliances that constrained and prevented superpower confrontations, international organizations such as the EU are imposing restrictions impacting both the domestic and the international arena. These checks are designed to foster interstate cooperation vis-à-vis transnational threats. Fragmegration has ushered in an innovative legitimacy formula for states. Not only must states garner legitimacy from their populations, but they must also gain support from the international community. Turkey discovered that it is too costly and ultimately ineffective to fight transnational terrorism alone. But cooperation comes at the price of convergence and a relinquishing of elements of sovereignty. Turkey required international assistance to arrest Öcalan, but then had to abide by the EU's rejection of Turkey's death penalty. As such, Turkish political culture began its arduous shift to converge its values with those of the European community.

Turkey's bid for EU membership, coupled with the advent of a moderate Islamic party, is propelling Turkey toward more liberal democratic values. The Spanish case exemplified how inclusive political measures under the guidance of enlightened leadership is the state's best strategy in its struggle to win legitimacy and decrease the ability of transnational terrorists to co-opt the population. Under Ataturk's leadership, strong institutions were developed laying the foundation for the development of a democratic political culture. Strengthening democracy not only allows states to win the domestic struggle for legitimacy, but also provides them with the best strategy to acquire international legitimacy allowing them to cooperate effectively and together defeat transnational threats.

CHAPTER 3

THE ETHNIC ALBANIANS IN MACEDONIA: CASE III

INTRODUCTION

Macedonia represents yet another interesting case of "fragmegration." At a National Endowment for Democracy forum, in Berlin Summer 2000, Madeleine Albright discussed the importance of Southeastern Europe, which faces the forces of globalization, fragmentation, and democratization:

> First, democracy may be the most stable form of government in the long run, but in the short run it is among the most fragile. The leaders of new democracies are often required to implement dramatic economic and political reform in countries with little democratic tradition and a host of inherited problems. In such situations, democratic processes must be relentlessly nurtured, for their success cannot be assumed. Second, as democracy has spread, truly global cooperation on its behalf has become possible. However, [globalization] has also made democracy more vulnerable in more places. Southeastern Europe is a prime example. So our new Community of Democracies will begin life with much work to do.[1]

Gjorge Ivanaov further highlights the importance of liberal democracy, namely the significance of substantial democracy over procedural democracy:

> The problem to organize a normal dialogue is within each ethnic group. That is why political leaders should be diplomats rather than pragmatic politicians. They should know how to negotiate and to respect the

counter partner because democracy is not a matter of procedure but it is a substantial as it depends on the participants themselves [note his earlier emphasis on the citizenry]. Procedure is also essential but not as much as it is with homogeneous societies.[2]

This case is somewhat messier than the Spanish case but perhaps similar with Turkey because like Turkey, it is an ongoing case, with Macedonia still democratizing. Its relevance and significance, however, offsets its messiness. One must be careful, however, not to haphazardly apply lessons from one case to another, recognizing that key differences are just as important as discovering important similarities. A key challenge in this case is understanding and analyzing the nature of the National Liberation Army (NLA). The NLA was a recent phenomenon that seemed to have evolved from the Kosovo Liberation Army (KLA).[3] While history and a plethora of information facilitated analysis of ETA and the PKK, quickly changing events and a lack of information make analysis of the NLA difficult. Based on the information available, this case treats the NLA as a transnational, terrorist organization born from the grievances of the Albanian community in Macedonia and possibly from the Albanian experience in Kosovo. Another key distinction among the cases is that Spain has a relatively peaceful neighborhood, Turkey has a conflicting, sometimes warring, neighborhood, while Macedonia has had a warring neighborhood for most of the last decade. Of course, Macedonia's leaders have witnessed an ethnic war at their doorstep, and it appears that their war aversion has played a key role in their search for a political solution.

Nevertheless, there are possibilities of learning lessons through case analysis. The Basque experience in Spain demonstrates how a state can foster the values of a liberal democracy as championed by Diamond, Almond, and Verba, such as tolerance, diversity, competence, trust, basic freedoms, rule of law, protection from political terror, and civilian authority over the military. Spain created a legitimate political community at the national and regional levels that enhanced state legitimacy. The Basque case revealed that fostering an inclusive political regime through power sharing, ethnic parties, leadership, reconciliation, and dialogue bolstered the state's legitimacy in the eyes of all the people. Additionally, the transnational nature of ETA required interstate cooperation, a cooperation that tended to have reflective properties. In other words, the foreign policies of the cooperating states had internal effects, which served to interlock the participating countries' domestic policies as well. To meet the challenge of a common transnational threat of terrorism, the involved states moved closer toward a common political culture that fostered the principles of liberal democracy. Hence, the states successfully won the fight for legitimacy and through cooperation were able to more effectively manage the terrorists' violent tactics. Turkey has not yet achieved a liberal democracy and is still transitioning. The case, however, reveals some promising political culture shifts as a result of the EU's influence, and with Turkey's new leadership, there may be a way ahead for real liberal democratic reform regarding the Kurds. The time frame for the Macedonian case begins with its independence in 1991 and ends during the summer of 2001, with the signing of the Ohrid Framework, which served to end the fighting between Slavs and Albanians in 2001.[4] As this case explores Macedonia's challenges, the question remains: Will the decisions and actions of Macedonia's leaders result in a stable, democratic, Macedonia, thus closely replicating the Spanish example?

BACKGROUND

Macedonia and its surrounding area are so rich in history that it is criminal to attempt to sum it up in a few pages. Kenneth Hill, a former Ambassador to Bulgaria remarked that "the Balkans has more history than it can consume."[5] Consequently, this section will focus on the relevant aspects of Ottoman influence, the Albanian and Macedonian peoples, and the significant events that led to Macedonian independence.

The Ottoman Empire reached its peak during the middle of the sixteenth century. It covered the Balkan Peninsula, Romania, a significant part of Hungary, all of the Aegean Islands, Cyprus, Algeria, Tunisia, Libya, Egypt, Syria, Arabia, Mesopotamia, Asia Minor, Georgia, and Crimea.[6] Interestingly, the Ottomans practiced religious tolerance. With the exception of the recruitment for the Janissaries[7] and early Islamization, for the most part, the Turks conducted very little proselytizing, although many Albanians, Rom, and Slavic-speaking people did convert to Islam.[8] The Turks believed that religion corresponded to nationality, which was the basis of their *millet* system. Non-Moslems throughout the Ottoman Empire enjoyed autonomy and religious freedom as long as they accepted the Sultan's sovereignty. Slavs in Macedonia were ruled by their fellow Slavs, who in turn were subject to Turkish governors. Political rights, however, were reserved for the Turks, but "religious toleration made possible the self perpetuation of national consciousness."[9] Alice Ackerman describes Ottoman rule similarly: "However repressive and exploitive, Turkish rule was also a time of peaceful coexistence. Turks, Slavs, Albanians, Greeks, Vlachs, Jews, and Rom often lived together in multiethnic communities."[10]

As the Ottoman Empire declined during the late nineteenth century, Macedonia became a pawn in the European balance of power politics. After the Turk–Russian War of 1878, Macedonia became part of Bulgaria as a means to counter Austria–Hungary. Four months later at the Congress of Berlin, Macedonia was sent back to the Ottomans. To counter Turkish rule, the Internal Macedonian Revolutionary Organization emerged in 1893.[11] Dimitrija Čupovski, in a 1913 article, describes the 35 years between the Congress of Berlin and the Balkan Wars as "one bloody page of continuous struggle of the Macedonian people for their liberation." Between 1898 and 1903, there were 400 Macedonian versus Turkish confrontations. European press reports confirm the terror and violence conducted by the Turks on Macedonians during the nineteenth century.[12]

The celebrated August 1903 Macedonian uprising lasted 2 months and ended in defeat. However, its significance that is recounted in Macedonia's constitution stems from the fact that 30,000 rebels held off a formidable 300,000 Turkish force and established a democratic commune called the Kruševo Republic. Dr. Nikola Karev was even elected as the Republic's first President.[13] Although this republic only existed for a short time, its government demonstrated tolerance for its Vlach, Bulgarian, Macedonian, and Albanian population. Its Manifesto is unwritten, and therefore, it is not a widely known event.[14] The First Balkan War (1912–1913) resulted in Macedonia and Albania's liberation; however, the Second Balkan War in 1913 ended in Macedonia's division: one-tenth to Bulgaria (Pirin Macedonia), one-half to Greece (Aegean Macedonia), and two-fifths to Serbia (Vardar Macedonia). World War I resulted in another Macedonian division, but by the end of World War II, Macedonia was a recognized republic with a distinct identity and language within the Yugoslav federation.[15]

Albanians' sense of nationalism was the last to develop among the Balkan peoples. In 1878, the Prizin League was established to protect Albanian lands, and it would later challenge Ottoman rule. Albanian guerrilla units emerged in 1906, and in 1908, Albanian leaders adopted the Latin alphabet for the Albanian language. In 1910, the Albanians revolted against the Ottomans in Priština, which spread throughout Kosovo, and in 1912, Albanians took over Skopje. The Treaty of Bucharest in 1913 established the Albanian state; however, almost half the Albanian population lived outside its borders.[16]

After World War I, Vardar Macedonia and Kosovo became part of the Kingdom of the Serbs, Croats, and Slovenes, but Albanians were never recognized as a separate nation. Macedonia was known as South Serbia and Kosovo as Old Serbia. The Serbs suppressed the Albanians, which fostered Albanian armed resistance in the 1920s and raised Albanian national awareness among Albanians. When Tito split from Stalin in 1948, relations between the Albanian state and Yugoslavia worsened, which made life for Yugoslav Albanians unbearable. Yugoslavia closed down Albanian schools and discriminated against them politically, economically, and socially. Albanians began identifying themselves as Turks just to escape this discrimination.[17]

Tito wanted a strong Macedonian identity in the Macedonian republic as a way to contain Albanians within Serbia and Macedonia, and he forfeited an earlier promise of creating a friendly Albanian state that united the entire Albanian population. The ethnic Macedonian population increased within the Yugoslav Republic of Macedonia as Greek Macedonian refugees fled from the Greek Civil War (1946–1949). Macedonia's state apparatus gained more authority when the 1974 Yugoslav constitution decentralized the Party and state administrations' activities for all the republics. Furthermore, the constitution reinforced Tito's contrived borders, which enhanced his own divide and conquer tactics, and the Yugoslav National Army served as the protector of Yugoslavia's unity. Tito's death unraveled all his efforts, and Yugoslavia became subject to eight political parties and eight fiefdoms.[18]

The events of 2001 in Macedonia turned the states,' regions,' and world's attention to the actions of the NLA, a self-appointed protector of Macedonia's ethnic Albanians. The NLA was a transnational organization, with many of its commanders KLA veterans from Kosovo. Some believe that during the Kosovo crisis, ethnic Albanians from Macedonia were among the KLA fighters, including Ali Ahmeti who led the NLA. He was raised in the city of Kičeva, Macedonia, and became politically active while studying at the University of Priština. His participation in a 1981 street demonstration landed him in an Idrižo prison for a year. In 1993, he and Emrush Xhemajli gained the approval of the Nationalist Movement of Kosova to create the KLA. By 1997, Ahmeti was living in Tirana, organizing groups to infiltrate and attack police in Kosovo. At this time, he was assisted by his uncle, Fazli Veliu, and by 1999, they established the NLA. Just as there were reports of arms smuggling from Macedonia to Kosovo during the Kosovo crisis, there were reports of arms smuggling from Kosovo to Macedonia during its crisis in 2001.[19] There were additional reports of other transnational efforts that helped build a clandestine logistics network within Macedonia in support of the KLA.[20]

Western analysts believe that the NLA had 1,500 members. The NLA recognized that any forceful overreaction by Macedonia would play to its advantage. Some observers believe that the NLA's actions were a result of frustration by the ethnic Albanian extremists in Kosovo based on the 2000 elections in Kosovo, which produced a moderate local government under the leadership of Ibrahim Rugova. The confrontations between the state and the NLA took place in Tetovo and other border towns that had mostly ethnic Albanian populations, before spreading to Aračinovo and Kumanovo and finally ending in the summer of 2001.[21]

While this study focuses on ethnic Albanian-ethnic Slav Macedonian relations, it is important to recognize that other inter- and intraethnic tensions existed. Upon Macedonia's independence, Greece withheld recognition of the new state's designation as the Republic of Macedonia. Greece based its nonrecognition policy on three points: first, the kindred community of Macedonians and historical Macedonian regions that extended into Greece could foster future expansionist desires of the new state; secondly, the name, Macedonia, belongs to Greece; and, thirdly, Greece objected to the new state's flag that depicted the Star of Vergina, a symbol that Alexander the Great used, and to the new state's currency that depicted the White Tower, a symbol of the Greek city of Thessaloniki. Greece not only tried to influence EU members to follow suit, but it also imposed an oil and commodity embargo, not including food and medicine, on the new state.[22]

In April 1993, the UN recognized the republic named "the Former Yugoslav Republic of Macedonia." EU members and the United States followed, and China, Russia, Turkey, Bulgaria, Slovenia, and Croatia recognized the new state with its chosen name, Republic of Macedonia.[23] However, Greece's embargo and the lethargic international recognition hurt Macedonia's economy; lack of recognition prevented receipt of foreign loans and capital. Once the compromise name, Former Yugoslav Republic of Macedonia was approved by the UN, the country was finally able to join the IMF and attain observer status in the Conference on Security and Co-operation in Europe (CSCE). Not only did Macedonia suffer from Greece's embargo, but it also suffered from the UN blockade imposed on Serbia, its main trading partner. Six weeks into the Greek blockade cost Macedonia $80 million per month, an estimated 85 percent of its total export income. By 1994, the anti-Yugoslav blockade cost Macedonia $3 billion.[24] From the beginning, Macedonia faced daunting internal and external challenges.

DEMOCRATIZATION

On September 8, 1991, Macedonia held a referendum concerning the establishment of an independent Macedonian state. The vote overwhelmingly was in favor of independence. Interestingly, the vote was extended to Macedonians who lived outside the Macedonian state. This extension of votes uncovers a core issue for many struggling countries consisting of ethnic groups that may compete for its members' loyalties vis-à-vis the state: the tension between a citizen of the Macedonian state and a member of the Macedonian nation, and the obligation of a citizen of a state versus a member of a nation. The Constitution reflects this tension as well. It refers to constitutional nationalism, which confers a special status for the dominant nation within the state versus the democratic principle that confers sovereignty on all citizens of the state.[25] The Constitution states:

> Taking as starting points the historical, cultural, spiritual and state-hood heritage of the Macedonian people and their struggle over centuries for national and social freedom . . . and particularly the traditions of statehood and legality of the Krushevo Republic . . . as well as the historical fact that Macedonia is established as a national state of the Macedonian people, in which full equality as citizens and permanent co-existence with the Macedonian people is provided for Albanians,

Turks, Vlachs, Romanics and other nationalities living in the Republic of Macedonia, and intent on the establishment of the Republic of
Macedonia as a sovereign and independent state, as well as a civil and
democratic one . . . [26]

Ivanov, an ethnic Slav Macedonian, states that the preamble allows for
other nationalities, thus making it a "civil and democratic state . . . "[27] and
that

> The Slav population in the Republic of Macedonia and its Macedonian
> national identity has always been both [an] ethnical and political or
> civil one. There are no contradictions for the Macedonians in this
> regard. As for the Macedonian Albanians, demanding their loyalty to
> the State is a problem in terms of the necessity to over bridge the gap
> between their ethnic origin and political reality in Macedonia.[28]

On the other hand, an ethnic Albanian party leader, Nevzat Halili, provides a different perspective: "What we need are radical changes in the
Macedonian Constitution. Albanians in Macedonia should be recognized as
a constitutive people. There are three categories of citizens in Macedonia.
Macedonians are first-class citizens, Albanians are second class, and Serbs,
and others are third class."[29]

Macedonia's area is about 25,000 square kilometers, and it has a population of just over 2 million people, with 66.6 percent ethnic Macedonians,
22.7 percent ethnic Albanian, 4 percent Turkish, 2.2 percent Roma, 2.1 percent Serb, and 2.4 percent of other minorities. These percentages are from
a highly disputed 1994 census, with Albanians insisting that they comprise
40–50 percent of the population.[30] For the year 1999, the U.S. Department of State gave Macedonia generally high marks concerning its human
rights practices. Macedonia is a coalition-led parliamentary democracy that
maintains an independent judiciary, freedom of the press, and "generally
[respects] the human rights of its citizens."[31] All these traits seem to support
Diamond's criteria of a liberal democracy. Additionally, while the report
documented problems, especially concerning irregularities based on ethnicity, it praised the government for its handling of over 335,000 ethnic Albanians from Kosovo during the Kosovo crisis. This situation, however, strained
political relations, as ethnic Slav Macedonians feared that the refugees would
permanently remain in Macedonia, thereby significantly changing the ethnic
balance within the country.[32]

Strained relations between ethnic Slav Macedonians and ethnic Albanians
marked the birth of Macedonia. The Albanians boycotted the referendum
on Macedonia's independence and the 1991 census, claiming that the census would not portray their true percentage of the population. However,
by 1993, the Albanian party, the Party for Democratic Prosperity (PDP)

announced that Albanian autonomy was not on its agenda. Instead the PDP wanted state and constitutional recognition of the Albanian nation. The ongoing university dispute concerning the Albanian university in Tetovo and the flying of Albanian flags on administrative buildings in Tetovo and Gostivar resulted in police intervention and three Albanian deaths in July 1997.[33] These unfortunate deaths were the beginnings of greater unrest.

The PDP's desire for partner nation status is based on the Albanian claim that their ancestors predate the Slavs as Macedonian inhabitants, that Albanians have peacefully coexisted with many minorities, and that they constitute the largest minority in Macedonia. Practically, the partner-nation status would establish joint decision-making mechanisms at the state and local levels; proportional representation on the police force, the military, the judiciary, and other such institutions; and, rights such as the state sanctioning of Albanian language, education, and the flag. Many Macedonians feel that Albanians are treated equally as evidenced by the political participation of Albanian parties and leaders.[34]

Given the historical context of ethnic relations in Macedonia, one must differentiate between Kosovar Albanians and Macedonian Albanians. From its start, Macedonia, unlike Serbia, copied Spain's political recipe for building an inclusive regime. In Macedonia, Albanians have been included in the state's politics; in Kosovo, the Albanians set up parallel state institutions. Albanian political parties in Macedonia have been instrumental government coalition partners. Between 1992 and 1998, the PDP served under the leadership of Branko Crvenkovski, Head of the Social Democratic Union of Macedonia (SDU). After 1998, the Democratic Party of Albanians (DPA) joined the government coalition of the Internal Macedonian Revolutionary Organization-Democratic Party of Macedonian Unity (VMRO-DPMNE) and the Democratic Alternative (DA).[35]

Moreover, like Spain's Basques and Turkey's Kurds, the Albanians in Macedonia are not monolithic. The splits within the PDP manifested this diversity of opinion within the Albanian community; after several splits producing the Party for Democratic Prosperity (PDPA) under the leadership of Arben Xhaferi and the National Democratic Party (NDP), Xhaferi emerged as the prominent political leader of the DPA. Interestingly, it was the increasingly nationalistic tones of regional neighbors, Albanian President Sali Berisha and Kosovar Albanian leader Rugova, which fostered the splits within the PDP in Macedonia.[36]

As the Basque case demonstrated, an effective governing coalition required leaders that were willing to compromise and foster dialogue to tackle the challenges of a newly democratizing state, especially if that state wanted to gain legitimacy from all the people. Macedonia has been fortunate to have such leaders. In 1998, when Ljupčo Georgievski, leader of the VMRO, included Arben Xhaferi and his party as a coalition partner, Xhaferi expressed moderation of his previous stance: "We can find common ground for ethnic integration through mutual understanding."[37] In fact, both Georgievski and Xhaferi's moderate stands are much different from past rhetoric.[38] Vasil Tupurkovski, leader of the Democratic Alternative (DA) observed, "They [VMRO and DPA] realized perfectly well they could never have won with the radical positions they used to hold, and they really wanted to win, and to hold power."[39]

The 1998 coalition was not the first expression of moderation. Four years earlier the government responded to the voters' desires, marking an important aspect of Almond and Verba's political culture, that being competence. Voters witnessed that they made a difference in the political system. In 1994, the voters rejected VMRO's nationalist agenda. Instead, voters elected a coalition of the Social Democratic Alliance of Macedonia (SDSM), the Socialist Party of Macedonia (SPM), the Liberal Party (LP), and the Party for Democratic Prosperity (PDP). Under the leadership of President Gligorov, the coalition maintained a pragmatic approach to its foreign and domestic policies. It skillfully managed relations with Serbia, Albania, Greece, and Bulgaria, and it maintained an accommodative approach toward Macedonia's ethnic Albanian population.[40]

This 1994 election result came after the Macedonia's first multiparty elections in 1990, which produced a nationalist coalition under the leadership of the VMRO. The 24-year-old poet and leader of VMRO, Ljupčo Georgeivski, articulated four aims: first, Macedonian independence; secondly, withdrawal of the Yugoslav National Army and the establishment of the Macedonian Defense Forces; thirdly, an independent currency; and, finally, world recognition as a sovereign state. The Party's message was that Macedonia was for Macedonians, which was not widely received by Macedonia's ethnic minorities.[41] Fortunately, other points of view were represented. For example, the SDSM pushed for a compromise solution with Yugoslavia such that Macedonia would have autonomous status as a Yugoslav republic.

Because the 1990 elections did not produce a majority, the government created a panel of experts, who had little party affiliation; this panel was designed to facilitate good governance that reflected compromise. Three ethnic Albanians were included on this panel, an early indication of the government's accommodation through power sharing, a technique witnessed in the Basque case. Also, even with the nationalist coalition's slight majority, Kiro Gligorov, a former communist, was appointed as President, while Georgievski was appointed as Vice President. An economics professor, Nikola Kljušev became the Prime Minister. This form of power sharing reflected the polls of the day. An April 1991 poll indicated that 60 percent of the people favored a restructured Yugoslavia as opposed to Macedonian independence. Also, people were concerned that a purely nationalist government may lead to a Slovenian and Croatian political outcome.[42] It appears that the values of toleration and diversity were important elements to the people and leaders of Macedonia.

Through the 1990s, Macedonia's political accommodation was able to avert the ethnic conflicts and disasters experienced by its regional neighbors. The ethnic parties helped to influence the governing coalition agenda. In June 1993, a constitutionally directed institution, the Council of Interethnic Relations, was stood up. The thirteen-member council, which had representatives from six ethnic groups, was charged with studying interethnic issues and making recommendations to Parliament. While its influence was questionable, it provided a forum for dialogue.[43]

Moreover, Macedonia's political leadership has been a significant factor for Macedonia's relative ethnic harmony, as mentioned earlier. In 1995, President Gligorov talked about the citizens of Macedonia: "We are all Macedonians. We are all citizens of this country and Albanians have a long-term interest to integrate themselves in this country. This does not mean that they should lose their national, cultural and linguistic characteristics." Furthermore, he stated that:

> In the ethnically-mixed Balkans, it is impossible to create compact national states in which only members of one nation can live. This is an absurdity which can hardly be realized in Europe.... Perhaps one nation can win a victory here and there, but then this would only lead to revanchism on the part of the others, and thus, there would never be an end [to warfare].[44]

According to Alice Ackerman, one way to defuse the problem of conflicting nationalities is to create a new nationality or identity. The idea of creating a European identity in Macedonia has influenced Macedonia's desire for membership in European institutions.[45] The idea of a federalized Europe resonates with citizens of Macedonia. They are used to a federalized system under the former Yugoslavia, and they view their inclusion in the European family as a way to bolster their status and way of life.[46] Just like Spain's overlapping state and local political communities, Macedonia seems like it, too, could incorporate overlapping identities and political communities. Some ethnic Albanians do feel Macedonian. Nusret Jakupi, a military officer in the Macedonian army said: "I, as an Albanian, feel I am in my country. I haven't come from another country. I am living in the same place where my grandfather, my great grandfather, and generations before have lived."[47] According to an ethnic Albanian leader, Sami Ibrahami:

> I think we have been lucky to establish this country without any conflict at all. And the contributions of [the ethnic] Albanians were a huge part because we know that we can talk to each other. The dialogue is going on in Macedonia. That is our priority. We respect each other, but the promises that are given are not realized. It was always said that things would be realized step by step but unfortunately there's still not a real

democracy here. But we have continued to preserve the peace. If we have not learned the lessons from Bosnia-Herzegovina then we are illiterate.[48]

And President Gligorov explained the balance that must be achieved to win legitimacy from not only ethnic Albanians, but also from the majority, Slavic Macedonians:

It's not possible to implement overnight a maximization program because there are other political entities in the country that have to accept those solutions. Two-thirds of the population in Macedonia are [Slavic] Macedonians, and one-third consists of all the [other] ethnic groups together. Therefore, if you want to improve some of the ethnic rights, then you have to convince the [Slavic] Macedonian population that that is good, and that it is to the benefit of the country and of the [Slavic] Macedonians of the nation. All this requires time, preparation, argumentation, patience.[49]

It seems that by first acknowledging overlapping identities and political communities, the state can better know how to foster legitimacy from the diverse population.

Polls conducted from March to May of 2000 support Gligorov's concern of attaining legitimacy among all ethnic groups. Ironically, it was the ethnic Albanians who seemed to have had more confidence in the government. Based on polls conducted in April 2000, political preferences had changed since the 1998 elections. The governing coalition (VMRO-DPMNE and DPA) lost public support, but that loss was mainly among the ethnic Slav Macedonians. Ethnic Albanians, however, increased their support for the coalition, and particularly showed increased support for DPA over PDP. The main opposition party, SDSM, had doubled its public support since the 1998 elections. This support was mainly from the ethnic Slav Macedonian and other-than Albanian ethnic communities. Also, SDSM supporters tended to have more urban, educated, and higher economic status than supporters of VMRO-DPMNE. Specifically, ethnic Slav Macedonians increased their support of SDSM from 15 percent to 27 percent, while their support of the VMRO-DPMNE coalition declined from 16 percent to 13 percent. Ethnic Albanian support remarkably grew for DPA from 31 percent to 50 percent, yet decreased for PDP from 32 percent to 13 percent. President Trajkovski received positive support from ethnic Albanians (62 percent) and mixed support from ethnic Slav Macedonians (46 percent). Prime Minister Ljupčo Georgievski, also from the VMRO-DPMNE, received more favorable support from ethnic Albanians (54 percent) than from ethnic Slav Macedonians (37 percent). The overall declining confidence in the ruling coalition may have been due to events in Kosovo, a presidential election scandal, and poor economic performance.[50] The leaders of the SDSM party, Tito Petkovski and Branko Crvenkovski, were gaining ethnic Slav Macedonian support while losing ethnic Albanian support. Former President Gligorov, whose views were in line with VMRO-DPMNE, continued to have great support among ethnic Slav Macedonians (72 percent) and limited support among ethnic Albanians (15 percent). Arben Xhaferi enjoyed widespread support among ethnic Albanians (83 percent) and minimal support from ethnic Slav Macedonians (21 percent).[51]

What do these polls mean? First, President Gligorov seemed to enjoy support based on his leadership. Even though his views reflected the views of the ruling coalition, the declining support for that coalition did not affect him. It appears that he enjoyed great power vis-à-vis his prime ministers during his time as President. Under President Trajkovski, the powers of the prime minister vis-à-vis the president seem more balanced. President Gligorov's personality and leadership seems to be the basis of this differentiation, as indicated by the polling data. Secondly, the ethnic Slav Macedonians and ethnic Albanians are not homogeneous in their opinions. Ethnic Slav Macedonians tended to be split between the VMRO and SDSM, while there were several Albanian parties. Although, the DPA was gaining more Albanian support, it was a party that reflected political accommodation and moderation. The DA party received the same support from the ethnic Albanians and ethnic Slav Macedonians, and ethnic Albanians gave ethnic Slav Macedonian President Trajkovski great support. Perhaps this pattern is a beginning of crosscutting cleavages such that future political parties would reflect issues that would override previous ethnic agendas.

Other indicators showed that there had been a decline in support of the police and army in both ethnic communities. However, ethnic Albanians increased their support for the judicial system from 7 percent to 20 percent favorable and for both the national, which rose from 24 percent to 50 percent, and local governments, which was at 51 percent from the previous year's 38 percent. Ethnic Slav Macedonians, however, had less support for the national government, declining from 46 percent to 27 percent, and the local government, dropping from 38 percent to 29 percent. Moreover, each community's views toward each other had changed. Ethnic Albanians' view of ethnic Slav Macedonians had improved from 17 percent as very favorable to 44 percent very favorable. In fact, a total of 76 percent responded as either very or somewhat favorable. Only 30 percent of ethnic Slav Macedonians viewed ethnic Albanians as either very favorable or somewhat favorable. However, only 9 percent of ethnic Albanians and 20 percent of ethnic Slav Macedonians felt that ethnic relations were very bad and that could result in a grave crisis. Indeed, both groups strongly backed a united Macedonia (ethnic Albanians at 82 percent and ethnic Slav Macedonians at 99 percent). Finally, 30 percent of Albanians only identified with their ethnic group and

50 percent viewed themselves as an ethnic Albanian and then as a Macedonian citizen. Ethnic Slav Macedonians viewed their residency in Macedonia as the most important factor of their identity (55 percent), followed by town (12 percent), occupation (13 percent), nationality (13 percent), and religion (5 percent).[52]

These polls also reflect increasing legitimacy for the government among the ethnic Albanians, and even increasing tolerance toward others, important criteria for a liberal democracy. The polls again demonstrate the importance of the government's ability to elicit legitimacy from all communities, even among the ethnic Slav Macedonians who were showing declining support for the government. These polls suggest that there may be crosscutting societal cleavages based on how people perceive themselves and others. State loyalties seem to be present and may help form the basis of a widespread civic identity; these loyalties and identity may help form the basis of a cohesive political community at the state level. Clearly, there are still polarized sentiments, but as Almond and Verba tell us, all societies will have some polarization.

Another set of polls indicate that ethnic Albanians appeared to be more optimistic about the economy than ethnic Slav Macedonians, with 65 percent of ethnic Albanians optimistic concerning the arrival of Western economic aid than the ethnic Slav Macedonians (34 percent). However, both ethnic Albanians and ethnic Slav Macedonians tended to favor the market economy with some restrictions. Overall, 77 percent of the public was in favor of private versus state ownership of small businesses, and 58 percent in favor of foreign investment. Supporters of VMRO-DPMNE and DPA tended to support the free market more than supporters of SDSM. Ethnic Slav Macedonians viewed trade (26 percent), foreign investment (26 percent), and fighting corruption (16 percent), as the top economic policy priorities, and ethnic Albanians relatively agreed, with foreign investment (31 percent), privatization (23 percent), trade (14 percent), and fighting corruption (12 percent).[53] Additionally both communities had put unemployment as their top election issue.[54] The importance of the economy will come to the fore again in the cooperation section of this study.

The political process still held promise as a viable alternative to ethnic violence. The DPA was increasingly asserting itself in government, attaining better job and bank loan access for Albanians. Additionally, the ethnic Albanian politicians in Kosovo were not supporting the ethnic Albanian extremists; they did, however, warn of western support for their Slavic rivals. Macedonia's neighbors have declared support. Albania reaffirmed its commitment to respect Macedonia's borders and rejected any call for a Greater Albania. Greece and Bulgaria offered military support to assist with border security between Macedonia and Kosovo.[55]

Furthermore, PM Ljupčo Georgievski's coalition continued to facilitate good relations between the Albanian and Slavic Macedonian communities, and in 2001, Tetovo University was scheduled to conduct education in the Albanian language with state approval. The Deputy Prime Minister Ibrahami and other ethnic Albanians held high posts in the government. *The Economist* reported that: "Despite this week's violence, the party [DPA] seemed keen to stay in government and uphold the tradition whereby patronage and political responsibility are shared out amicably."[56] DPA rejected the extremist goal of a "greater Albania," and even Mr. Ibrahimi claimed that Albanians could live in several countries, just as German-speakers live in Germany, Austria, and Switzerland.[57]

The NLA, however, challenged Xhaferi's political efforts, and in response, Xhaferi pressed for more rapid improvement concerning ethnic Albanian rights using the political process. Most Albanians just want stability and opportunity, and they have no desires for a Greater Albania. Generally, Albanians want their language officially sanctioned, more decentralization, constitutional amendments guaranteeing equality, a change in the preamble of the constitution, an internationally monitored census, and an Albanian language university. The EU's security chief, Javier Solana tried to discourage use of force from all sides, and he encouraged President Trajkovski to step up negotiations. However, Solana noted that Macedonia's democracy was strong enough and that it did not need direct international mediation for its political dialogue. Solana observed: "Xhahferi is part of the government."[58]

Xhaferi warned: "People must not generalize and criminalize everyone and create some Satanic idea about the Albanians." Moreover, "They must talk about concrete positions of real people, and not make false presumptions. And you cannot buy loyalty to the state with the repression of its citizens."[59] Xhaferi rejected the NLA's violence and has had no contact with its leader, Ali Ahmeti. However, Xhaferi attributed his warning to the NLA that increased violence would damage any gains on the political front, led to the NLA's recent restraint. Xhaferi acknowledged the delicate balance he must attain: "The boys in the hills have a collectivist ideology. But if I don't succeed in opening the process of real change, I will have failed, and I will be responsible for the change in people's heads. I want to civilize the conflict, not militarize it. But I must succeed."[60]

The West wanted Xhaferi to succeed as well and pressured President Trajkovski to use restraint against the NLA forces, intensify negotiations, and address Albanian grievances. According to Nikola Dimitrov, Macedonia's Ambassador to the United States in 2001, "This is a fight against terrorists, not against any single ethnic community." An ethnic Albanian villager called the government attacks against the NLA "a tragedy and a crime." But he also added that the Albanians wanted "only justice" and as opposed to a separate state.[61]

According to Branko Geroski, the editor of *Dnevnik*, Macedonia's largest newspaper, the state sanctioned language status for the Albanian language and a change in the constitution's preamble that clearly articulates equal citizenry status for all people were imminent. The state, with the OSCE's help, had accredited a new university, albeit not the Tetovo University, with Albanian as the primary language.[62] While movement was occurring on a political front, action had to be taken against the NLA. According to a senior Macedonian official, "we needed to do it to keep ordinary Macedonians from losing faith in the government and turning to private vendettas." He noted that even with the killing of a Macedonian policeman, "not one single Albanian shop window has been smashed." And a senior Western diplomat remarked that the government "had to do something to stop the Macedonians from melting down in this crisis, because they're all frightened and critical of inaction."[63] Was the government just fulfilling its obligation of protecting its population from political terror, a tenet of liberal democracy as discussed by Diamond?

COOPERATION

Macedonia's cooperation with International Governmental Organizations (IGOs) and other states have helped counter the NLA actions. This case differs from the Spanish and Turkish cases because of the plethora and increased robustness of IGOs in Macedonia. Such cooperation, nevertheless, was required to defuse the transnational NLA, especially on the regional level. According to Carl Bildt, "There will not be stable peace in the region until a political arrangement for this area is accepted by the peoples of Kosovo, all the countries of the region, including Serbia, and the U.N. Security Council."[64] Moreover, Macedonia's leadership realized that the redrawing of borders to accommodate ethnic populations was dangerous. According to President Trajkovski: "We cannot redraw borders and boundaries, making smaller units of even purer ethnic states. We cannot survive as a region if ethnicity becomes the sole defining justification of statehood."[65] The alternative is to turn toward a transnational and integrative Europe. The desire to join Europe is a regional unifying factor. Interestingly, Bildt describes the road to EU membership as to "likely be a long one for most of these countries."[66] However, on April 9, 2001, Macedonia became the first Southeast European country to sign the Stabilization and Association Agreement (SAA) Pact. This Pact confers the status of potential EU candidacy to Macedonia, with a transition period of 10 years toward full EU membership. For Macedonia, the SAA is concrete EU recognition of Macedonia's political and economic progress, especially in the areas of regional cooperation and respect of fundamental rights.[67]

According to the Stability Pact Coordinator, Bodo Hambach, regional neighbors' support for Macedonia helped to quell the conflict in Macedonia that was ongoing in 2001. His view was that the "terrorists" were politically isolated "as never before, from the government of Albania, from the official Kosovo Albanians, and from the political parties of the Albanians in Macedonia." In fact when asked in an interview: "Who is supposed to keep in check these UÇK (NLA) fighters from Kosovo?" Hambach replied:

> Whoever holds power in Kosovo. And that is Kfor. It has the obligation under international law to ensure that no threat to a neighboring country comes from this territory. Kfor has to draw a line in the sand.

Furthermore, he stated,

> Not all violence shown on TV means war. We are dealing with armed confrontations, but these are not crossing the threshold of war. I consider it a controllable conflict. This includes clear opposition terrorism. . . . These terrorists now notice how isolated they are. They now want to present themselves as freedom fighters and portray the terrorist actions as a popular uprising in Macedonia.

Mr. Hambach made clear the importance of the Stability Pact as a means toward regional cooperation: "We have made demonstrable progress, precisely in the area of regional cooperation. Since Slobodan Milošević's departure there has been no head of state in the region who considers military aggression to be a means of policy."[68]

Interestingly, polls indicate that ethnic Albanians supported NATO and felt more secure with NATO troops in Macedonia. However, ethnic Macedonians did not favor a NATO presence and half had an unfavorable view toward the United States. VMRO-DPMNE supported NATO presence in Macedonia, but SDSM did not. However, ethnic Slav Macedonians responded favorably to joining NATO, with perhaps the hope that NATO membership could help secure economic benefits. Confidence in the EU, UN, and OSCE decreased from 1999 to 2000 among ethnic Slav Macedonians (41 percent to 33 percent, 44 percent to 34 percent, and 42 percent to 30 percent, respectively). Ethnic Albanians, however, consistently held these organizations in high regard (82 percent, 79 percent, and 85 percent).[69] According to Keith Brown, there is great support within Macedonia for being included among the European family of states. In fact, the idea of the European welfare state is much more attractive than the model of the United States.[70]

Furthermore, the Commissioner for External Relations, Chris Patten, had repeatedly called for Albanian Kosovar leaders to reject NLA actions, which they did.[71] He warned the Kosovar leaders that an absence of such rejections would harm the continuance of the substantial EU aid to Kosovo. The EU doubled its aid to Kosovo, providing 900,000 euros, during a visit by Serbian Deputy Prime Minister Njeboša Cović to Brussels. The EU has also discussed plans for additional aid for the Preševo Valley area. As of

2001, the Commission had provided 470 million euros to Macedonia in the form of government assistance with interethnic issues via education, road construction, refugee shelters, and establishing border-crossing points.[72]

Interstate cooperation occurred between Serbia and Macedonia. Both countries agreed that the best way to manage the ethnic Albanian extremists is with restraint. As the Basque case demonstrated, state restraint vis-à-vis terrorists seemed to help elicit state legitimacy from the population. President Trajkovski and Serbian President Vojislav Koštunica signed treaties that delineated the border between their countries.[73] Furthermore, Koštunica rejects the idea of a "Greater Serbia" and believes that political accommodation will produce a future stable and decentralized Yugoslav state.[74] Unfortunately for Koštunica, the task of producing such a state is formidable. Bernard Kouchner, the high representative of the UN Secretary General in Kosovo during its first 18 months as an international protectorate, concluded at the end of his term in late 2000: "Kosovo remains a violent society in which guns are used to resolve arguments and exact revenge." He added: "The Kosovo Albanians have already damaged their reputation in the eyes of the world and undercut international sympathy by the culture of impunity and tolerance for reverse ethnic cleansing."[75] Albanian insurgents have posed a security problem for Koštunica with their killings and kidnappings of local Serbs. President Koštunica asked for increased UN patrols to combat Albanian "terrorism," which spilled into the buffer zone that borders on Macedonia.[76]

On the process of democratization, Koštunica realized that it is a process that takes time. In 1996 and 1997 at civic protests, he said, "For people who have not experienced democracy it is important that democracy grow in this country. If it was somehow imported, it would not give people the right idea." He also talked about his attraction to U.S. democracy.[77] Just like Macedonia, Koštunica's Serbia has had to face many challenges as it forges its path to democracy: most notably a corrupt and mismanaged economic system that lasted 13 years under Milošević; the effects of U.S. sanctions that were only lifted in January 2001; and, lethargic and delayed foreign investment and aid. But democratic progress has occurred. There has been a noticeable change in political culture: more pluralism, freedom of expression, and an unhindered media. The police have shed their heavy-handed ominous presence, the state has reestablished its international contacts, the value of the currency has remained steady, and wages are increasing. And as Leonard Cohen observes, "... the more virulent xenophobic and authoritarian aspects of Serbian political culture have waned considerably."[78] It appears that Koštunica has directed Serbia (also known as Serbia and Montenegro) on the path toward greater tolerance and acceptance of diversity. The election of a moderate Kosovo government, which has also renounced violence, seemed to validate Koštunica's efforts. As the Basque case highlighted, however, such transitional efforts by a democratizing state may be met with increased violence from terrorist groups. Koštunica must stay the course to effectively and politically marginalize the KLA. A marginalized KLA will not only cause fewer problems for Serbia, but it will also be less of an asset for the NLA.

Serbia has also made strides toward the rule of law and greater tolerance. Over 100 Kosovar Albanians were freed from Serbian jails. They were arrested in 1999 on suspicion of terrorism and were serving sentences that ranged from 7 to 13 years.[79] Condemning an attack on several Macedonian soldiers by extremists, the former head of the United Nations Interim Administration Mission in Kosovo (UNMIK), Hans Haekkerup, remarked that political, religious, and community leaders in Kosovo, support Macedonia's government and citizens because "People ... want to live in peace for a better future."[80] President Koštunica has been working with UNMIK to help foster the work of Kosovo's committee to design a legal framework for a provisional self-government, and specifically, he has encouraged Kosovo Serb representation.[81]

Other countries, as mentioned earlier, also manifested signs of democratization and a willingness to cooperate. Specifically, Albania rejected the idea of a Greater Albania and championed its own democratization. Albania's Prime Minister Ilir Meta seemed to be committed to Albania's democratization. He was able to cut crime, improve the customs service, and regulate taxes. Nevertheless, poverty remained pervasive and extreme (GDP per capita is $1,000). During the run-up to the June 2001 elections, Prime Minister Meta said that his goal was to expand the Albanian economy into the Balkan market and foster ties with the EU. Albania's restraint during the Kosovo conflict won great approval from the EU.[82] Greater regional interethnic tolerance has helped to foster a domestic intraethnic tolerance as well. The promise of a future EU inclusion seems to entice states to pursue a liberal democratic path.

By spring 2001, at issue was the smuggling between the Macedonian and Kosovo border. Unemployment was high at 32 percent, and many unemployed Slavic Macedonians were not enamored with ethnic Albanians who were attaining wealth through illegal activities, namely smuggling. The good news was that Macedonia had been able to curb inflation, obtain $250 million of Greek investment, attain a budget surplus, and foster job-creating investments. The continued path toward economic prosperity may help defuse potential ethnic tensions.[83] And as mentioned earlier, Greece and Bulgaria had even volunteered to patrol the border, which would help thwart the smuggling activities.

Concerned about the transnational nature of the NLA, President Trajkovski urged KFOR and UNMIK to help with border control. The President called the violence of 2001 in his country a "direct export from Kosovo." He claimed that the armed extremists were trying to destroy Macedonia's multicultural democracy, charging that they were guided by "racist ideology" and engaged in "trafficking in drugs and women."[84]

In Peter Liotta's book, *Dismembering the State*, he discusses two key lessons from Kosovo that may shed light on Macedonia's situation. First, he insists that American avoidance of the Kosovo situation at the Dayton Peace Talks in the hopes of making a compromise on Bosnia more appealing to the ruthless Milošević led to the legitimization of the KLA. Secondly, the West's lack of support to legitimate democratic opposition in Kosovo and Serbia led to increased violence. The message received by many Kosovars was that nonviolence did not produce international support. Instead, violence hardened ethnic identity and increased legitimacy within those ethnic groups for perpetrators of violence.[85]

The September 2002 elections that produced the coalition of SDSM and Democratic Union for Integration, Ali Ahmeti's party, has a lot to prove and overcome. On the one hand, it may be the way ahead if indeed the NLA is gone and the SDSM-DUI coalition can produce results through the political system. Real gains across the population will be necessary to elicit legitimacy. However, Biljana Vankovska claims that with this coalition, "one can hardly talk about undivided legitimacy." For now, "SDSM cannot talk on behalf of the Albanian population, which is also true for DUI regarding the Macedonian voters."[86] While Macedonia passed through these elections peacefully, the fact that the DUI is not distinguishable for some from the NLA, may have reinforced the lesson that violence works. A former NLA General and now DUI politician remarked that using weapons in war is easier than using words in politics.[87] Politics is hard. For the people of Macedonia, let's hope that their leaders and the region's leaders choose the "harder right" and not "the easier wrong."

Unfortunately since the 2002 elections, both Serbia and Macedonia lost their leaders during these trying times. On February 26, 2004, President Trajkovoski's plane crashed while enroute to a conference to discuss investment opportunities in the Balkan.[88] Since his tragic death, Branko Crvenkovski has been elected President, while Vlado Buckovski serves as Prime Minister holding together the ethnic Albanian party (DUI) and Liberal Democratic Party (LDP) coalition.[89] Meanwhile in Serbia, Prime Minister Djindjic was assassinated in March 2003. Currently, Voislav Koštunica is serving as Prime Minister, and Boris Tadic serves as President. Hard work lies ahead for both elites and society, and as the next chapter will further highlight, the international community.

IMPLICATIONS

Following the horrific events of September 11, 2001, the security dilemma of the former Yugoslavia virtually vanished before the eyes of many policymakers. Understandably, the United States and Europe felt compelled to divert resources away from the region and into their mutual struggle against global terrorism. Yet for over a decade, the Balkans presented the

West with one of its greatest strategic and policy challenges; the prosecution and aftermath of four violent conflicts—including the first military intervention by NATO—consumed billions of dollars and involved exhaustive diplomatic and regional initiatives.

The Balkans no longer constitutes a primary foreign policy challenge; this does not mean, however, that the international community can afford to look in all directions other than Southeast Europe. The region itself is in a period of difficult, painful transition, and stands the chance of rapidly succumbing to transnational criminal influences and becoming a "black hole" of terrorism such as happened in Afghanistan, which became not a sponsor of terrorism but rather a terrorist-sponsored state. Even as halting progress toward representative government and institution building takes place in Croatia, Serbia, and Kosovo, internal corruption, black market activities, and illegal arms shipments threaten the stability of the region. When $25 can buy anyone a real, not a counterfeit, passport, the area has increasingly become attractive to those who easily escape the notice of already overstretched internal security forces. Nowhere has this security dilemma entered a more crucial period than in Macedonia.

Much of this changed security environment, inevitably, has left Macedonia both scarred and distorted. Indeed, as Robert Hislope has noted, "The Macedonian state itself encompasses a thoroughly corrupt set of institutions that has stymied democratic development, alienated ordinary citizens, and delegitimized the idea of an ethnically neutral, citizen-based, liberal state, especially among Albanians."[90] Yet given these negative outcomes, it seems worth remembering what Samuel Huntington emphasized in *Political Order in Changing Societies*: "Corruption provides a means to assimilate new groups and new influences into a structured system."[91] Macedonia is a perfect example of an assimilating system, transitioning from the Socialist apparatchik of Yugoslavia to a state struggling with the tenuous transition to democracy. Corruption in "moderate doses"—if one could live with such a euphemism—can in truth help overcome static bureaucracy and actually act as an instrument of progress.

Moreover, it seems worth emphasizing, as Huntington did, that corruption is a less extreme form of alienation than violence: "He who corrupts a system's police officers is more likely to identify with the system than he who storms the system's police stations."[92] In Macedonia, corruption is so pervasive that it actually perversely supports the stability of the government. That said, it remains a security issue that such a porous region has the potential—especially if it becomes increasingly overlooked by external actors—to become of thriving cesspool of criminal activity; 70 to 90 percent of heroin seizures in Europe, for example, have transited either through Kosovo, Albania, or Macedonia.[93]

To be sure, given the election results of September 2002, the citizens of Macedonia were ready for change. As a result, the coälition government of so-called "national unity" that had weathered the storm of the 2001 insurgency was thrown out of office 1 year later. Yet whether or not Macedonia survives truly does depend on "external" forces and actors. Clearly, the root solutions for all Southeast Europe will prove problematic, and at times seem overwhelming. And Macedonia may represent the greatest challenge as well as represent the last best hope for the Balkans.[94]

The Macedonian case reveals some of the same patterns discovered in the Spanish case. Specifically, Macedonia has been able to survive and continue its democratization because of the state's adherence to liberal democratic principles and the more recent regional cooperation from its neighbors and international organizations. With the advent of regional cooperation, the participating states, namely Serbia and Macedonia, also saw shifts in their political cultures toward the Larry Diamond, Gabriel Almond, and Sidney Verba criteria. The NLA, just like the ETA in Spain, increased its activities during the very vulnerable transitioning period for Macedonia's democratization.

It appears that Macedonia marginalized the NLA and attained legitimacy by following a similarly elite-driven political development path as Spain. Both countries used an inclusive approach to democratization; allowed ethnically based political parties; established a parliamentary system that implements a proportional representative electoral system with a cap; used power sharing techniques; and, had the fortune of good political leadership. For both countries, the ethnically based political parties served a representative function, not a governing function; however, in both cases the ethnically based parties influenced the governing coalition and were able to get ethnic issues on the political agenda. Because each country required parties to attain a certain percentage of the vote in order to get a seat, both countries avoided the problem of overrepresentation at the expense of effective governance. In other words, they were able to limit the number of political parties in their multiparty system, and therefore, produced representative governments that could, indeed, govern. While it can be argued that Spain had a more developed civic culture than Macedonia, the people of Macedonia had an ethnic war at their doorstep. War aversion seemed to have kept points of disagreement and despair in the political process.

Legitimacy for the government of Macedonia was at an acceptable level. The state provided for freedom of expression, organization, demonstration, institutional accountability, citizens' votes matter, a flourishing media, and rule of law. There were still controversies concerning language rights and the constitutional definition of a citizen. The polls seemed to indicate that ethnic Albanians were satisfied. Perhaps the pace of democratization was delayed by the ethnic Slav Macedonians who had been less tolerant of the ethnic Albanian community as indicated by declining rates of satisfaction with the government. However, it appeared that through the leadership of Gligorov, Trajkovski, and Xhaferi, political accommodation was the path of choice and accepted by most citizens of Macedonia. At the time, Ali Ahmeti appeared to be stepping aside from assuming a leadership role in government as a gesture of compromise.[95] While the 2002 government had many challenges, it resulted from a relatively violence-free election. And perhaps, Macedonia will see more political development of its party system so that one day, ethnicity will become a lesser priority on the agendas of political parties and more pressing problems such as the economy and corruption may be addressed.[96] However, the West must resist the temptation to make Macedonia like itself. As Koštunica had remarked, imported democratic models will not work. For example, the countries of Southeastern Europe must ascertain a satisfactory definition of a citizen vis-à-vis a nationality. They must find their own way of attaining those liberal democratic values that will secure them the legitimacy of their population that will overcome terrorist challenges.

Liberal democratic states must also, according to Diamond, protect their population from political terror. Serbia required cooperation, especially at the regional level in order to effectively protect its population from the transnational NLA. Also, its neighbors helped defuse ethnic tension by adopting liberal democratic values themselves, especially those of tolerance and diversity. Examples include Albania's renouncement of a Greater Albania; Koštunica's rejection of a Greater Serbia; Bulgaria and Greece's contribution to border patrols between Macedonia and Kosovo; and, Greece's open acceptance of Macedonia and subsequent trade. The elected leaders in Kosovo denounced violence and have been working toward a legal framework for self-government. Both Serbia and Macedonia need each other to prevent cross-border activities that enhance terrorist acts by Albanian extremists in either country. By halting arms smuggling and denying safe havens, both countries have a better opportunity to mute extremist activities. Trajkovski and Kostunica's policies of restraint have served them well, to the disappointment of both the NLA and KLA.

What was the NLA? Was it a terrorist group, a rebel group, freedom fighters, or just a criminal organization? It appears that Macedonia, with the help of the regional and world community, marginalized the NLA. The Kosovar leaders have renounced the NLA as have all the other regional and world players. The NLA still made headlines with its violent activities, but Xhaferi continued to use the political process, and the government was praised for its restraint. However, the government must still protect its people, so it took action in 2001, which is further explained in the next chapter. One point that deserves further investigation is the possible organized criminal goals of the NLA. Based on the goals of Ahmeti, the NLA's former leader, the NLA only wanted more political rights for ethnic Albanians. Yet, some reports indicated increased smuggling, drug trafficking, and other illegal cross-border operations. What became of the NLA, and was it linked to these activities? Did these activities become an end, not just a means that supported the NLA's activities?

Another key difference between the Basque Case and this one is that the EU is much more robust today. Macedonia seems to have many international organizations that may help its democratization process. And this last point may be a good sign. With all the gloomy predictions for Macedonia's demise, it remains a pillar for Southeastern Europe, signing a Stabilization and Association Agreement and a Interim Agreement with the EU on April 9, 2001. It is also interesting that this agreement was signed in the wake of the NLA's attacks. It perhaps was a reward for Macedonia's restraint and continued political efforts concerning the rights of its ethnic Albanians. Furthermore, the economic benefits of increased EU integration may help to appease the ethnic Slav Macedonian population, which according to recent polls, were most worried about their economic plight. If Macedonia makes economic progress, then perhaps the ruling coalition will regain support among the ethnic Slav Macedonians and ethnic Albanians, alike.

Through cooperation and an increasingly developed civic culture, Macedonia was able to stay the course given its rough beginnings and ringside view of the last decade's terrible ethnic wars. Its neighbors also experienced political culture shifts as everyone saw the connection between domestic intraethnic and regional interethnic relations. This transnational relationship requires a regional perspective for analysis and policy. As the next cases highlight, the regional neighborhood matters.

CHAPTER 4

THE FAILURE OF RUSSIAN DEMOCRATIZATION AND THE TRAGEDY OF CHECHNYA: CASE IV

When Spain began the process of democratization in 1975 after the death of Francisco Franco, it faced a determined separatist movement dedicated to achieving independence for the Basque region. When Russia emerged as an independent and democratizing state in late 1991, it too faced a committed separatist movement in the breakaway province of Chechnya. Within 10 years, Spain had become a stable democracy and had effectively contained the danger of Basque separatism and terrorism. Over a roughly similar period of time, Russia's transition was upended. In 2004, *Freedom House* downgraded Russia to "Unfree" from "Partly Free," placing it alongside Pakistan and Chad, among other nondemocratic countries. *Freedom House* also rated Chechnya in 2005 as one of two territories (the other is Tibet) receiving the lowest possible rating in terms of political rights and civil liberties.[1] Over the past 12 years, tens of thousands of Chechen civilians and rebels have been killed in the violence.[2] Hundreds of thousands more have been uprooted from their homes and remain displaced in Chechnya or live in refugee camps in neighboring regions. According to official Russian statistics, over 5,000 Russian servicemen have lost their lives in the conflict. Independent sources suggest the number is much higher. But Russia has yet to eliminate the Chechen insurgency, which has become increasingly terroristic in strategy and tactics, expanding regionally but also to Moscow itself.

Russia's failure at democratization has severely weakened its ability to counter Chechen terrorism and resolve the problem of Chechen separatism.

Understanding why Russia has failed to democratize is clearly important, beyond the suffering inflicted on untold innocents. Respected analysts suggest
that the next "soft" target of Chechen terrorism—following the hostage
crisis of the Beslan schoolhouse in September 2004 where hundreds of
Russian schoolchildren and adults died after the building was seized by
Chechen terrorists and then stormed by Russian forces—could be a Western one. Equally important, the widespread violation of Chechen human
and civil rights by Russian forces confirms for many Muslims in Europe,
the Middle East, and Asia the hostility of the "West" toward Islamic
peoples.

Why did Spain succeed but Russia fail in the linked tasks of democratization and counterterrorism? Are there lessons from the Spanish case that
may point the way to renewed democratization in Russia and to an effective
Russian policy in Chechnya? The argument of this chapter is that the Spanish and Russian cases differ in terms of several domestic and international
factors, making "success" in Spain much more likely in the areas of democratization and counterterrorism. Unlike Russia, Spain began democratization
as a stable state with a functioning market economy. Furthermore, a significant segment—perhaps a majority—of its political elites were committed to
democratic change. Perhaps most important, Spain was embedded in an international, and particularly regional, environment that provided important
incentives for Spain to proceed with democratization and effective counterterrorism. Although such advantages were either absent or much diminished
in the case of Russia, lessons from the Spanish case are still important for
Russia, particularly in the international dimension. The chapter will examine these lessons and attendant policy proposals for Western governments
in its concluding section.

THE FAILURE OF STATE-BUILDING AND MARKETIZATION: THE IMPACT ON DEMOCRATIZATION

Any analysis of political change in post-Soviet Russia should recognize that
the failure of democratization—and the disabilities of Moscow's policies in
Chechnya—were "overdetermined" by a number of disadvantageous factors. An obvious but important observation is that geography matters. The
pull and lure of European democracies was strong in the case of Spain, but
weak in the case of Russia. Independent political parties and trade unions,
crucial manifestations of civil and political society, had been suppressed or
controlled by Franco, but were still part of recent Spanish history and memory, and could be resurrected rather quickly after the death of the dictator.
In the Russian case, however, society did not have any memory of a vibrant
civil society due to the decades of totalitarian communist rule that followed
centuries of tsarist oppression. Unlike Spain, political and civil society had
to be created *de novo* in the Russian case.

Two other core obstacles to successful democratization in Russia—that were missing in Spain—are particularly important: the collapse of the antecedent Soviet state and the absence of a market economy or private property. We will first examine the problem of the weak Russian state and how this disability undermined democratization in Russia. The chapter then turns to how the breakneck introduction of capitalism and private ownership into post-Communist Russia profoundly disrupted a social and political system long used to the public ownership of property.

The weakness of the Russian state in the immediate post-Soviet period was a serious obstacle to successful democratization given the difficulty if not impossibility of creating a democratic polity if the state cannot establish public order or deliver other essential public goods. Theda Skocpol offers a minimalist definition of the state as the "set of administrative, policing, and military organizations headed, and more or less well coordinated by an executive authority."[3] For Max Weber, the state is an administrative and legal order that claims "binding authority" over all individuals within its borders and a monopoly on the legitimate use of force.[4]

Three dimensions of state capacity comprise the requisites of an effective and legitimate state.[5] Each of these dimensions has a significant influence on the course of transitional polities. First, the institutional dimension encompasses national political institutions and measures the capacity of the state to formulate and enforce political and economic rules. Most important is the legitimacy of these rules, particularly among political elites.[6] The institutional dimension also measures the degree of state autonomy from pressure groups.[7] Polarized elite conflict is more likely in transitional than stable regimes because the political and economic rules of the game or even the boundaries of the state may not yet be defined. If intra-elite conflict is polarized, it is also likely that attempts to build state capacity (or state-building) will falter, victimized by the efforts of politicians to allocate state resources on the basis of expectations of political support.

Second, the political dimension refers to the linkages between state and society and their impact on state capacity. A state's effectiveness depends on cooperative links with society and on the capacities of society itself. Strong societies are vital supports for state capacity in democratic polities.[8] However, when the organizational support of society is weak and intra-elite conflict is polarized, politicians have incentives to neglect state building in favor of exchanging state resources for political support. Given that society in this setting contains few strong potential allies, such political exchange relationships are likely to cluster at the level of political and economic elites. The concentration of state largesse at the elite level favors the emergence of an economic oligarchy.

Third, the administrative dimension refers to the ability of the state to provide essential public goods, including law and order, education, and the infrastructure of market economies. This task depends on the fiscal resources and extractive capabilities of the state, and the professional competencies of the state's bureaucracies. The organizational coherence of these bureaucracies and their compliance to the directives of central authorities strongly affects the provision of public goods.

An effective state will exhibit significant capabilities in the institutional, societal, and administrative dimensions of state capacity. Weakly institutionalized states have less capacity, but not necessarily equivalent deficits in each of the separate dimensions. Unlike earlier transitional cases, including Spain, but also the countries in East Central Europe, the new Russian state was profoundly weak in all of the dimensions of capacity outlined above. To make matters much worse, Russia was forced to embark on dramatic economic reforms that seriously damaged the legitimacy of the new political system.

Comparativists commonly argue that transitional polities should first create effective states and institutionalize democratic politics before launching painful economic reforms. Building consensus and infrastructure for economic reform ensure that marketization strikes deep roots without undermining democratization. Reflecting the central perspectives of comparative transitology, Juan Linz and Alfred Stepan stress the importance of crafting effective political institutions, which in turn depends on the choices and skills of political leaders and elites.[9] Other theorists stress the importance of "pacts" or "concertation" between regime and society to ease the social distress caused by structural change in the economy. They also maintain that dual transitions—tackling democratization and marketization—are more likely to achieve institutionalization if democracy is consolidated first. Spain is cited as a model of intelligent sequencing and concertation applicable to post-Communist polities, including Russia.[10] From this perspective, the unwillingness of Boris Yeltsin, as Russia's first executive, to forge a new constitution, found a political party, or hold early elections—actions that might have strengthened the state and legitimated reforms—represents a profound failure of political intelligence and provides a central explanation for Russia's current difficulties.

Notable Russian area specialists, such as Jerry Hough and Michael McFaul, maintain that Yeltsin's errors were compounded by the fact that the president's first reformist government, led by Yegor Gaidar, embraced an ideology of radical economic reform. Influenced by the failures of the Soviet command economy and by neoclassical economic thought, Gaidar's team paid little initial attention to market-supporting institutions, believing that they would emerge spontaneously from the process of marketization. This unyielding commitment to neoclassical economics is held equally responsible for the neglect of state building and the pursuit of breakneck privatization.[11] According to Linz and Stepan, Yeltsin's decision to privilege radical economic reform, while neglecting the democratic restructuring of the parliament, the constitution, and the state "weakened an already weak state" and swelled the ranks of the opponents of democracy and markets.[12]

The neglect of state building is an important reason for the failure of economic and political reform in Russia, but it cannot be traced solely or even primarily to the reformers' technocratic strategies, authoritarian tendencies, or embrace of neoclassical economics. Rather the explanation must begin with two powerful constraints on both the *ability* and the *willingness* of governing elites to build state capacity. First and most immediately, the economic crisis and breakdown of state institutions attending the collapse of the Soviet Union forced the reformers to launch economic reform without adequate political, economic, and administrative supports.[13] Short on time to build basic institutions and market infrastructure to support comprehensive economic restructuring, the reformers lost control of much of the process. Not surprisingly, Russia has been plagued by pervasive corruption and rent-seeking.[14] Second, sharp elite conflict and weak links between state and society dramatically reduced the incentives of incumbents to devote the political capital and resources necessary to build state capacity and counter efforts by the winners of initial economic reforms to stave off further reforms that would reduce their advantageous positions.

Facing an escalating economic crisis amid state weakness, the Russian reformers pursued radical restructuring at the outset. By mid-1992, mass privatization emerged as the most dramatic component of the reforms. The scope of privatization and the speed with which it was implemented were unprecedented. By the beginning of 1996, 17,937 industrial firms, 72 percent of large and mid-sized enterprises had been privatized, accounting for 88.3 percent of the industrial output of the Russian Federation. Roughly 82 percent of small shops and retail stores were also privatized, including 900,000 new small businesses started by Russian entrepreneurs.[15] By contrast, Great Britain took 7 years to sell off forty-three state enterprises in its "large-scale" privatization of the 1980s.[16]

Yeltsin's government had little choice but to pursue rapid de-etatization given the bankruptcy of the Russian state, which was due to Gorbachev's failure to launch authentic economic reforms during perestroika. Between 1985 and 1991 the budget deficit had skyrocketed from roughly 2 percent to 30 percent of GDP, while domestic production shrank 12.8 percent in 1991 alone. Although the republics were starting to withold tax revenues, Gorbachev kept sending money to enterprises and regions, and together with populist politicians in the Congress of People's Deputies, financed extravagant growth in wages and social benefits through deficit spending, igniting a serious surge in inflation.[17]

Rapid privatization was also spurred by the reformers' recognition that they were incapable of controlling Russia's vast bureaucracies and enterprises. These "agency problems" pointed to the low and rapidly eroding capacity of the state in the administrative dimension.[18] Yeltsin underlined this second crisis in his speech of October 28, 1991: "Bribery, privatization for the sake of and by the nomenklatura, the plunder of natural resources, and nomenklatura separatism threaten the disintegration of Russia."[19] Thus, the scope and pace of privatization was determined as much by a strong sense of crisis among the reformers as their conviction that the state's role in the economy was predatory and had to be reduced.[20]

In short, the facts of the Russian case raise doubts about the feasibility of the sequential strategies adopted in the Spanish transition. Given the extent of the economic crisis it would have been self-defeating to delay liberalization, stabilization, and privatization until the institutions of an effective state had been put in place. As Robert Putnam observes, "most institutional history moves slowly. Where institution building (and not mere constitution writing) is concerned, time is measured in decades."[21] Case studies such as South Korea suggest that the reform of inefficient, self-regarding bureaucratic structures requires years of sustained effort.[22]

In the absence of a strong, autonomous Russian state, the breakneck privatization and marketization under Yeltsin produced extreme political and economic distortions. A form of "oligarchical capitalism" was created, in which large companies controlled the huge swaths of economic production and also wielded significant political influence over foreign and domestic policy. They had amassed their initial wealth in 1991–1993 from currency speculation and massive subsidized credits.[23] Export arbitrage, based on the purchase of commodities at government-controlled prices, which are then sold at great profit on unregulated foreign markets, was another favorite activity of business elites. In 1992 alone, export arbitrage in metal, oil, and natural gas accounted for roughly 30 percent of Russia's GDP.[24] The rigged privatization auctions of 1995 ("loans for shares" deals) accelerated the already dramatic growth of these conglomerates, allowing them to capture important segments of the Russian economy, particularly fuel and extractive industries, real estate, and the media.

Much of this accumulation was facilitated by privileged access to state officials. Factions within the government provide "krysha" ("roof") or protection and favors for economic groups loosely organized into "clans" in exchange for private gain.[25] These arrangements demonstrate the absence of any significant distinction between public and private behavior on the part of government officials, who view self-enrichment while in office as a justified perquisite. While Viktor Chernomyrdin provided aid and comfort for Gazprom, the gas giant he headed before his appointment as prime minister, Anatoly Chubais served as the patron of Vladimir Potanin, the President of Oneximbank, one of the big winners in the loans-for-shares auction.

Self-regarding behavior, however, is not the only explanation for interlocking ties between Russian business and the state. Such connections have served another purpose: providing crucial political support for the regime. Facing intense political opposition, Yeltsin promoted the dense web of ties between the state and economic interests as part of a broad political strategy. Since the toleration of corruption and rent-seeking behavior is one of the currencies with which the leadership purchases elite support, Yeltsin's camp readily justified the loans-for-shares scheme (and breakneck privatization as a whole) as a political necessity.[26] Similarly, conglomerates that enjoy political favor have often successfully evaded taxes.[27] This political strategy worked to keep the Yeltsin administration in power.

Drawing on both oligarchical capitalism and bureaucratic capitalism for political strength, Yeltsin's strategy necessarily weakened the Russian state and effective market reform as it augmented his personal power in the short term. The penetration of the state by oligarchic and bureaucratic interests enabled these forces to oppose government regulation and a competitive market, condemning Russia to intermittent periods of feeble reforms. Other post-Communist transitions, in conditions of partial reform, also experienced the rise of powerful private economic groups which then opposed comprehensive reform in order to maintain profitable distortions in the economy. Although partial reforms in Russia created similar groups, the Russian administration fostered these interests and worked to create linkages between them and the state. This difference helps account for significant variations in the economic and political power of such groups across transitional cases.

ZERO-SUM POLITICAL STRUGGLE

Russia specialists often argue that the gross distortions of economic restructuring in Russia were largely avoidable and that the leadership could have secured both political survival as well as effective reform and state building. Linz and Stepan argue that an interregnum devoted to cultivating societal forces and building bridges to moderates would have allowed for comprehensive economic transformation. The convocation of elections when he was most popular would have permitted Yeltsin to mobilize support for economic change and driven many of his antireform opponents from the Supreme Soviet and from local soviets. In short, intra-elite bargaining and linkages with society increase the capacity of the state to implement reforms.

Other analysts, however, recognize that state collapse and economic crisis left the reformers with no opportunity for careful democratization and state building prior to economic restructuring. Nevertheless, they criticize Yeltsin for not *simultaneously* restructuring the state, the political system, and the economy. According to Anders Aslund, Yeltsin succumbed to his preference for personalistic rule, and by turning his back on early elections and a new constitution, squandered his store of legitimacy.[28] This scenario of lost opportunities is attractive and seemingly plausible because it reflects many of the successful elite choices that were made in transitional cases in South America and Southern and Central Europe. However, some of its basic assumptions are faulty, particularly in assuming sufficient malleability of confining conditions at the hands of astute elites. In Russia, divisions among elites were significantly sharper than in earlier transitions, blocking agreement on new constitutional arrangements or a program of economic reform. Thus, the frequent use by political scientists of post-Franco Spain as a transitional model is particularly inappropriate.[29] Regarding elite conflict, Russia in the immediate post-Soviet period more closely resembled Spain in the 1930s when extreme ideological divisions were accompanied by a highly confrontational political style. By the time of the Spanish transition 40 years later, this original ideological divide had virtually disappeared.[30] Even in more turbulent cases, such as Argentina, decades of political unrest finally led elites and interest groups to value cooperation.[31]

At the heart of the process of depolarization in Spain were two conditions absent from post-Soviet Russia: (1) a higher level of elite security grounded in organized and coherent social groups; and (2) relatively stable market economics.[32] In Russia, by contrast, the collapse of the Soviet Union deeply exacerbated the ideological divisions in the country over markets and democracy that had initially developed under Mikhail Gorbachev in the late Soviet period. Furthermore, battling elites, particularly liberals, were politically insecure because their newly won power did not rest on strong or stable bases of societal support.

This is not to deny that the radical Russian reformers alienated moderates with their arrogance, aloofness from coalition-building, and inclination to polarize the debate over reform. Yet these faults were common to virtually all political elites in Russia. According to John Lowenhardt, Russia's political elites failed to reach agreement on institutional choices, particularly a constitution, due in large measure to their venality, lack of patience and equanimity, and above all their weak commitment to democratic procedures.[33] While Gaidar's radical policies further deepened elite divisions, the fundamental contours of elite conflict predated—and were not caused by—the economic policy of the radical reformers.

These deep splits among elites were cemented by the holdover institutions of the late Soviet period. As Linz and Stepan and other scholars point out, political institutions, if properly crafted, can promote elite accommodation and cooperation. But dysfunctional institutional design makes agreement on the political and economic rules among fractious elites improbable. The weak political institutions inherited by Russia from the Soviet period cemented the deep elite splits in post-Soviet Russia, making agreement on the political and economic rules of the game even less likely. These holdover institutions comprised an assembly and a presidency, which were created sequentially—the assembly in 1990 and the presidency in 1991. As Gorbachev's perestroika unraveled, institutional self-interest dictated that both branches cooperate to undermine the power of both the union CPSU and the central government. But this cobbled institutional design lacked clearly defined powers for the different branches, ensuring the escalation of turf battles between the legislature and the President (Yeltsin) after the dissolution of the Soviet Union.[34]

Thus, in the context of polarized elite competition, rapid mass-privatization was driven not only by a weak state seeking to create economic efficiencies and stem the looting of its assets by self-regarding bureaucratic elites, but it was also shaped by reformers intent on creating socioeconomic foundations of support that would offset the perceived strengths of the communist and growing ultranationalist opposition.[35] These different objectives created fundamental tensions within the reform process, increasingly pitting political expediency against sound economic policies. Such tensions were usually resolved in favor of political expediency. The administration exchanged state assets for political support, enabling concentrated private interests to amass wealth and power.

RUSSIAN SOCIETY: WASTED ASSET OR WEAK ALLY?

Some analysts contend that these momentous struggles between elites could have been resolved in favor of the reformers had they forged political links with Russian society. Furthermore, a number of area specialists, whom Linz and Stepan follow, argue that Yeltsin had the opportunity to stand at the head of Democratic Russia, the political movement, which had supported him since 1990. Although Yeltsin eventually demurred, Democratic Russia might have been transformed into a presidential party dedicated to democratization and structural economic reform.[36]

In *Democracy From Scratch*, Steven Fish helps us evaluate the argument that the reformers wasted societal assets. The work is an intelligent study whose examination of state-society interaction during the late Gorbachev period is linked to the problems of the post-Soviet period. Fish asks why the emerging organizations in Soviet "political" society were weak in the following areas: interest articulation and aggregation; channels to the government; coherent agendas; rational intra-organizational hierarchies; and effective infrastructures. Perhaps most important, he explores why the new societal organizations failed to secure stable, mass memberships.[37]

Fish convincingly argues against the use of political culture to explain the inchoate nature of political society during late perestroika. He adopts an institutional approach that focuses on the constraints created by the legacy and policies of Soviet state institutions. His argument, in brief, is that the totalitarian nature of the Soviet system and its etatization of the economy left society naked before the state. Although the advent of perestroika provided society with opportunities to mobilize against the Leninist state, the growth of an authentic civil society and independent political associations was checked by continued state resistance and by the absence of a middle class skilled in self-organization. Elections were eventually sanctioned by the

Soviet regime, but their convocation before political parties were allowed
to exist reduced their importance as mechanisms of political mobilization.
According to Fish, "To a far greater degree than in other contemporary
transitions, the most basic elements of collective political identities had to
be invented and assembled entirely from scratch."[38]

For the reasons that Fish elaborates, party building in Russia, even from
above, confronts enormous obstacles. Democratic Russia, like all mass
movements, was congenitally unstable, becoming more so after the collapse
of Soviet communism and the loss of the organization's founding logic.[39]
This pattern of demobilization and fragmentation was also evident among
mass movements in Poland and Czechoslovakia.

Given the weakness of civil society in Russia, the reformers had fewer
political opportunities than Linz and Stepan suggest. Not only were the
reformers weak in terms of political organization and growing weaker; they
confronted relatively disciplined Communist forces that remained strong in
Russia's regions. Furthermore, in the year following the Soviet collapse, a
"red-brown" alliance was forged, joining Russian Communists and extreme
nationalists. Even at this early stage, when the popularity of the reformers
was at its height, the unity of "red-brown" groups within and outside the
national legislature was significantly greater than that found among Russia's
anemic liberal parties.[40]

For these reasons, it is unlikely that early elections would have significantly
altered the composition of the legislature. Sending Russia to the polls may
have undermined, not strengthened, the reformers. Elections also would
have enhanced the legitimacy of the hostile legislature, threatening to tip the
struggle between president and assembly in the latter's favor.[41]

THE COSTS OF POLITICAL SURVIVAL

The damage that Russia's pattern of political conflict inflicted on the Russian
state and the project of political and economic reform may be assessed
by returning to the three dimensions of state capacity. At the institutional
level, which encompasses the legitimacy of the state as well as the ability
of governing elites to frame the rules of the game, the Russian state under
Yeltsin suffered a severe loss of capacity. If one measures the effectiveness of
a state by its insulation from pressure groups, the autonomy of the Russian
state must also be judged to be very low.

Political combat also negatively affected the institutional framework of
the political system. In a context of zero-sum conflict, Yeltsin had strong
incentives to favor a super presidential system. When this system was put
in place after the violent disbandment of the parliament in October 1993,
state capacity further eroded. The Russian presidency was subject to little
oversight by the new (and weak) parliament, encouraging corruption and
rent-seeking. The weakness of the parliament also discouraged politicians

from investing time and resources in nurturing Russia's nascent political parties. Furthermore, by insulating the executive from the parliament, super presidentialism worked against intra-elite bargaining and sharpened political conflict, while reinforcing the foundation for "delegative" democracy.[42]

In the political dimension of state capacity, zero-sum conflict and Yeltsin's strategy further eroded society's capacity for political self-organization. Although the political utility of early national elections may have been low for Yeltsin, his decision to forego them arrested the long-term development of political parties and undermined popular perceptions of political efficacy. In one survey administered in the late Yeltsin period, only 8 percent of the respondents felt that the influence of ordinary citizens was greater in the post-Soviet period than under the communist regime.[43]

Finally, the Russian state suffered a continuous and significant decline in administrative capacity during the Yeltsin year. The administration's toleration of corruption and rent-seeking seriously damaged the state, and encouraged similar behavior at all levels of the bureaucracy. Inevitably, such practices undermined the legitimacy of the state, crippling public-spirited behavior and the desire to obey the state.

THE RISE OF VLADIMIR PUTIN, THE REVIVAL OF THE RUSSIAN STATE, AND THE ASSAULT ON PLURALISM

In the Russian case, situational (economic crisis) and particularly structural constraints set the country apart from earlier, successful transitions like Spain. Yeltsin did little to ameliorate these negative conditions, allowing the country to drift from crisis to crisis in the second half of the 1990s. Facing poor health and single-digit ratings in public opinion polls at the end of the decade, Yeltsin abruptly resigned his office, in December 1999, thereby moving Vladimir Putin, his Prime Minister and former member of the KGB and FSB, into the position of Acting President. Putin won the subsequent presidential election of 2000 handily.

If Russian democratization under Yeltsin suffered from extreme neglect as well as frequent abuse, under Putin it has been brutally assaulted. An important development of the Yeltsin period had been the gradual acceptance by most Russian elites—at least in principle—of elections, markets, and private property. However, the most influential elites under Yeltsin—the oligarchs—did much to corrupt each of these institutions, in part through their ability to pressure the Russian state to protect and favor their interests. Nevertheless, the Russian oligarchs were closely tied to the West through their business interests and cultural tastes, and felt it necessary to at least publicly support free markets and elections. A few of the oligarchs—such as the oil tycoon Mikhail Khodarkovsky—eventually if belatedly lent their support to authentic efforts at democratization in Russia.

Putin has done much to diminish the political influence of this group, transferring it to the *silovki*, top state officials with backgrounds in the Interior Ministry, the military, or the Federal Security Service (FSB). These "uniformed bureacrats" form a nascent "militocracy" that shares Putin's interest in restoring a strong Russian state and reviving Russian patriotism.

Given the debilitation of the Russian state under Yeltsin, the restoration of its autonomy was a logical priority for Putin. However, Putin's approach to reviving the Russian state strengthens institutions (the "power ministries") that for the most part are hostile to authentic pluralism. This prejudice is supported by their institutional interest in vigilance against domestic and external enemies, real or imagined. This perspective is shared by Putin, who has referred to his critics in the Russian media as "traitors" and has worked to constrain Russian civil society, most recently by restricting the activities of nongovernmental organizations. After the politicized arrest and conviction of Mikhail Khodarkovsky on economic charges, even the once-powerful Russian oligarchs have been driven from any oppositional role in politics.

Putin seeks to revive the Russian state in part because of its important role as provider of essential public goods, above all public security. But Putin's view of the state is also strongly influenced by his understanding of the path to modernity and of what a modern society should look like. Adhering to Russia's centuries' old conceptualization of political and socioeconomic development, Putin's approach to modernization is dominated by the idea of a strong state that mobilizes society to achieve the goals of the state.

In order to better understand this threat to Russia pluralism, it is useful to compare Putin's view of the international environment to that of Stalin. In 1931 Stalin sought to mobilize the Party and the nation for his forced-draft economic program by stressing the need to defend the Russian homeland against foreign threats:

> We have a fatherland and shall defend its independence. Do you want our fatherland to be beaten and lose its independence? If not, then you must abolish its backwardness. . . . We are fifty or a hundred years behind the advanced countries. We must make good this lag in ten years. Either we accomplish this or we will be crushed.[44]

On May 16, 2003, Putin delivered his annual address to the Russian Federal Assembly. Putin told the gathering that Russia must concentrate all its energy in ensuring that Russia will take its rightful place among the ranks of the "truly strong, economically advanced and influential nations. . . . Not only will people feel proud of such a country. . . . They will remember and respect our great history." In order to achieve this objective, "we must consolidate, we must mobilize our intellectual forces and unite the efforts of the state authorities, civil society, and all the people of this land." Putin told the audience that Russia's modernization must not be delayed:

[History demonstrates that] when Russia is weak...it threatens the collapse of the country....We [now] face serious threats....We are surrounded by countries with highly developed economies. We need to face the fact that these countries push Russia out of promising world markets whenever they have the chance. And their obvious economic advantages serve as fuel for their growing geopolitical ambitions....It is my conviction that without consolidation at a minimum around basic national values and objectives, we will not withstand these threats. [45]

Reminding the gathering that Russia had always surmounted serious challenges to its existence in the past, Putin stated that the historical task of maintaining the immense Russian state and preserving Russia's international position was "not just an immense labor, it is also a task that has cost our people untold victims and sacrifice."[46]

There is little evidence to suggest that Putin wants to return to extreme, Soviet methods of controlling society or that his proclaimed goal of intergrating Russia into the global economy is not authentic. However, Putin's refusal to condemn the brutal character of Soviet modernization, and his apparent willingness to trace the human losses under Stalinism to the requirements of state survival, mark an important shift in official discourse that further reconstructs and simplifies the past through deliberate forgetfulness. Putin apparently seeks integration with the West on his own terms, which do not include the adoption of Western democratic institutions.

Putin's threat to Russian democratization is particularly dangerous because he remains overwhelmingly popular. A number of factors explain this phenomenon, and it would be unwise to assume that it is due simply to an authoritarian political culture bred in Russia by centuries of political oppression. To the contrary, polling evidence suggests that a majority of Russians value democracy in normative terms, embrace the importance of elections, and hope that Russia will one day develop strong democratic institutions. Nevertheless, the basis of Putin's popularity is the long-awaited provision under his government of social, economic, and political stability – public goods that were in very short supply under Yeltsin. Indeed, many Russians now associate the "democracy" and "capitalism" that emerged under Yeltsin with the weak Russian state, the rapacious oligarchs, and the economic hardships of the 1990s.

THE WARS IN CHECHNYA AND THE DECAY OF RUSSIAN DEMOCRATIZATION

The crisis in Chechnya, which has deeply scarred the political landscape of post-Soviet Russia, both reflects and promotes the withering of democratization. The chapter now turns to how the weakness of democratic institutions in Russia has exacerbated the Chechen conflict, and how the Chechen conflict has, in turn, further weakened the prospects for democracy in Russia.

It is not surprising that the most unstable region in post-Soviet Russia is the North Caucasus, which had been a fiercely contested outpost of tsarist expansion in the nineteenth century. Over a period of four decades (1816–1856) the Russian state encountered strong resistance from the mountain nationalities of the region, particularly the Chechens. The Chechens, who are a distinct ethnic group (but closely related to the neighboring Ingush) are the largest group in the North Caucasus (with around 1 million inhabitants according to the 1989 census) and the second largest ethnic group in the Caucasus as a whole (after the Georgians).

In this initial, brutal encounter with Russia, Chechen civilian casualties were high, and forced, mass deportations from the Caucasus to the interior of Russia were common. Hundreds of thousands of members of the autochthonous communities fled to Turkey and other regional states. This pattern of extreme violence by the Russian state against the Chechens recurred in early 1944, when the Chechen nation, now part of the Soviet Union, was accused by the Stalin's regime of mass collaboration with the Nazi invaders. The Chechens were deported *en masse* to Siberia, Kazakhstan, and Kyrgyzstan. The collective memories of these calamitous events have shaped Chechen identity and the Chechen "othering" of the Russian state and the Russian people.

At no point in the post-Soviet period has Russian policy toward Chechnya been guided by a consistent recognition that the Chechen people suffered greater political, physical, cultural, and economic repression under the tsars and Communists than perhaps any other ethnic or religious group in the Russian empire or the Soviet Union. This legacy of almost two centuries of historical grievances against Russia largely accounts for Chechen secessionism in the 1990s and for the ferocity of Chechen resistance to Russian attempts to quell the Chechen rebellion.

Although memories of tsarist and Soviet oppression fueled the Chechen bid for independence from Russia, it was the weakness of the Russian state as it emerged from the collapse of the Soviet Union that permitted Chechen separatists to calculate that secession had good prospects for success. This movement had gathered strength in 1990 and 1991 under former Soviet air force general Dzhokhar Dudaev, although it is unclear precisely how widespread the support for secession was in the republic. Dudaev refused to negotiate a federal treaty with Yeltsin's administration that would have provided Chechnya full autonomy within the Russian Federation similar to arrangements negotiated with Tatarstan.

In late 1994 the Russian government under Yeltsin launched the first of two invasions of Chechnya. It is likely that the first conflict was a case of "diversionary war," motivated more by political considerations than concerns for territorial integrity.[47] According to the literature on diversionary war, embattled leaders and elites may instigate hypernationalist programs and perhaps initiate war to attract elite and popular support. For example, Sergei Witte remarked on the eve of the Russo–Japanese War that what the tsar needed was "a short, victorious war" to restore his prestige and weaken the growing revolutionary movement in Russia.

Edward Mansfield and Jack Snyder suggest that similar political motives were at work in Russia's First Chechen War (1994–1996). In their discussion of "Weimar Russia," Mansfield and Snyder argue that recently empowered voters injured by Yeltsin's market reforms and privatization cast their ballots in droves for ultranationalists like Vladimir Zhirinovsky, putting ostensible liberals like Yeltsin and Foreign Minister Andrey Kozyrev on the defensive and contributing "to the climate that led to [first] war in Chechnya."[48] At the same time, embattled old elites, particularly from the Army and the security forces, saw an invasion of Chechnya as a means to restore their sagging legitimacy and advance their standing in the budgetary struggle in post-Soviet society.[49] Other factors doubtless also played a role in the decision to invade, including Moscow's desire to reclaim the significant oil resources of the region.

Expecting a quick victory, the Russian Army entered Chechnya overconfident and unprepared both in terms of planning and provisions. Chechen fighters inflicted a series of humiliating defeats on Russian forces, eventually leading to a political settlement in August 1996. That agreement, signed for the Chechens by Aslan Maskhadov, the most famous of the Chechen generals, stipulated the withdrawal of Russian troops, followed by long-term negotiations as to the future status of relations between Russia and Chechnya. Chechnya's status was not to be determined before December 31, 2001.

THE SECOND CHECHEN CONFLICT: JUST WAR OR DIVERSIONARY CONFLICT?

The price of the Chechen victory was high. The war caused widespread devastation and social dislocation in Chechnya, and the reparations for reconstruction promised by Russia were not forthcoming, not least because Moscow had difficulty keeping its own fiscal house in order. Although Chechens elected Maskhadov as president in fair elections in 1997, he was unable to govern the territory with any effectiveness. The collapse of civil order in Chechnya was evident in rampant smuggling operations, trade in white slavery, and ransom kidnapping of Russian citizens and journalists by numerous Chechen gangs. During the period 1996 to 1999, over 1,300 Russian citizens, mostly Dagestanis, were abducted.[50]

The primary source of instability was the struggle among political elites over the future of Chechnya. Prominent Chechens who were commanders in the first Chechen War, including Shamil Basaev, increasingly denounced

Maskhadov, who envisioned a nominally independent Chechnya but with close political and economic ties to Russia, as a traitor to the Chechen cause. The wave of kidnappings was partly due to the efforts of radical Chechens to undermine Maskhadov's efforts at cooperation with Russia and the Western organizations. Twenty-two aid workers were assassinated and twenty-two were kidnapped during this period. The culmination of these kidnappings occurred on March 5, 1999, when General Gennady Shpigun, the Russian Interior Ministry representative in Chechnya, was seized at the Grozny airport by masked gunmen. As NGOs began to leave Chechnya in fear and disgust, President Maskhadov failed to restore order.

Conviction but also political expedience led many of Maskhadov's opponents to embrace Muslim fundamentalism and form alliances with the numerous mujahedeen from the Middle East and elsewhere who were drawn to Chechnya by the Russian invasion and the prospect of a holy war against Russia and the West. In 1998, a political and military union was struck between three forces: Basaev and his Chechen followers; Ibn-ul-Khattab, the Arab leader of international mujahedeen in Chechnya; and Islamic radicals from neighboring Daghestan. The Arab mujahedeen were primarily of Saudi Wahhabi background, and many were also veterans of the Afghan war against the Soviet Union. They had financial resources, battle experience, and a fervent commitment to undermining Russian rule throughout the Caucasus. Although Maskhadov attempted to counter the spread of radicalism by more publicly embracing Islamism himself, this defensive measure promoted an unintended spiral of political outbidding which ultimately strengthened Islamic radicalism, while also alienating the West and moderates in Russia. For example, after his election Maskhadov introduced Islamic law (sharia), leading to widespread and public corporal punishment and even to executions broadcast on local television.[51]

Islamic militancy in Chechnya was also buoyed by the tentative spread of Islamic radicalism among ordinary Chechens made desperate by the socioeconomic and political disorder that followed the war with Russia. Their search for security led some of them to embrace the idea of an "Islamic order," weakening Chechnya's strong traditions of secularism and moderate Sufism. Yet another source of destabilization was the growth of radical Wahhabism in a number of villages in neighboring Daghestan. In April 1998, these extremists formed the Congress of Peoples of Chechnya and Daghestan for the purpose of joining the two Russian republics in an Islamic state.

Border skirmishes beginning in April 1999 between Russian and Chechen forces culminated in early August 1999 with the invasion of neighboring Daghestan by several hundred Chechen, Daghestani Wahhabis, and other Muslim fighters who seized a number of villages. Yeltsin dispatched Vladimir Putin, his newly appointed Prime Minister, to restore order in Daghestan.[52] On September 5 it was reported that 2,000 additional Chechen fighters had crossed the Daghestani border to support the initial invasion. However by mid-September all of the invaders had been dislodged from Daghestan by massive Russian air and ground assaults, which laid waste too much of the contested area.

Amid the crisis in Daghestan a bombing campaign was launched against civilian targets in Russian cities. On August 31 a bomb exploded in the Manezh shopping area near Red Square. On September 9 and September 13 powerful bombs destroyed two apartment buildings in Moscow. On September 16 another bomb exploded near an apartment building in the city of Volgodonsk. Almost 300 people died in these explosions.

Although no group claimed responsibility for these terrorist acts, the bombings served as the proximate cause for Russia's second invasion of Chechnya. Russian authorities blamed Chechen rebels for the explosions, and declared they would wipe out the source of terrorism in Chechnya. Military operations commenced against Chechnya and Grozny was bombed on September 23. Nevertheless, Russian journalists and Western analysts remained unconvinced, accusing the government of responsibility for the blasts in an effort to provoke popular outrage and justify a second invasion of Chechnya.[53]

Did the Second Chechen War begin as a just war or as a diversionary conflict? The bombings *did* galvanize Russian public opinion for military action, and invasion of Chechnya *did* serve the political interests of the Kremlin. Most important, the invasion provided Yeltsin with an exit strategy from his failing Presidency. Allegations of corruption had dogged Yeltsin in 1999, and members of his family and circle of advisors were placed under investigation abroad. In May 1999, the Duma started impeachment proceedings against Yeltsin, accusing him of high treason and other crimes. Although Yeltsin survived this ordeal, only 12 percent of Russians were happy with the outcome.[54]

On New Year's Eve Yeltsin resigned his office, making Putin, his appointee as Prime Minister, the acting President according to the provisions of the Russian constitution. Within 24 hours, Putin extended immunity to Yeltsin and his family, who had been threatened with corruption investigations both at home and abroad.[55] By this time the war in Chechnya had made Putin enormously popular and the ideal shield for Yeltsin. A former Lieutenant Colonel of the FSB (the domestic successor to the KGB), Putin had been plucked from obscurity to head that agency in 1988 and was then appointed prime minister in 1999. The surprise of Yeltsin's resignation also made it unlikely that Russian political society would have sufficient time to field a viable challenge to Putin in the presidential elections now rescheduled for March 2000. Thus, the Second Chechen War created conditions that protected Yeltsin from criminal investigations and all but ensured the election of Putin, his protege and presumed protector, as president.

Despite the continued belief of many Russians and Western analysts in a government conspiracy, it is more likely that the bombs were set off by

Islamic militants, such as Basaev and Khattab, to advance their campaign to create a united Chechen–Daghestani Muslim state.[56] Convinced that Russia was a paper tiger after its defeats in Afghanistan and in the First Chechen War, the Chechen militants believed that a second war with Russia would destroy the political center in Chechen politics and propel them to power at the head of an independent trans-Caucasus Islamic state.

The steady descent of Chechnya into anarchy over the preceding 2 years and the dramatic incursions into Daghestan from Chechnya, followed by the bombings, were ample justifications for a military response from Moscow to curb Chechen radicalism and bring a semblance of order to a region still legally part of the Russian state (the only states to recognize Chechen independence were Afghanistan under the Taliban and the Turkish Republic of Northern Cyprus, which itself was recognized only by Turkey). However, Russian conduct in the second Chechen conflict was strongly influenced by domestic politics. Yeltsin and Putin quickly abandoned the initial goal of fighting terrorism soon after the beginning of the invasion. Moscow refused to exploit the deep political rifts in Chechen ranks or to join forces with President Maskhadov against the Chechen militants despite Maskhadlov's repeated entreaties to the Kremlin for support in his struggle with Chechen militants like Basayev. Nor did Moscow demonstrate any interest in tapping the war-weariness of the average Chechen, who was either indifferent or hostile to Muslim radicalism, the proclaimed target of the Russian invasion. Instead, Moscow prosecuted a war of unrestrained brutality, which it justified by the demonization of the Chechen people in the state-controlled media. Putin refused to rein in the Russian Army, whose rampage in Chechnya was clearly retribution for its humiliating defeats in the First Chechen War. Indeed, Putin encouraged the brutality of the army by coarsening public discourse ("We will kill them in the outhouse") and by placing strict limitations on Russian and foreign press coverage. In the words of Sergey Parkhomenko, the editor-in-chief of the Russian magazine *Itogi*, "The wonder and triumph of Putin rest not only on the blood of innocent people who have perished in Chechnya ... but on a cold-blooded policy aimed at exploiting the gloomy shadows residing in the hidden corners ... of 'everyday' nationalism."[57] Thus, the Second Chechen War was launched in response to Chechen provocations, but the political interests of Yeltsin and Putin and the prestige considerations of the Russian Army dramatically broadened the scope and objectives of the war.

Just as the terror bombings in Moscow and the incursions of Chechen and Daghestani radicals into Daghestan in 1999 helped Yeltsin hand-pick Putin as his successor at a time when all other political options appeared exhausted, the launching of the Second Chechen War by the Kremlin enabled Putin as president to use Russia's "war on terror" to legitimate the Kremlin's attacks on democratic institutions and freedoms in Russia.

Russian civil society, including the independent media, has suffered significant losses during this period and remains under constant political pressure. One of the notable features of the First Chechen War was the determination of Russian journalists to expose the lies of the government and the military as well as the vast cost of the war in terms of blood and treasure.[58] By contrast, the Second Chechen War has seen a much higher degree of support among the Russia media. This support is partly due to the widespread belief—after the apartment bombings in September 1999 in Moscow and elsewhere—that Chechnya now poses a serious threat to the national security and constitutional integrity of Russia. But direct and indirect government pressure on the media has also played an important role in marginalizing criticism of the government in its efforts to use the war in Chechnya to generate political support. Although the evidence does not support the accusation that Yeltsin and Putin manufactured pretexts for the invasion of Chechnya in September 1999, it is clear that the Kremlin seized the opportunity for war once it presented itself in the form of the terror bombings the previous month. Kremlin spokesman, Sergei Yastrzhembsky, spelled out the politicized nature of the war: "When the nation mobilizes its forces to achieve some task, that imposes obligations on everyone, including the media."[59]

The Russian state has used the cover of antiterrorism to attack other segments of Russian civil society in order to stifle the growth of potential political opposition and dissent. In December 2005 the Duma (legislature) approved a bill that places strict curbs on nongovernmental organizations in Russia. The bill, which was signed into law by Putin the following month, provides for a new state agency to oversee the registration, financing and activities of thousands of foreign and domestic NGOs. The new agency, not the courts, would determine the legal status of an NGO. Supporters of the proposed law, which would require NGOs to continually account for their activities to the government, argue that the measure is necessary to identify groups that support terrorism and extremism. But opponents say the law will further cripple Russian civil society. They maintain that the legislation stems from the Kremlin's hostility to NGOs that criticize the government's authoritarian practices and might support a Russian "color revolution," as was the case in Ukraine, Georgia, and Kyrgyzstan.[60] Pro-government commentators openly admit that the law was meant to forestall efforts to establish a "Western version of democracy in Russia."[61]

ONE STEP FORWARD, ONE STEP BACK: PUTIN'S CHECHENIZATION STRATEGY

Using overwhelming and often indiscriminate firepower in the Second Chechen War against a Chechen force that was internally divided (unlike the First Chechen War), the Kremlin eventually achieved a measure of success in its struggle to conquer Chechnya. By 2001 a harsh militarized peace had been imposed: Government or pro-government republican forces controlled the urban areas and a pro-Kremlin Chechen administration was installed in Grozny, the capital.

Although the shrinking numbers of Chechen insurgents were forced into the rugged countryside, they ranged freely after nightfall, attacking the Russian "occupiers" and the militias of the Chechen "puppet" government and its supporters. Underlining the fragility of the occupation, Akhmad Kadyrov, the Chechen mufti who was appointed by Putin in 2000 to head the interim civilian administration and later elected president of the republic in October 2003, was assassinated in May 2000. Equally important, the radical wing of the Chechen insurgents continued to launch spectacular and gruesome terror assaults against Russian civilian targets not only in neighboring regions but also in Moscow.

The most tragic episode of terrorism was the attack by Shamil Basayev, the most effective and brutal of the Chechen rebels, on the schoolhouse in the town of Beslan, in the Russian republic of North Ossetia, which took the lives of over 350 adults and children. Ruslan Aushev, the former president of the neighboring republic of Ingushetiia, served as an intermediary during the siege, and later provided a sobering assessment of the prospects for peace in the region. According to Aushev, the continued brutal treatment of the Chechen population by Russian forces and their proxies was constantly replenishing the insurgency with new, ever more fanatical, recruits. Only if the Kremlin is willing to negotiate in good faith with moderate insurgents could the new "fanatics" be isolated and the cycle of violence be arrested. Otherwise, political unrest and terrorism would continue to spread to other parts of the Caucasus, and perhaps beyond.[62] Similarly, other Russian observers argue that revenge—not radical Islamism—is the primary source of terrorism—and support for terrorism—in the Caucasus. Oleg Orlov of the *Memorial Society*, Russia's leading human rights organization, followed this line of thinking in his explanation for why Chechen women were becoming suicide bombers, detonating their explosives on Russian commercial airliners and in Moscow's subway and on its streets.

Orlov places much of the blame on the *zachistki*, the violent operations conducted by Russian forces and their Chechen allies searching for rebel forces, which have inflict widespread murder, rape, and torture on the local population. Another important catalyst for rebellion are the undocumented kidnappings of suspected Chechen rebels or sympathizers by security forces, which according to Orlov, now equal the number of similar abuses committed at the peak of the Stalinist repression in 1937–1938. These intolerable conditions have left Chechen society "completely unprotected.... People are angry. Some of them start sympathizing with terrorists; others . . . start helping them. There is a mass of insulted, humiliated, and desperate people."

Increasing numbers of Chechen women who had lost their husbands, parents, or children to "state terror" often see suicide bombing "as the "only recourse."[63]

Khassan Baiev, a Chechen physician who risked his life treating both insurgent and Russian casualties in the Second Chechen War and who later received political asylum in the United States, provides a more complete picture of the losses suffered by Chechen society since the first Chechen War:

> About one-quarter of our population has been killed since 1994. Fifty percent of the Chechen nation now live outside Chechnya. . . . Estimates claim that 75 percent of the Chechen environment is contaminated. . . . Pediatricians report that one-third of children are born with birth defects.[64]

Despite its support for the brutal conduct of the Russian Army in the Second Chechen War, the Russian government under Putin has gradually moved closer to understanding that brutality breeds extremism, and that a political solution—not simply fear and violence—must be part of any plan to pacify Chechnya. To that end, the Kremlin inaugurated a policy of "Chechenization" in 2001 that sought to draw Chechens into Moscow-supported institutions that would govern the republic and direct its reconstruction. Elections for a new president were held in 2003 and parliamentary elections took place in December 2005. To support this process, Putin criticized the gross mistreatment of the Chechen nation by the Soviet and then post-Soviet Russian state, and has suggested that such abuse was partly to explain for the extreme hostility many Chechens felt for Russia. Most important, in an address before Chechnya's newly elected republican parliament, Putin publicly deplored Stalin's deportation of the Chechen nation to the steppes of Central Asia in 1944.[65] Shortly after the tragedy at Beslan, Putin also admitted to a group of journalists that the First Chechen War "was probably a mistake," and seemed to grasp the importance of political compromise in resolving the problem of Chechen separatism.

For some Chechens, Putin's willingness to tell the truth about the deportations seemed open to the door to political reconciliation. Indeed, Moscow's greatest potential asset in finding a political solution in Chechnya is the Chechen people, who have been traumatized by more than a decade of conflict, insecurity, and deprivation. Understanding the hard choices before them, most Chechens now reject secession and the goal of an independent Chechnya. In a recent authoritative survey, 78 percent of Chechens said that Chechnya should remain one of the eighty-nine regions of Russia.[66] Only 19 percent of those polled felt that Chechnya should pursue independence.

The complication for the Kremlin is that 61 percent of the respondents would support Chechnya remaining part of Russia only if Chechnya was given more autonomy than any other constituent part of Russia. Responding to this widespread opinion, Putin has promised that a policy of "Chechenization" would establish authentic autonomy based on electoral legitimation as well as the devolution from the center of significant powers to the republic, even to the point of "violating the Russian constitution."[67]

Despite the extensive publicity given to Chechenization by the Kremlin, it is doubtful that Putin's plan will yield positive results. In fact, Chechenization is likely to fuel Chechen terrorism rather than extinguish it. While it is true that the new Chechen constitution sponsored by the Kremlin in 2003 provides more autonomy to Chechnya than to any other regional government in Russia, many Chechens question the durability of such powers at a time when the federal center has been aggressively reducing the rights of the other federal "subjects." Skeptics need look no further than next door, to the Russian republic of Ingushetiia, where Ruslan Aushev, the popular but independent-minded president of that republic, had demonstrated considerable skill in weakening local radical Islamism and more generally keeping the potentially explosive multiethnic republic at peace with itself through effective policies. Despite this impressive record, the Kremlin forced Aushev to resign in December 2001 and engineered the election of Murat Ziazikov, a general in the FSB, as the new president of Ingushetiia.

Even if Chechnya is exempted from Putin's efforts to recentralize power in the Kremlin, reducing federalism in Russia to window-dressing, there is much else that is flawed in his plan for stabilizing Chechnya. The essential missing ingredient in this political process is inclusiveness: not only rebels but also peaceful advocates of separatism have been excluded from participation in the elections. Yet as the experience of the IRA in Northern Ireland and other separatist movements has shown, progress becomes possible only when the staunchest opponents of compromise are offered a role in the political process.

To make matters worse, by all accounts the presidential and parliamentary elections that Russia supervised in Chechnya were not free and fair even in terms of the limited field of candidates that were permitted to run. The Kremlin threw its weight behind Alu Alkhanov and Ramzan Kadyrov, the son of the assassinated president. After the electoral victory of Alkhanov, Ramzan Kadyrov was appointed his deputy prime minister and it became clear that Kadyrov was the real power in the government, not least because he commanded perhaps the largest of the private militias that now vied with Russian forces for control of key sectors of Grozny, the capital, and other parts of the country. Kadyrov and his militia are often blamed by Chechens and knowledgeable Russian and foreign observers for widespread kidnapping, extortion, and other crimes. However, Putin has received Kadyrov in the Kremlin and honored him with a high Russian decoration.

The death of Aslan Maskhadov in Chechnya at the hands of Russian security forces in March 2005 marked the loss of another opportunity to work for a durable peace in Chechnya. The killing of Maskhadov, who was elected president of Chechnya in 1997 and had led Chechnya's underground separatist government after 1999, was dramatic evidence that the Kremlin held fast to imposing, not negotiating, a political settlement in Chechnya. Although Maskhadov's death was hailed by the Kremlin as a victory in the war against terrorism, Russian human rights groups pointed out that Maskhadov had consistently opposed the use of terrorism as a political tool and had never abandoned his efforts to negotiate with the Kremlin. Although Maskhadov had fought a losing battle with Chechen extremists such as Basayev from 1997 to 1999, and did not possess sufficient authority to speak for all of the rebel factions fighting Russian forces after the outbreak of the Second Chechen War in August 1999, he did represent authentic moderation and still commanded widespread respect among the Chechen population. While in office, Maskhadov had spoken in favor of secular education in Chechnya and against Moslem fundamentalism. With the rise of Muslim radicalism and terrorism in 1999, Maskhadov sought Russian help to defeat the alliance of Muslim fundamentalists and radical secular separatists, but Moscow rejected his appeals.

A brief window of opportunity to broker a peace deal between Russia and Chechnya opened in August 2001 when delegations from the Russian Duma (legislature) and Maskhadov's underground government met for secret talks in Caux, Switzerland, and the following year in Liechtenstein. The meetings were sponsored by the American Committee for Peace in Chechnya (ACPC), an American NGO chaired by former National Security Advisor Zbigniew Brzezinski, former Secretary of State Alexander M. Haig, Jr., and former Congressman Stephen J. Solarz. The organization is dedicated to finding a peaceful solution to the Chechen conflict, but nevertheless remains extremely critical of Russia.

The ACPC-sponsored talks produced a draft agreement that stipulated that Chechnya would remain legally a part of Russia, but would enjoy a maximum degree of authentic self-rule. Although plans were made to present the draft formally to the Kremlin, Putin suddenly and inexplicably disowned the plan as the work of Boris Berezovsky, the rogue Russia oligarch in self-exile in the United Kingdom.[68] With the killing of Maskhadov 3 years later by Russian forces in Chechnya, the legitimately elected leader of Chechnya passed from the scene. Tanya Lokshina, a program director at the Moscow Helsinki Group, a human rights organization, observed that the moderates in the separatist movement had now lost their leader and face a choice: "Quit or join Basayev. And I think most will join Basayev."[69]

The legacy of Russian brutality and the inevitable repercussions of the Kremlin's refusal to implement an inclusive political settlement are compounded by the Kremlin's failure to address adequately the disastrous social and economic conditions that beset the republic. Disease is rampant, and the lack of basic necessities is a chronic and widespread problem. Alu Alkhanov, the pro-Russian president of Chechnya, openly complained that the "70 per cent jobless rate [in Chechnya] drives young men desperate to earn money into the arms of rebels fighting Russia."[70]

Andreas Gross, the Swiss representative of the Parliamentary Assembly of the Council of Europe (PACE), traveled to Chechnya in November 2005 to observe unofficially the Chechen parliamentary elections. Gross did not find it surprising that the elections were "not free of fair." Stating that the ordinary voters he spoke to on election-day were wracked by constant fear for their lives, Gross traced the multiple problems facing Chechnya to Russia's wrong-headed policies and to the unrestrained power of Kadyrov and his followers:

> The absence of security can undermine any election. That is why it is so important to include opponents in the process and to take over the control of security forces that do not obey the elected government and are not under the jurisdiction of the Courts. Moreover, a majority of the population is unemployed. That is why it is so important to restore the economy, the village, and the spirit of the people. There is money for these goals, but . . . it is stolen by corrupt officials.[71]

WHAT IS TO BE DONE?

Promoting democratization in Russia and working to resolve the crisis in Chechnya are important goals for the West. Yet the West must recognize the limits of its influence in both areas. Russia is too large and also geographically too distant for the democratic international community to have a decisive impact on either of these problems. If a state is self-sufficient, or nearly so (as is Russia), and possesses a vast base of natural resources, its rulers can more easily refuse to consider political reforms that might improve state capacity but may also weaken their rule. Such rulers can also skillfully exploit the reliance of external actors on trade or strategic cooperation with their country (in Russia's case, European reliance on its energy resources or America's desire for Russian acceptance of U.S. bases in Central Asia) to moderate or fend off international demands for internal reforms. A dramatic illustration of this point was the decision of Helmut Schroeder, the recently defeated German chancellor, to take a job with the Gazprom, the huge Russian energy conglomerate.

Furthermore, location matters, even in the era of globalization. The considerable distance of Russia from European institutionalized democracy also reduces the ability of the West to pressure or encourage Russia to change. It must also be doubted whether core Western institutions such as the EU and NATO have the capacity to absorb a country as large as Russia into their ranks. By contrast, Spain, as it started its own democratization, enjoyed an advantageous size and a propitious location, being close by a stable, wealthy, democratic community of fellow European states. Spain was invited to join that group as an equal member so long as it undertook democratization. This was an offer that most Spaniards could not refuse.

Russia lacks the possibility of a similar embrace by stable, wealthy democracies; the recent, unexpected, and tumultuous "revolutions" on Russia's borders are viewed as threats by Russia's ruling elites, who are drawn in large part from the security services and who worry that Russian influence is yet again receding in post-Soviet space. Democratization in Ukraine, Georgia, and Kyrgyzstan may very well be the harbinger of new, stable democracies on Russia's borders—with the potential one day for powerful, positive demonstration effects on domestic politics in Russia itself. That would be an historical irony indeed, as the former subservient republics of the Soviet empire help advance political change in the former metropole. But for now the "color revolutions" are stark reminders for Russia's rulers of the inability of the Russian state to control events in contiguous states that were recently constituent parts of the Russian and then Soviet empires. Such perceptions of vulnerability strengthen the desire to treat the problem of Chechnya as a completely "internal" matter.

Given the realities noted above, the Kremlin is unlikely to heed Western calls to explicitly "internationalize" the Chechen problem – either through the United Nations or another transnational agency that would supply peacekeepers and police.[72] This is especially so given the altered configuration of elites under Putin and the installation of officials who are deeply suspicious of the West. Although the Russian leadership was particularly sensitive to Western pressures and preferences in the early years of the Yeltsin administration, that time, for the most part, has passed.

Dedicated human rights advocates both in Russia and the West respond that the West has never adopted a consistent hard-line toward Russia on the question of Chechnya, and that sustained pressure and threats of ostracism stand a good chance of yielding results. Yet even sympathetic policymakers in the West must weigh the potential costs and benefits of such a strategy, fearing that Russia may decide to weaken its support for global security norms, particularly the prohibition on the spread of weapons of mass destruction (WMD). Specifically, Russia might complicate Western efforts to pressure North Korea or Iran to abide by international regimes.

This does not mean that no useful policies or leverage are available to the West, but it does mean that the West should have a balanced and consistent approach to the twin problems of Russian democratization and Chechen separatism. The West should not oscillate between condemnation and approval of Russian behavior in Chechnya, even in the face of dramatic intervening events, such as the terror attacks of 9/11, which led Washington to adopt generally supportive language regarding Kremlin policies in Chechnya.

While holding Russia publicly and privately accountable for atrocities committed in Chechnya by Russian and pro-Russian Chechen forces, the

West should repeatedly reassure the Kremlin of its support for Russia's territorial integrity. Although Putin has politicized and "instrumentalized" the crisis in Chechnya, it is also clear that Putin and Russia's political elites— already shaken by the "color revolutions"—fear that instability in Chechnya will spread throughout the Caucasus. As noted above, these fears are not unfounded, given the increased political unrest and violence in the Russian republics of the North Caucasus.

Clear support for Russia's territorial integrity is in the interest of the West but also in the interest of the vast majority of Chechens. Chechnya is far from possessing the political, civic, or administrative institutions to support an independent state. An independent Chechnya would quickly descend further into the anarchy that marked the period 1996–1999, but with a difference. The stillborn Chechen state would be home to even larger numbers of criminals, traffickers, and predatory politicians and bureaucrats. Perhaps most important, radical Islamists, both Chechen and non-Chechen, would have a secure base from which to spread the gospel of jihad throughout the Caucasus.

The policy options available to the West are familiar but nevertheless important. The expansion of NATO eastward since the fall of communism has fostered political stability and democratization in its prospective members. NATO should continue this advance and open discussion with Ukraine and Georgia over the terms for entry into the organization. This will not only help anchor both countries to the West, but also bring the West and its democratic culture closer to Russia. If done with care and transparency, the further expansion of NATO to Georgia and Ukraine is likely to be accepted, however grudgingly, by Russia's elites.

The West must relearn the importance of human-to-human contacts between Russia and the West as an important means to develop further a democratic culture in Russia. The West should also step up its business investments in Russia for two important reasons. Such investments will help nurture the Russian middle class and hopefully stimulate a stronger attachment to democratic political culture. Investment is also important for its injection of Western managerial and business culture and its attendant emphasis on transparency and good governance in the market place.

The West could also accomplish much on the issue of Chechnya, but patience and the willingness to marshal financial resources would be essential prerequisites. Perhaps most important, the West should engage Russia in talks over how to craft and fund a reconstruction program for the North Caucasus region that would make human security an immediate priority. Putin himself has suggested the possibility of securing the support of international assistance for this vital task. This opportunity should be coupled with the creation of an international working group similar to those that advanced the peace process in Ireland and in Tajikistan, where Russia itself played a role. Such a group would best be created in the United Nations

Security Council or perhaps the G8 organizations, which Russia values and in which Russia is unlikely to encounter harsh criticism on the sensitive issue of Chechnya.[73]

It is clear that such policies would be costly and require significant and sustained political will to accomplish. However, they would be important investments that would hopefully promote democracy in Russia as well as security and justice in Chechnya.

CHAPTER 5

PALESTINIANS, ISRAELIS, AND A FUTURE PALESTINIAN STATE: CASE V

INTRODUCTION

The final case analyzes state formation in the Palestinian territories where a nation is transitioning to democracy, while simultaneously continuing its struggle for national liberation to determine the final boundaries of a Palestinian state. The chapter explores whether or not the Palestinian authority, led by the Islamic militant group Hamas, has the capability to address genuine Palestinian grievances and continue the democratic transition. Additionally, the Palestinian Authority's ability and willingness to combat terrorism emanating from its territory during the unstable and volatile period of democratic transition remains questionable because Hamas does not recognize Israel's right to exist. Although this case diverges significantly from that of Spain's as it does not deal with an ethnic minority or a state that has determined boundaries, there are still lessons to be gleaned from Spain's successful transition to democracy. Since 1967, when Israel occupied the West Bank and the Gaza Strip, the Palestinians have witnessed democracy firsthand as they served as laborers in Israel. Yet how the Palestinian leadership approaches building democratic institutions will determine its future and whether or not terrorist activity will decrease. The United States and its European allies should support the Palestinian transition, while simultaneously taking an active role to restart the Palestinian–Israeli peace process.

Hamas gained power through democratic elections, but liberal democracy's fate under its tutelage is unknown. As an Islamic party, part of its ideological core is to create an Islamic state. As such questions emerge regarding the role of women and individual rights under such a regime. Furthermore, since Hamas' platform and rhetoric discount negotiations with Israel and retain the option of armed, violent struggle, the entire future of the peace process remains precarious.[1] As this chapter argues, the peace process, democratization, and the decrease of terrorism are interconnected. Therefore, there is a possibility that if Hamas continues and strengthens the democratic process, the Palestinian population, despite Hamas' public stand that it will not negotiate with Israel, might find the prospect of increased violence with Israel as detrimental to their interests. This chapter explores the pitfalls of the Palestinian's transition to democracy under the prior ruling party, Fatah, which contributed to Hamas popularity and concludes with a discussion of the implications of Hamas' victory for both democracy and terrorism.

Since the creation of Israel in 1948, Palestinians and Israelis have missed many opportunities for peace. Without a solution to the Palestinian issue and the determination of final borders, the Palestinians will be incapable of nurturing a working democracy. The death of Palestinian leader and national symbol Yasir Arafat in November 2004, coupled with the waning of the Al Aqsa Intifada that began in September 2000, ushered in a period with the potential for both peace and the consolidation of a democratic Palestine. The PA under Fatah had an interest in curbing terrorism to propel the peace process with Israel forward and to garner legitimacy within its borders and with the international community. The PA sought to stem the appeal of more violent organizations such as Hamas, the Palestinian Islamic Jihad, and the Al Aqsa Martyrs Brigade, a secular group. Unfortunately, the PA did not reform sufficiently before the January 2006 elections leading to Hamas' victory at the polls.

Undoubtedly, the advent of Hamas, which refuses to engage in a peace process or even recognize the Israel's right to exist, complicates the relationship between Palestinians and the international community. The United States has said that it would not deal with a government that vows the destruction of Israel and the European Union (EU) proclaimed that it would not engage a Hamas government unless it renounces terrorism.[2] Without international cooperation and financial aid, any Palestinian government will face difficulties in transforming its society. As the Spanish case illustrated, international cooperation is essential in fostering a convergence of political culture.

THE BACKGROUND

The nineteenth century saw the emergence and competition of political Zionism and Arab nationalism that led to the increasingly acrimonious and violent conflict between the two groups for political sovereignty in Palestine. The Zionists' claim historical, biblical, and ideological connections to the land, while the Arabs attribute their right to Palestine to continued habitation in the land for hundreds of years, along with great power promises for Arab independence after World War I. The potency of these historical and emotional connections has created one of the most complex and enigmatic questions of this century. During the late nineteenth century many Jews began to immigrate to Palestine due primarily to the growing anti-Semitism in Europe.[3] Once in Palestine, the Jews prepared for statehood by building a strong community with roots for political, social, and military institutions.

In 1917, the proclamation of the Balfour Declaration by the British supporting a national home for the Jewish people in Palestine exacerbated the conflict. A significant problem was that the British had been vacillating in their policies toward both Jews and Arabs.[4] Consequently, both groups believed that they were promised statehood in the same territory. Nascent Palestinian nationalism emerged prior to the collapse of the Ottoman Empire, though it was only after the Balfour Declaration that a more distinct Palestinian nationalism began to take root. As Jewish immigration continued to climb, more frequent and intense conflagrations between the two groups erupted in Palestine.[5] The heightened tension generated by the increased effort of both groups to control the land, culminated in the 3-year period of Arab unrest beginning in 1936.[6] Notwithstanding increasing hostilies, the Zionists continued to build a political, economic, and military infrastructure in preparation for statehood.[7]

The partition of Palestine by the United Nations in 1947 was an attempt by the international community to alleviate the tensions between the two groups. This UN action, however, only heightened the level of violence in the region. The Arabs rejected the proposal to create two states, while the Jews reluctantly accepted.[8] Despite repeated Arab threats to declare war on the Jews if a Jewish state was erected, David Ben-Gurion proclaimed the creation of the state of Israel on May 14, 1948, and became the embryonic nation's first Prime Minister. The following day violence ensued and the first of many Arab–Israeli wars began. A result of the war was that the Palestinians acquired less territory than was granted them under the UN partition. Transjordan, now Jordan, gained control of the West Bank and Egypt maintained control of the Gaza Strip.

On June 5, 1967, Israel preempted what it perceived as an imminent attack by the Arab countries on its borders and won a stunning victory. The Arab states' defeat during the Six-Day War resolved several problems for Israel, while generating others. Israel's acquisition of the Golan Heights, the Sinai Desert, the West Bank, and the Gaza Strip created more secure borders for Israel; however, the retention of the West Bank and the Gaza Strip left the Israelis in control of 1 million Palestinians who were hostile to the notion of Israeli domination. As expected, once Israel controlled these areas, Palestinians and Israelis could not avoid almost daily contact. Not only did the Palestinians interact with Israelis in the occupied territories, but Israeli policy also permitted Palestinian employment within Israel. This increased contact shifted the conflict more explicitly to one between Israelis and Palestinians than one between Israel and other Arab states.

In 1973, the Arab states made one last attempt to defeat Israel by exe-cuting a surprise attack to retrieve the territories lost during the Six-Day War. Although the Arab states inflicted severe casualties on the Israelis, they were unable to regain control of their territories, but perceived the event as a victory.[9] By instigating a surprise assault, the Arab states caused an enor-mous number of Israeli casualties.[10] In the eyes of the Arabs and especially those of the Palestinians, Israel's deterrent power was waning.

Again, the war in 1973 convinced the Palestinians that they could not depend on the Arab states to liberate their land. Rather than relying on military strategies alone, the Palestinian Liberation Organization (PLO) be-came more interested in pursuing both diplomatic and military strategies. Although many peace proposals had been advanced over the years, real movement toward an Israeli–Palestinian agreement did not occur until the uprising in the Gaza Strip and West Bank in 1987.

The Palestinian uprising in the Gaza Strip and West Bank, also known as the *intifada,* reflected a changed Palestinian. After 20 years of Israeli con-trol of the West Bank and the Gaza Strip, Palestinian frustration reached a zenith. The majority of the population was young and as such, had grown up under Israeli control without experiencing political freedom. When the territories were occupied in 1967, Palestinians had lived either under Jor-danian or Egyptian rule, and although these states were not democracies, Palestinians compared themselves to their Arab brethren. After the occu-pation, the Palestinians, appeased by their increased standard of living and continued relationship with the Jordanian economy, realized that their Is-raeli counterparts earned higher wages for similar work.[11] Furthermore, Palestinians experienced economic growth without corresponding politi-cal freedom. Because Israel controlled most aspects of their lives, Pales-tinians were unable to obtain complete political freedom, which they per-ceived as a right despite the occupation. In addition, daily contact with Israelis magnified their deprivation under occupation, while the growth of a more educated Palestinian population heightened people's expecta-tions for better opportunities and civil rights. The eventual creation of a severely dependent region on Israel due to the lack of an economic infrastructure increased the population's rage over time. A strong Pales-tinian national identity, one separate from being Arab, continued to de-velop. This growth of a potent national identity was crucial in influencing the eruption of the *intifada* in 1987 and impelling the process of nation building.

By late 1990, large riots within the territories that characterized the first *intifada* had lost momentum because of successful Israeli countermeasures, extreme Palestinian infighting, and Saddam Hussein's invasion of Kuwait in August 1990. The Gulf War propelled the United States into the domi-nant position in the Middle East and led to its direct role in convening the Madrid conference. By forcing Saddam Hussein to withdraw from Kuwait, the United States achieved new credibility within the Arab world. More-over, the end of the cold war between the United States and the Soviet Union enhanced opportunities for peace. With the Soviets' diluted global position, they did not oppose the U.S.-led coalition's war with Iraq leaving the United States in a strong position to pursue the peace process. In a speech to Congress in March 1991, President George Bush proclaimed that "the time has come to put an end to the Arab–Israeli conflict" based on Resolution 242 and 338.[12] Additionally, Palestinian leader Yasir Arafat's weakened stance in the Arab world worked to America's advantage in propelling peace talks. With Arafat disparaged by the Gulf states and reeling from the lack of financial assistance, the United States pressed for an international peace conference to resolve the Arab–Israeli conflict and eventually arranged the Madrid Conference on October 30, 1991.

Although there was little progress between the Palestinian and Israeli adversaries during Madrid, the Oslo accords infused fresh hope that a "new world order" was on the horizon.[13] Notwithstanding difficulties in adhering to the accords' nebulous timeline, noteworthy advancement occurred. By May 1994, the Palestinians controlled most of Gaza and portions of the West with the Palestinian Authority running the civil affairs of Palestinian daily life. Yet by 2000, 2 years after the Palestinians were supposed to have reached final status agreements with Israel, they still lacked an independent state. The slow pace of the peace process along with the deteriorating economic and political situation of Palestinians, due not only to Israeli policies, but also to corrupt and authoritarian practices of the Palestinian Authority, set the stage for another rebellion. In this charged environment, on September 28, 2000, Ariel Sharon, then head of the Likud party, entered the Temple Mount or Haram al-Sharif despite warnings from other players that his visit would exacerbate tensions with Palestinians.[14] When the second uprising erupted—also known as the Al Aqsa Intifada—it was apparent that it diverged drastically from its antecedent especially from a tactical perspective. Palestinians abandoned their policy of avoiding firearms as they did during the first *intifada* and began to use more violent means. It was clear that the Oslo Accords were in their final throes.

To stem the heightened violence in the Middle East, the United States, Russia, the European Union, and the United Nations—also known as the Quartet—drafted a road map for peace in December 2002. The proposal called for a Palestinian state by 2005, while deferring complex issues such as the return of refugees or the status of Jerusalem.[15] Although discussed prior to the beginning of war with Iraq on March 19, 2003, the road map was not introduced until after the overthrow of Saddam Hussein. In June 2003, President George Bush, met in Aqaba, Jordan for a summit between Israeli Prime Minister Ariel Sharon and Palestinian Authority Prime Minister Mahmoud Abbas to begin implementation of the road map.[16] An indication of President Bush's commitment to the peace process was the creation of a monitoring team headed by Ambassador John Wolf.[17] The road map led to a ceasefire that began on June 29, 2003. But on August 14, Israel assassinated a Palestinian militant—a member of Islamic Jihad—who Israel claimed was responsible for planning suicide attacks and who was in the midst of planning a new assault.[18] In response, Hamas, the Islamic Resistance Movement, carried out an attack on August 19, which killed twenty Israelis. By August 21, 2003 the ceasefire was over.[19] Once again the peace process was in tatters.

There was little movement in the peace process despite repeated calls from the international community to implement the road map. The cycle of terrorist attacks in Israel and within the Israeli settlements continued followed by harsh Israeli countermeasures. It was not until the death of Yasir Arafat in November 2004 that momentum for the process reemerged. Additionally, in 2003, Ariel Sharon announced his plan for a unilateral withdrawal from the Gaza Strip. This move was heralded by some as a real indication of Israel's willingness for peace and by others as a ploy to withdraw from "Gaza first, Gaza last."[20] The tepid response by Palestinians reflected their trepidation that without a coordinated effort to withdraw, chaos would ensue.

Despite anxiety from both the Israeli and Palestinian sides, Israel began its withdrawal from Gaza and parts of the West Bank on August 15, 2005, without serious incident. In a rare show of cooperation, but in an atmosphere of distrust, Palestinian and Israeli security forces were in place during the pullout to deter any attacks from militant groups. Israel's withdrawal has given Palestinians an opportunity to govern their own territory in preparation for statehood. Clearly, the Palestinian Authority's ability to govern is complicated by the continued Israeli occupation and, as will be discussed below, its incomplete authority over its territory.

PALESTINIAN DEMOCRATIC TRANSITION[21]

The Palestinian Authority, under any party leadership, faces several challenges to its ability to transition and subsequently consolidate democracy in its state. First, the final borders of the Palestinian state have not yet been determined. Therefore, not only does the government need to develop democratic institutions, but it must also continue to negotiate or fight for its independence. The consolidation of democracy is dependent upon whether or not a state exists. According to Juan J. Linz and Alfred Stepan, if there is no state, there is no democracy.[22] Second, the PA is not the only governing power in its territory. Because of the continuing occupation, it competes with Israel for actual control of the areas under Palestinian jurisdiction. Prior to the outbreak of hostilities in September 2000, Palestinians in the Gaza Strip and most West Bank cities controlled several aspects of their daily life including taxation, health issues, tourism, education, and culture. Nevertheless, a crucial result of the Al Aqsa Intifada was the vivid illustration that Palestinians lacked powers of a truly sovereign nation.

For example, following terrorist attacks in Israel in 2002, the IDF reoccupied areas that were relinquished to the Palestinians during the Oslo process confirming that the territory under Palestinian authority was not sovereign either in the eyes of the Israelis or in the international community. Furthermore, Israel's withholding of funds from the Palestinians reiterated that Palestinians remained subject to the vagaries of Israeli policy. The Palestinian challenges differ significantly from those confronted by Spain. Spain needed to garner legitimacy from the Basque population because Basque separatism was, at least from the Spanish government's perspective, an unacceptable solution to its terrorist problem. In the Palestinian case, the foundation for an independent Palestinian state has been established and most people accept the two-state solution as inevitable, despite the protestations of rejectionists on both sides.

For the Palestinians, this inability to retain final authority over Palestinian land humiliated them, fueling their radicalization and increasing the use of violence during the second uprising. Notwithstanding their new power over some areas of their daily life, the Palestinians wanted nothing less than a state with complete jurisdiction including maintaining a military, providing security for their population and conducting foreign affairs. According to the Declaration of Principles (DOP), the Palestinians could form a limited police force with specified types and amounts of weapons. Additionally, they were barred from having a military.[23] The accords state that, "Israel will continue to carry the responsibility for defending against external threats, as well as the responsibility for overall security of Israelis for the purpose of safeguarding their internal security and public order."[24] From an Israeli perspective, its security would be severely jeopardized if Israel allowed an armed Palestinian state on its borders until sincere confidence building mechanisms were in place. From a Palestinian perspective, however, their broadening independence was nothing more than a sham.

A third factor hampering the Palestinian transition to democracy was that following the Al Aqsa Intifada; the Palestinian economy was all but destroyed. More than half of the population live below the poverty line and there remains little, if any, economic infrastructure. Although the correlation between terrorism and economic disparity is disputed, it is apparent that an inability to meet the economic demands of a population can lead people to find effective governance elsewhere.

As Palestinians secured control over aspects of their daily lives after Israel withdrew from several areas of the West Bank and the Gaza Strip following the Oslo Accords, they began to establish democratic institutions. The signing of the Gaza–Jericho Accord on May 4, 1994, also known as the Cairo Agreement, called for Israeli withdrawal from the Gaza Strip and Jericho and established provisions for the creation of an elected Palestinian legislature in the Palestinian territories.[25] Despite the growth of institutions, old patterns of politics persisted making the formal transition to democracy challenging. Palestinian President Yasir Arafat proved to be a patrimonial leader whose government was plagued with corruption and glaring authoritarian leadership. David Schenker argues that although inclusive, the PLO had never been a democratic organization. "It is a nepotistic and autocratic institution in which loyalty is valued above all else."[26] Some scholars argue that although formal democratic institutions were developing within the territories, they were "emptied of substantive content."[27]

In a patrimonial system, all political functions are concentrated around the ruler: in this case, Palestinian Authority President Yasir Arafat. Patrimonialism is characterized, in part, by personalism where even the formal structures do not apply to the ruler.[28] Far from a meritocracy, Arafat placed people in positions of power based on their personal loyalty to him. Aside from breeding corruption and incompetence, the bloated bureaucracy took a toll on the Palestinians financially. Moreover, the marginal role of the judiciary and the legislature under Arafat's tenure allowed the authoritarian leadership to bypass any scrutiny for corrupt actions. Scholars such as Linz and Stepan argue that even if executives are elected freely, if they do not govern within the rules of law and violate the constitution, the regimes are not democratic.[29]

During implementation of the Oslo Accords, aside from the patrimonial structure plaguing democratic transition in the territories, the Palestinian Authority constituted an interim government. As such, it "was caught between its endeavors towards independence on the one hand, and the establishment of a stable and legitimate regime on the other."[30] The PA under Fatah was required to balance three extremely complex activities: building institutional legitimacy, battling militant groups calling for the liberation of more land and, negotiating with the Israelis for a continuation of the peace process. The intricate juggle required to succeed in these undertakings complicated the PA's ability to fight terrorism and meet the population's political and economic expectations.

The legislative and presidential elections in 1996 provided a crucial indicator of the direction the Palestinian political system would follow during the Oslo years and beyond. The PLO leadership encouraged elections as a way of legitimizing its authority in the eyes of the Palestinian population. Moreover, PLO support for elections stemmed from an understanding that impeding elections would hamper the creation of a democratic Palestine and would reflect the PLO's intent to retain the "reins of power."[31] Judging from the population's expectation that a more democratic system would evolve as Israel retreated, any obstacle—including the PLO—would be perceived negatively by the population. The elections held on January 26, 1996, registered an impressive 75 percent of eligible voters at the polls. According to Ziad Abu-Amr, several reasons account for the high voter participation including an interest in transforming the corrupt and inefficient Palestinian Authority into a more legitimate organization and the ability for Palestinians to exercise the legitimate right to vote.[32]

Although decried as the initial step toward the Palestinian transition to democracy, a close analysis of election results reveals significant systemic flaws carrying the potential to stifle real progress toward a democratic Palestine. At the outset of negotiations between the Israelis and Palestinians, both Israel and Yasir Arafat favored an exclusive political system as evidenced in the early electoral laws.[33] By setting both the legislative and presidential elections for January 20, a day before the start of the Muslim holy month of Ramadan, the Palestinian Central Election committee removed a potentially crucial recruiting period for Hamas. With attendance at mosques higher during Ramadan, the group could have preached political ideas to a larger number of people.

Additionally, the form of electoral system selected affected the results of the election. Arafat preferred a majoritarian or first-past-the-post system, which favored his Fatah party.[34] In contrast, a proportional system allows for broader representation and produces more diverse parties affording minorities a voice in the political process. Had a proportional system been implemented, Hamas candidates would have gained several more seats in the legislature.[35] To ensure Fatah's success, Arafat manipulated the electoral system to create very small districts, which elevated local, not national issues. The interest in local issues exacerbates cleavages as "it does little to encourage bridge-building among political, religious, or ethnic communities."[36] Moreover, the small districts allowed the system of family patronage and patrimonialism to flourish.[37] One other drawback of the electoral system was the implementation of a quota granting Christians 7 percent of the Council seats.[38] According to some scholars, the creation of an electoral quota system is detrimental to the development of a healthy democracy.

In addition to research positing that the type of electoral system affects election results, it also influences whether or not an increase or decrease in terrorist activities occurs. In other words, in some types of democracy, there is an increase in terrorist activities depending on the structure of the regime. According to Quan Li, countries with a proportional representation system have fewer transnational terrorists incidents than those with a majoritarian or mixed system because of the fact that "the proportional system is more likely to resolve political grievances than either the majoritarian or the mixed system, reducing incentives to resort to terrorism."[39] Li also found that democratic participation decreases terrorist activities providing the population with avenues to air their grievances and to influence reform in their political system. Political participation, "increases satisfaction and political efficacy of citizens, reduces their grievances, thwarts terrorist recruitment, and raised public tolerance of counterterrorist policies."[40]

Despite the assessment by international observers that the elections were "free and fair" the evolution of genuine political opposition was stifled. Ostensibly, the elections produced a one-party system with almost two-thirds of the elected Parliament Fatah or Fatah sympathizers.[41] According to many democratization scholars, a crucial component of democracy is the presence of real and competitive opposition. Opposition is important for a variety of reasons including the fact that the consolidation of democracy involves a peaceful turnover of government and an opposition provides a real choice for the population. Without opposition, legitimate avenues to articulate dissent are stifled. Opposition groups also force the government in power to be more transparent.[42] In actuality, Yasir Arafat ignored primary elections in which the local population voted for particular candidates. Arafat rejected those results and handpicked his own Fatah candidates despite the fact that local candidates were popularly elected to run in the parliamentary elections.[43]

Notwithstanding Arafat's manipulation of the electoral system, he publicly courted opposition parties to participate in elections in order to legitimize the outcome. From Israel's perspective, its government was concerned with the Jewish state's security and therefore wanted groups contesting the peace process including Hamas, Islamic Jihad, the Palestinian Front for the Liberation of Palestine (PFLP), and the Democratic Front for the liberation of Palestine (DFLP) expelled from the political arena. Despite Arafat's public statements, his interest in maintaining ultimate control did not lead him to lament the exclusion of the opposition parties from politics.

During the initial phase of the Palestinian Legislative Council's (PLC) tenure, it was hindered in its abilities to fulfill its legislative mandate and to supervise executive power.[44] Regardless of the Oslo Accords and the Palestinian expectation of a democratic, independent state, the Palestinian Authority ignored the popularly elected PLC that became synonymous with a "rubber stamp parliament."[45] The PLC adopted significant legislation including the Basic Law, which refers to the separation of the executive, judicial, and legislative powers along with covering civil rights. President Arafat did not ratify this bill that was intended to serve as an interim constitution until the creation of an independent Palestinian state.[46] Arafat's refusal to sign the bill reflected his reluctance to diminish his authority in any capacity.[47] Consequently, the absence of any type of constitutional document obfuscated the role of the branches of government. Confounding the problem further, the West Bank's legal system was derived from Jordanian law, while Gaza's fell under the Egyptian system.[48]

Although the interim agreement blurred the lines between governmental functions and made the separation of powers virtually impossible, Arafat exacerbated this situation by exploiting the Interim agreement's ambiguity on the separation of powers issue.[49] For instance, Arafat would not allow the cabinet to meet alone, but rather convened broad-based "leadership meetings" that included the cabinet (Executive Authority), PLO executive, Fatah Central Committee members, security service heads, and the speaker of the PLC. According to Abu-Amr, "This confusion of functions, entirely consistent with PA President Yasir Arafat's individualistic leadership style, makes it virtually impossible to hold the cabinet accountable for implementing the government's program."[50]

Because of the fact that President Arafat did not enact the Basic Law until 2002, he did not submit a legitimate budget to the PLC as called for in both the Basic Law and council bylaws. According to Azmi Shu'aybi, a former member of the PLC, although the PA did submit budgets beginning in 1996, the PA refused to submit it to the PLC unless the legislators promised to approve it in advance. Other budgets raised confusion on a variety of issues and were rife with unaccounted funds.[51] As such, transparency was nonexistent and public funds were undeniably misappropriated.[52] The PLC formed an investigative group, the Public Monitoring Body (PMB), to explore the financial practices of the PA. A report issued by the PMB in May 1997 detailed, "financial and administrative malpractices carried out by public servants."[53] The PMB also called for submission of an on-time budget in which the PA would be forced to adhere to its articles. Vociferous appeals for reform in the PA continued to mount and in 1999, nine PLC members along with a former Palestinian minister and several mayors, signed the "Statement of the 20," protesting the autocratic and corrupt procedures of Arafat's regime. After Arafat's death, many news reports documented the corruption and fiscal irresponsibility of his regime. According to polls conducted in March and April 2000, 71 percent of Palestinians believed that the PA was corrupt, a number that had steadily increased since the PA's creation in 1994.[54]

The Palestinian Authority also cracked down on free speech. Journalists including Daoud Kuttab, Director of the Institute of Modern Media at Al-Quds University, were arrested for criticizing the government's stifling of opposition and ban on free speech.[55] Security services invaded most aspects of people's lives. The PLC issued resolutions demanding monitoring mechanisms to prevent human rights abuses by the eight security services. Moreover, almost half of all PA employees were involved in some type of internal security activities in order to neutralize any dissent.[56] Arafat's tight control of the media impeded the growth of any true opposition, a crucial element for the growth of a vibrant civil society. The Palestinian Authority also retained a series of security courts, staffed by military officers who were accused of serious human rights abuses.[57] Scholars argue that an independent judiciary would be a crucial step in creating a more just, democratic society. Although the PLC passed resolutions to create an independent judiciary, their efforts were disregarded. Human rights abuses in the areas under PA control were well documented as evidenced by a 2000 Amnesty

International of Arafat's regime's use of torture, unjust imprisonment, and repression.[58]

The continued constriction of individual freedoms increased the level of discontent and violence within the Palestinian community. Khalil Shikaki of Bir Zeit University, argued that the eruption and duration of the Al Aqsa Intifada was not only a response to Israel's continued occupation, but also represented a struggle between the Palestinian "young and old guard."[59] The younger, local leadership within the territories resented the corrupt and undemocratic practices of those Palestinian leaders, who prior to the Oslo Accords directed the occupation from Tunisia. Moreover, the growth of an elite class and patronage structure represented by Arafat's supporters further increased dissatisfaction with the Palestinian Authority.

The Al Aqsa Intifada, aside from representing a reaction to continued Israeli occupation and a rejection of the Oslo process, reflected a schism between rival Palestinian groups' philosophies of how to create a Palestinian state. When Arafat and PLO members living in exile returned to the Gaza Strip and the West Bank under the terms of the Interim agreement, they conflicted with the local political elite on both the type of governmental system that was necessary and how to end the Israeli occupation. First, the local elites recognized the authoritarian political culture of the PLO, which placed those loyal to Arafat in positions of authority.[60] Second, the "young guard" contended that the confluence of violence and negotiations would deliver the best deal for the Palestinians. The "old guard" maintained that diplomacy and political means would prove the most expedient method to an independent state. Groups such as Hamas and Islamic Jihad rejected and continue to reject the two-state solution by calling for the liberation of all of Palestine. In March 2005, at President Abbas' request, Hamas agreed to a ceasefire with Israel and supported its withdrawal from the Gaza Strip in August 2005.

According to Abu-Amr, Yasir Arafat's regime was not solely responsible for failing to create legitimate institutions during the Interim Period. Abu-Amr criticizes the PLC for lacking self-confidence and initiative during the early period and for not taking a vote of no confidence in the government, a duty that fell within its purview.[61] Although a vote of no confidence was no guarantee that Arafat would have implemented reforms, internal pressure on the president to make changes would have been significant.

Furthermore, the Palestinian Authority faced crucial challenges to its legitimacy and its ability to govern the population in the areas ceded by the Israelis. Prior to the Oslo Accord, the Palestinian Liberation Organization had the "luxury" of providing a philosophical and theoretical motivation for the Palestinians without having to deliver on tangible aspects of daily life under occupation. In other words, the organization fought for the liberation of the Palestinian homeland, but was not required to provide services in the territories. Once the Oslo Accords were signed, the Palestinian leadership, namely Arafat, had to shift "the center of Palestinian life from the 'outside' to the 'inside'—this is, from abroad to Palestine itself."[62] While little attention was paid to the political system in the territories prior to the peace negotiations, Arafat was now obligated to confront the type of governmental structure that would best serve the Palestinian people. It became insufficient to preach about independence; the fulfillment of the population's economic and political needs became paramount. Yet Yasir Arafat adhered to the PLO's authoritarian legacy where "the PLO means revolution and there is no transparency in a revolution."[63]

Additionally, whereas a broad civil society flourished in the occupied territories prior to 1993, the authoritarian nature of the PLO and PA all but killed its growth. A result of the first *intifada* and Israel's harsh countermeasures was the development of alternative economic and social groups. In actuality, the 20 years of Israeli occupation forced the expansion of a civil society. To survive, social organizations, women's groups and student unions gave the majority of the population a noteworthy part in the 1987 uprising. When the Israelis blocked businesses from opening or denied Palestinians access to jobs in Israel, various social organizations set up parallel economic systems. More significant with regard to Palestinian civil society than the occupation's role in its expansion, however, was the process that occurred after the Oslo Accord with the development of a nascent Palestinian state. Arafat quelled any real opposition to his Fatah party with his vast internal security apparatus and these actions have had clear ramifications for the choice of Palestinian tactics during the Al Aqsa rebellion. In 1999, several Palestinian legislators signed a petition criticizing the undemocratic practices of Arafat's regime.[64] In response, Arafat jailed the dissidents and cracked down on dissent.

With the increase of violence between Israel and the Palestinians after the eruption of the Al Aqsa Intifada, many Palestinians clamored for more internal reform. According to Shikaki, one event that catalyzed an impetus for change was the Israeli reoccupation in 2002 of parts of the West Bank that had been relinquished previously to the Palestinian Authority. Because of the hardships of Palestinian daily life under Israeli reoccupation with increased curfews, Palestinian frustration escalated when the Palestinian Authority did not deliver on basic services to ease the strain of occupation.[65] Although a push by the masses to democratize is crucial for the consolidation of democracy, genuine change cannot occur without a democratizing elite. With growing internal and international pressure to reform, by 2002, President Arafat agreed to some important modifications in the political system. He finally signed the Basic Law, along with the Law of the Judiciary. Nevertheless, both continued Israeli occupation and PA corruption "opened the way for lawlessness and a rise in the authority of Hamas and other Islamists."[66] The inability of the PA to gain legitimacy from its population led to the increased popularity of militant groups and their terrorist activities.

According to a poll in 2002, 52 percent of the Palestinian population supported attacks on Israeli civilians within Israel. With regard to attacks on Israeli civilians within the West Bank and Gaza, 89 percent supported a continuation of these activities.[67]

The increasing discontent with the Palestinian Authority's harsh rule and human rights abuses made it more challenging to mobilize large numbers of the population. As such, the absence of a wider civil insurrection might be the Al Aqsa Intifada's "Achilles' heel."[68] The PA's corruption and lack of political development led to a demobilization of the population along with a crackdown on any type of discord. Student groups, unions, and other symbols of civil society ceased to flourish under PA tutelage. As a result, the Palestinian community witnessed the unraveling of crucial advancements in political development due to both Israeli and Palestinian actions. The inability of the Palestinians to achieve self-determination despite their raised expectations contributed to the intensity and duration of the Al Aqsa Intifada. Therefore, although the lack of democratic reform contributed to the increase of terrorist activities emanating from the areas under Palestinian control, the continuing Israeli occupation, which hampered reform, was a key cause of terrorist activity.

The final years of Arafat's rule saw an even greater move by Arafat not to share his power and appeared "paranoid" if there was any challenge to his authority.[69] For most of his life, Arafat's leadership style can be summed up as follows: "While never the cruel dictator, Arafat epitomized one-man rule."[70] Although Arafat retained his aura as the symbol of Palestinian resistance and nationhood, many Palestinians were clamoring for internal reform. In February 2003, Arafat agreed to create the position of prime minister, which at that point, was more symbolic than actual. Creation of the post was ratified by the PLC in March 2003 granting the Prime Minister the right to name cabinet members and to oversee the security and financial matters. Mahmoud Abbas became the first Prime Minister, but quit after several months due to an inability to implement genuine reform. As Arafat lay on his deathbed, the position of Prime Minister was considerably strengthened.

Some scholars posit that the reforms in the Palestinian Authority stemmed mainly from external pressure and did not reflect internal changes. Acceptance of this view connotes that the Palestinians have not yet embraced a more democratic political culture and that "the essential dynamic or reform remains endogenous to Palestinian society."[71] Yet according to As'ad Ghanem and Aziz Khayed, the Palestinian national movement has undergone a series of internal reform that has led to a push for political changes.[72] To challenge Israeli occupation, Palestinians in the territories created community organizations, voluntary associations, rival parties and other groups, which reflected the growth of civil society.[73] Clearly, the internal political development of the Palestinians differed significantly between those living in the West Bank and the Gaza Strip and those who resided in the diaspora.

Early on, after Arafat's ascension to power as the head of the Palestinian Liberation Organization and the Fatah faction, he consulted widely with other PLO factions. By 1970, however, Arafat consolidated power and dominated all aspects of decision making in the PLO.[74] Although other factions protested and demanded that the organization be more accountable to all groups, the reforms never materialized. It is this legacy of patrimonial politics that permeated all aspects of the governmental structure of the Palestinian Authority created after the Oslo Accords. It was during this period that Hamas emerged as a true parallel government for many Palestinians by providing services to the population.

During the first *intifada*, Hamas played a role peripheral to that of the nationalist groups, but counted on the disillusionment of the Palestinians with the nationalist groups' ability to deliver on their promises to increase its popularity. And, when the Palestinian population recognized that the Palestinian Authority was not improving their political and economic situation, Hamas' esteem soared. Hamas was an outgrowth of the Muslim Brotherhood that had existed in the Palestinian community since 1935 when its founder, Hasan al-Banna from Egypt, sent his brother, Abd al Rahman al-Banna, to the Palestinian community. After the Six-Day War, the Brotherhood operated in the territories by establishing schools and religious organizations, though it had tepid appeal for a population concerned with national liberation.[75] With the eruption of the *intifada* in 1987, leading members of the Muslim Brotherhood including Ahmad Yasin and Abd al-Azziz al-Rantisi met to discuss their approach to the uprising. By January 1988, the organization calling itself Hamas began issuing leaflets to direct the *intifada*. Although the charter Hamas issued in August 1988 denounced peace initiatives with Israel and called for jihad, the organization did not implement violent tactics during the first 2 years of the uprising.[76] By the Al Aqsa Intifada, Hamas opened the floodgates of violence and increased its use of firearms and suicide bombings.

After Arafat's death, the presidential elections of January 2005 named Mahmoud Abbas, also known as Abu Mazen, President of the Palestinian Authority. Although the elections were open and fair, Hamas boycotted the process, detracting from the legitimacy of the results. However, in May 2005, Hamas participated in the municipal elections throughout the Palestinian territories taking 30 percent of the seats compared to Fatah's 60 percent. Interestingly, in some Gaza municipalities, Hamas grabbed the majority of seats, reflecting not an ideological convergence by Hamas supporters, but more likely reflecting a vote against Fatah's corrupt policies and a ballot for those who had been delivering daily services and making progress by resisting the occupation.[77]

Nonetheless analysts believed that if the Palestinian Authority managed to garner effective legitimacy by providing services to the population and developing an efficient and transparent government, the number of recruits available for suicide bombings would most likely decrease. According to

Mark Tessler, in the years following the eruption of the Al Aqsa Intifada, almost 70 percent of Palestinians supported Hamas and other Islamic groups, which advocated violence, but also provided services to the population. Yet espousal of the militant groups was due less "on the appeal of their ideology than on their role in delivering services at the grassroots level and, equally, on the absence of any credible and appealing alternative."[78] Although there is a core group of ideologues that desires an Islamic state based on a strict interpretation of the Quran,[79] many Palestinians support a secular democracy. According to Joseph Nye, "prospects for democracy and free expression may help to reduce some of the sources of anger. But there are other sources of anger besides the absence of democracy."[80] Undoubtedly terrorism cannot be completely eradicated, yet democracy can lessen the appeal of more radical activists and provide more nonviolent avenues to express discontent.

During periods when the Palestinian population perceived that the PA progressed in the peace process—consequently forcing the government to focus on state building—support for violent resistance decreased and support for Fatah increased at the expense of Hamas. Following Israel's withdrawal from the Gaza Strip in August 2005, a poll conducted in September in the West Bank and the Gaza Strip revealed that 62 percent polled opposed continued violence emanating from Gaza into Israel. Finding solutions to unemployment and poverty became the priority for 40 percent of the Palestinians rather than support for the occupation, which was at 25 percent. Additionally, corruption and internal reforms was also a priority for 25 percent of those polled. In a June 2005 poll, 34 percent of the population placed unemployment and poverty as their priority, while 33 percent selected the occupation. Clearly, the progress on the peace process influenced Palestinian priorities. Additionally, the polls reflected the shifting priorities of the population during that period from fighting the occupation to dealing with economic issues and internal reform.[81] The PA, at that juncture, was viewed as possessing the ability to reform the economic system better than Hamas.

Interestingly, during municipal elections in December 2005, Hamas did well at the polls gaining control of Nablus, a traditional Fatah stronghold, although Fatah retained the majority of seats throughout Palestinian territory.[82] Hamas' increased popularity at the municipal polls did not bode well for the health of Fatah, which continues to suffer from severe infighting, disorganization, and corruption.

COOPERATION: ISRAEL AND PALESTINE

An important factor that can still work to the Palestinians' advantage during its transition to democracy is the fact that their neighbor is one of the only democracies in the Middle East. Undoubtedly, since 1967, the democratic political culture that Palestinian laborers witnessed in Israel proper—not the occupied territories—has influenced their approach to politics. Palestinians in the territories are a young population who no longer compare themselves to the Arab states, but to the Israelis. "As much as they may abhor Israeli occupation policies, they have seen what a free press can do, witnessed a working parliamentary system, and seen mobilized electorates oust governments that failed to deliver on promises."[83] Over the years, the Palestinians have pushed their leaders for a more open political system. The second *intifada* was due, in part, to the failure of the Palestinian leadership to establish democratic institutions in the areas from which Israel withdrew.

Nonetheless, for a variety of reasons, the Israelis have not supported the growth of democracy in the Palestinian territories. As mentioned above, Israel wanted groups opposed to the peace process barred from the Palestinian political process. Israel initially stated that it would contest Hamas' participation in the January 2006 parliamentary elections, but has since modified its posture. Israel did not retreat from its stance that President Abbas should disarm terrorist groups prior to elections.[84]

During Arafat's regime, Israel weighed its short- and long-term security concerns and concluded that presenting Arafat with a strong security force to repel and destroy opposition groups trumped any move toward democracy.[85] Yet offering the Palestinians the option of a harsh state response to terrorism eroded the PA's ability to transition to democracy. Under Arafat's tenure, the security regime turned on the local population and hampered any moves toward true opposition and freedom of expression. For some scholars, Israel's disinterest in democracy appears perplexing. According to William Quandt, "Israelis have shown little interest in this crucial issue. This is a strange posture for citizens of a democracy to adopt, but it stems from Israel's primary concern with its own security and widespread skepticism among Israelis about the possibility of democracy anywhere in the Arab world."[86] Obviously, Israel recognizes the advantages of having a democratic neighbor since the DOP and the subsequent Oslo agreements called for the creation of elected Palestinian political entities. However, despite this recognition, the reality for Israel is that, historically, authoritarian rulers were easier to negotiate with than those "accountable to the vagaries of public opinion."[87] Egypt is a case in point. Much of the Egyptian population did not support President Anwar Sadat's overture and eventual peace with Israel, yet under an authoritarian regime President Sadat did not require popular approval to sign a peace treaty with his neighbor.[88]

Undoubtedly, continued Israeli control of Palestinian territory has circumscribed Palestinian efforts at state building. Any successful operation to combat terrorism from the Palestinian-controlled areas requires intimate cooperation between the PA and Israel. Thus far, collaboration has been fraught with significant tribulations as both sides underscore the reluctance of the other to sincerely support the effort. Since the Oslo Accords were signed, Israel pressured the Palestinian leadership to crack down on terrorists within its borders. When the Al Aqsa Intifada erupted and broadened, Israeli Prime Minister Ariel Sharon held that Israel would not negotiate with the Palestinians until a week of calm ensued. He insisted that Yasir Arafat attack the perpetrators, especially those executing suicide attacks within Israel. Arafat, however, was either unwilling or unable to stop the terrorist attacks. From the Palestinian perspective, if Arafat cooperated with the Israelis, he was accused of being their stooge.

From the outset, Palestinians perceived cooperation with the Israelis in the security realm as an asymmetric power struggle. According to terms of the Oslo II Agreement, Palestinian police are obligated to act against Palestinian terror and arrest the perpetrators. They are not, however, allowed to arrest Israelis who retain freedom of movement throughout Gaza and the West Bank.[89] Furthermore, the Palestinians are barred from creating an army, which leaves Israel in control of its security. For the Israelis, a Palestinian transition to democracy continues to be relegated to second place after Israeli security. The DOP and subsequent agreements reflected, "a carefully crafted security agenda, propelled chiefly by Israeli rather than Palestinian concerns in this area, which encourages strong hegemonic control, limited democratic rights, and is sympathetic to a monopoly of political control by the Palestinian executive."[90] According to Graham Usher, the relationship between Israel and Palestinians with regard to security services as stipulated in the Oslo Accords reflects Israel's continued domination and hegemony of Palestinians.[91]

At the outset of the deployment of the Palestinian police in areas under PA control, there was feeling of pride among the population who perceived an armed police force as an important step in the process of state-building.[92] Yet, Palestinian assessments of the police force changed drastically on November 18, 1994, known as Black Friday, when Palestinian police fired on demonstrators leaving a mosque in Gaza, killing thirteen. During the summer of 1994, subsequent to this incident, tensions increased between police and various Palestinian factions when Israel pushed for militant groups to disarm. The resulting discord between the groups brought to the fore the increased possibility of civil war among the Palestinian factions. After Black Friday, the Palestinian police were used more frequently to crack down on opposition—not just suspected terrorists—and were perceived as executing Israel's dirty work. For many, "the repressive measures of the Palestinian Authority (PA) against opposition elements led to suspicion that it was more an instrument for Israeli security than a precursor to an independent Palestinian state."[93] From then on, the police were seen as tools for a corrupt ruler intent on maintaining a firm grip on power. Instead of keeping order in the streets and protecting Palestinian citizens, the police force was utilized to brutally quell opposition. Israeli pressure on Arafat and the PA to eliminate terrorist activities continued and in 1996, the Palestinian police were ordered to raid universities and social institutions. This led to a pervasive opinion that "the security situation under Palestinian control was becoming more repressive than under Israeli control."[94] As tensions between the PA and militant groups heated up, more terrorist attacks were launched into Israel.

For most of the Al Aqsa Intifada, Israel targeted the Palestinian Authority infrastructure as retaliation for suicide attacks in Israel. Whether or not the PA retained the will to combat terrorism, this action rendered the Palestinian regime impotent to respond militarily to the violence. Israel's rationale for its persistent raids into Palestinian-controlled territories was twofold. Aside from destroying infrastructure, Israel was sending the Palestinians a strong message: despite the Oslo Accords, we are still in control. Instead of forcing the Palestinians to curb attacks, Israel's incursion into Palestinian-controlled territory increased confrontations. The IDF destroyed symbols of the Palestinian Authority's power such as police stations and PA headquarters.

By March 2002, the frequent suicide bombings of Israeli civilians in the heart of the Jewish state convinced Israel that the PA either lacked the resolve or competence to control the militant groups. Whether or not the PA under Arafat had the institutional capacity to combat terrorism was hotly debated. In fact, Ariel Sharon's government insisted that Arafat ordered the deadly attacks. Along with this allegation, Israel contended that Arafat was indisposed to curb Palestinian violence and as such, both the Israelis and Americans rendered Arafat *persona non grata*. By surrounding his compound in Ramallah and severely limiting his mobility, Israel held Arafat prisoner in the very territory he was supposed to control.

After considerable restraint following repeated suicide bombings where 124 Israelis were killed throughout March 2002, Israel launched Operation "Defensive Shield" during which the IDF conducted house-to-house searches to eradicate the terrorist infrastructure. Some argued that the objective of this operation was to undermine the Palestinian Authority and cause its collapse. If indeed this was Ariel Sharon's intention, the growth of Arafat's popularity during this operation did not lead to the outcome sought by Israel.[95] Undeniably, the price paid by Israel in the international media was high. Clearly, "another positive result from the Palestinian perspective was that Israel was perceived—nearly everywhere except in the U.S.—as the heavy-handed aggressor trampling human rights, while using disproportionate force against the weak Palestinians."[96] This was exactly the reaction that Palestinians had desired.

Although Israel did achieve some of its objectives—capture of wanted terrorists, arms and documents linking Arafat to terrorism—the costs outweighed the benefits.[97] The destruction of most of the Palestinian Authority's infrastructure and institutions rendered the authority completely unable to control violence even if it retained the determination to do so.[98] Additionally, most Palestinians were touched, either directly or tangentially, by the

operation leaving the door wide open to a backlash. In fact, a spate of suicide bombings after Israel's withdrawal from most towns in the West Bank
was proof that life for Israelis had not improved significantly as a result of
the operation.

Without cooperation between Israelis and Palestinian leaders, the move
to both create a democratic Palestinian state and reduce terrorism is severely
undermined. With Hamas in power, the prospects for cooperation are dim,
unless Hamas completely reframes it ideological stance regarding Israel.

IMPLICATIONS

Terrorism poses a vexing problem for the fledgling Palestinian state. As
long as the Palestinians remain under the ultimate control of the Israelis,
their ability to transition to democracy will be severely curtailed. Hamas'
declarations rejecting cooperation with Israel on any level render bilateral
decisions regarding the occupied territories highly improbable. In such a
volatile and confrontational situation, it is doubtful whether Israel would
withdraw unilaterally from sections of the West Bank. Just a day before
the Palestinian legislative elections, acting Prime Minister Ehud Olmert said
that Israel would need to relinquish some West Bank territory in order to
retain a Jewish state with a Jewish majority.[99]

After the withdrawal from Gaza and a small section of the West Bank in
August 2005, the Israelis pressed President Abbas to disarm all Palestinian
factions prior to any legislative elections reiterating that a monopoly on
force is key in the nation-building process. President Abbas refused to do so
claiming that disarming the groups should occur after the elections. Abbas
contended that the road to gaining legitimacy from the opposition groups
is through co-optation into the new political system. At the time of Abbas'
remarks, most analysts did not foresee that Hamas would emerge as the
ruling faction in the PA.

Moreover, Abbas was aware that attempts to disarm the groups would
require force, a move that could have led to a civil war and completely derail
the nation-building process. Israel's insistence that Abbas reject Hamas'
request to participate in the political arena generated a challenging dilemma
for Abbas, but one that he rejected. He recognized that if he cracked down on
the militant groups, forcing them to relinquish their arms, he ran the risk of
alienating a significant portion of the population who would regard him, as
Arafat was considered in the past, as bending to Israeli demands. In contrast,
by allowing Hamas to participate, despite understanding that Fatah could
lose significant power, the government perceived an increase in its legitimacy.
From Abbas' perspective, shutting out Hamas from the process would have
led to a backlash by those who champion Palestinian democracy. When
asked, prior to the elections, why he did not confront Hamas, President
Abbas responded that, "we prefer the safe way to cooperate with them

in order that they will be diverted into a political party. In the beginning they accepted the truce. After that, they participated in local elections. Now they're aiming to participate in legislative elections."[100]

Although known for its very brutal and well-publicized terrorist attacks on civilians, Hamas has also provided social services for the Palestinian population since its inception especially during the challenging Oslo period and the Al Aqsa Intifada. By providing medical services, education, and other "good works," and by providing services that the Palestinian Authority could not, Hamas built "a wide power base beyond its natural ideological constituency."[101] Some scholars and states have differentiated between Hamas' political and armed wings. This separation allowed governments to meet with Hamas leadership, while still condemning terrorist activities.[102] Jeroen Gunning argues that although there may be some overlap in personnel and ideology, "there are two functionally and spatially distinguishable wings."[103] Yet Matthew Levitt cautions that Hamas leaders themselves have not distinguished between the military and political wings.[104] For much of the Palestinian population, the Palestinian Authority was viewed as corrupt and inefficient, while Hamas bolstered its legitimacy as a group that could effectively run a state by providing effective support. Clearly, if Abbas imparted required services to the Palestinians, along with granting them a political voice, there is a strong possibility that Hamas' popularity would have waned.

Although Hamas' ultimate goal is to create a Palestinian state in *all* of Palestine, its leadership has professed its acceptance of a state in the 1967 borders as an *interim* solution. Additionally, Hamas has claimed its willingness to implement *hudna*, or long-term truce, reflecting "a pragmatic and flexible approach to the conflict."[105] The movement's leadership, however, has made it clear that incorporation into the political system does not portend a renunciation of violence.

A noteworthy factor that has led some scholars to believe that increased political activity and participation can moderate more militant groups such as Hamas is the movement's concentration on its active political wing. "Continuing to marginalize Hamas, which represents a significant portion of Palestinian society, will ensure that the movement will continue terrorist activities, thwarting any future political agreement with Israel and dashing any prospects for the creation of a vibrant Palestinian democracy."[106] Under the Oslo Accords, Hamas' decision not to recognize the process left it with no political voice to protest the lack of credible economic and political reform.[107] According to Haim Malka, Hamas should be incorporated into any political system since it has exhibited a readiness, albeit at times reluctant, to participate in the political process. Although this assessment might be overly optimistic, Malka argues that if the stakes become high enough in the long-term, the organization might eventually renounce terrorism completely.[108] As the PLO found out following the Oslo Accords, running a country on a daily basis differs significantly from providing ideological motivations to gain independence.

On March 17, 2005, several Palestinian factions met in Cairo, Egypt, to temporarily suspend attacks in Israel in order to give President Abbas the chance to move the Peace Process and subsequently the state-building process, forward. The number of suicide attacks in Israel declined dramatically since the March 2005 cease-fire agreement in Cairo and the August 2005 Israeli withdrawal from the Gaza Strip. The PA's move to strengthen political participation with municipal, presidential, and parliamentary elections cannot be ruled out as an important factor in terrorism's decline. "Any long-term delay of parliamentary elections without the agreement of Hamas could lead to an outbreak of violence between the two rival organizations as well as to a resumption of full-scale terrorist operations against Israel."[109] Although it is impossible to separate whether the decline in terrorist activities owes more to the peace process or to the transition to a more democratic polity, it is clear that the two go hand in hand. But Fatah's moves toward democracy and its continued corruption came too late for it to retain control of the Palestinian territory.

Undoubtedly, any lasting peace requires cooperation between Israel and any Palestinian government, which would subsequently aid the growth of Palestinian democracy. Nonetheless, the prospect of the two governments cooperating in the near future remains uncertain. Consequently, the new PA must create an efficient and transparent government that meets the economic, political, and social needs of its population. Under any party, the PA needs to develop the population's allegiance to the regime and ultimately to a democratic system. For the Palestinians, the peace process, state building and the transition to democracy are all intricately entangled. Without movement on the peace process and a resolution of key issues, the PA's ability to gain legitimacy will be curtailed. Israelis must recognize that unless the Palestinians reap peace dividends, the discontent and tendency toward violence will continue.

Despite the fact that Hamas won the recent election, the United States and Europeans should continue to support the Palestinian transition to democracy, while concurrently taking an active role in pushing negotiations between Palestinians and Israelis. Hamas ascended to power on its platform of reform and rule of law and less for its stance on the peace process. Withholding economic aid from the Palestinians, as the EU has threatened, will broaden Palestinian frustration increasing the likelihood of a resumption of terrorism. Clearly, the international community must put tight restrictions on aid recipients to ensure that it is not funding terrorists. Former U.S. President Jimmy Carter, recognizes that the United States is legally bound to cut off funding to the PA once the Hamas-led government assumes power, but recommends circumventing the PA to get funds to the Palestinian people by increasing donations to the United Nations and other aid organizations.[110]

At the very least, the international community should convince Hamas to prolong its truce with Israel in the hope that future dialogue can be implemented. Some local Hamas leaders have intimated in the past that they would speak with Israelis regarding municipal issues leaving the door ajar, however slightly, to a future opportunity for negotiations.[111] Hamas leader, Mahmood Zahar, although fiery in his rhetoric that Israel is not a partner for negotiations, also added that, "negotiation is not a taboo."[112] Gunning argues that there are several factors in Hamas' composition that would allow it a "de facto" recognition of Israel including the fact that they derive much of their support "from its domestic reputation, rather than its stance on Israel."[113]

President Abbas has 3 years remaining on his term and is already searching for creative ways to renew discussions with Israel. Abbas said that he might "reactivate the role of the Palestine Liberation," perhaps implying a way to hold talks with Israel, without Israel and Hamas dealing directly with each other.[114] Abbas also declared that any new Palestinian government would be bound by the previous agreements with Israel. Unquestionably, empowering Hamas through international recognition and economic assistance is an enormous gamble because its future intentions regarding both Israel and democracy are unclear. Yet for the near term, Hamas will be preoccupied with daily governance and meeting the expectations of the Palestinian majority who favor democratic reform. If Hamas fails to implement significant democratic restructuring, the result will be violence directed toward Israel. At this juncture, the best chance that Israel and the international community have for decreasing terrorism is to aid Palestinian society in expanding liberal, democratic values in the Palestinian territories. Although the Oslo peace process failed on many levels, the foundations for functioning democratic institutions, along with changes in the Palestinian political culture, were cultivated. People expect democratic reform. Perhaps through its struggle for legitimacy based on the implementation of democratic values, Hamas will be forced to moderate its policies.

Conclusion

This study provides evidence that combating terrorism requires a multidimensional approach. Most importantly, states must be able to address real societal grievances to mitigate the legitimacy of terrorist groups who try to offer an alternative to the political process. This task is most difficult for those states that are in the unstable state of transition, yet this study demonstrates that even such transitioning states can succeed. The key to their success is the cooperation of neighboring states and IGOs who are necessary in the fight against terrorism, a transnational force. In short, we argue that states can accomplish both democracy and security. In truth, democracy and its liberal values, are a security imperative as they bolster state legitimacy vis-à-vis terrorist organizations.

The significance of these cases underscores the importance of analyzing terrorism in a strategic, political, and regional context. The March 2004 bombings in Madrid highlight how terrorism, whether ethnically or extremist Islamic based, challenges democracy. Although the perpetrators responsible for the most gruesome attack since Spain's civil war were not from ETA, but rather from Al-Qaida, the attack appears to have directly affected the elections in Spain. Some argue that the vote against the government at the time, led by Prime Minister Aznar, was a reaction to the government's insistence that ETA was responsible; the Aznar government lost legitimacy in the eyes of the Spanish electorate. Although the Al-Qaida attack contributed to the electoral surprise, the government's untruthful reaction was also a factor.[1] As such, the dramatic shift in public sentiment demonstrates that compromising democratic principles such as institutional transparency can only result in a loss of legitimacy. It is for this reason that governments must understand what they are facing before taking action; otherwise, they play right into the terrorist's scheme.

By highlighting the importance of the regional context to guide a state's strategic approach, the insights from this study are applicable to other regions not covered in this book. While the lessons from Spain are not germane everywhere, recognizing key similarities and differences as one moves further from the European context is critical, especially because a major pillar of the U.S. national security policy includes democratic state building. Greater insights by U.S. policymakers into the challenges faced by various states and regions prepares the United States to effectively craft strategic responses and initiatives both for the short and long term.

Perhaps a key question to emerge from this discussion is whether or not the United States is equipped at all for promoting democracy in certain regions of the world? P. H. Liotta and Jim Miskel ask, "Will or should [a] region's governance resemble American or Western forms, and does any external entity have the authority to demand or even actively promote change in governance of another state?"[2] They argue for an "adaptive democracy," one that resonates with a regional population. For example, their study of the Near East concludes that focusing on political and individual rights, rather than governing structures, is necessary to establish a successful path toward democracy.[3] They advocate a democracy for the Near East that flourishes in a cultural context. "And while we certainly do not agree that 'benign despotism' is a proper model, we do agree that individual states and peoples within them will need to adapt in various, sometimes, dissimilar, degrees."[4]

Transitions to democracy are dangerous. Success depends on a government's ability to address real societal grievances and by being accountable to the people. As our cases demonstrate, no "one-size-fits-all" democracy exists and that must be understood to avoid policy pitfalls. Regime transitions are inherently dangerous. As such, if the United States is in the business of combating terrorism, then it must focus on unique state, regional, and societal frameworks prior to addressing security issues. Combating terrorism is not for the fainthearted, and it requires a profound grasp of the political context of terrorism, coupled with insights into the intellectual tasks required for informed strategic planning in concert with the international community.

Of all the cases, Macedonia seems closest to Spain. Both governments addressed the concerns of their respective ethnic communities through their inclusive democratization efforts. Additionally, both regimes built the foundations for a civic culture as a precursor to democratization. Spain legitimized the Basque political community, and has so far created compatible, yet overlapping political communities at the state and regional levels. Macedonia is in the process of hopefully achieving a similar result by acknowledging the ethnic Albanian desire for a regional political community. As such, the state is crafting its constitution and laws to satisfy both ethnic

Albanians and ethnic Slavs in Macedonia. Macedonia seems committed to finding a legitimate, political solution to its challenges as evident by the signing of the Ohrid Framework and the successful 2002 elections. Ljupčo Georgievski, who was defeated in those elections proclaimed, "These were the most democratic elections in the history of Macedonia."[5] And as the discussion on the spillover effects indicated, due to Macedonia's success, there is hope for the situation in Serbia and Kosovo.

Interstate and regional cooperation was essential for the positive outcomes in both cases. By cultivating legitimacy, Spain contained ETA, and with France's cooperation, Spain effectively protected its society. Moreover, France bolstered its liberal democracy and reassessed its views on justice and its approach to terrorism. Clearly, the convergence of political cultures is a slow process, but the Basque case reveals some convergence of political cultures in both Spain and France. Likewise, in the Balkans, with the Ohrid Framework and with Serbia's continued steps toward democratization, regional cooperation may have helped mitigate the activities of extremist ethnic Albanians in both Kosovo and Macedonia. With courage and continued regional and international cooperation, Macedonia can marginalize and overcome future extremist activities. By some reports, the NLA is now largely nonexistent.

Unlike Spain, Turkey has consistently linked terrorism to the Kurdish population and has made no distinction between the ethnic community and the PKK. However several factors have lately improved the Turkish state's ability to gain legitimacy from most elements of its population, strengthen its democratic institutions, and decrease the appeal of terrorist groups. First, the PKK violence frustrated a majority of Turkish Kurds who suffered at the hands of both the Turkish military and the PKK. The violent tactics by the PKK and the Turkish state cost both groups internal legitimacy. Harsh military operations fostered international sympathy for the PKK and elevated the Kurdish plight to international attention. Turkey's initial reluctance to recognize the cultural rights of minority groups served as a significant source of tension in Turkey's bid for EU membership and underscores the potential for international influence on a state's domestic politics. With the advent of a moderate Islamist party professing social justice and lobbying hard for inclusion into the European club, Turkey is modifying significant policies to strengthen the nature of its democracy. Clearly, a democratic Turkey can only bode well for the future of Iraq. Each country will need to continue to work hard to cultivate overlapping identities for the minorities, namely the Kurds, such that subnational and national loyalties do not conflict.

The Russian case demonstrates the impact of a legacy of "hard constraints" on democratization. Shaped by centuries of autocratic and totalitarian rule under tsars and commissars, Russian political culture—with its prejudice against organized pluralism and dissent—stood firmly in the way of democratization when the Russian state emerged from under the rubble of the Soviet Union. The collapse of the Soviet empire also severely weakened the prospects for democracy, forcing the new Russian state to build many institutions of the government from scratch in conditions of extreme elite conflict.

Chechen separatism emerged from this political chaos, and helped spark two brutal wars with the Kremlin, the former imperial center. The terrorist ideology and program that was forged in this crucible of wartime destruction and brutality is now an almost intractable problem due to Moscow's unwillingness to recognize and address the political, social, and economic grievance of the Chechen people. Given the political forces on both sides of the conflict who oppose a political settlement, the Russian and Chechen tragedy is unlikely to be resolved from within the Russian political system.

Russia is also too large, too autonomous, and too distant for external actors like the United States or the European Union to force Moscow to change its policies toward Chechnya, much less induce the Kremlin to support democratization. Nevertheless, the West seems to possess sufficient influence over Russia to press the Kremlin to halt its attacks on the remaining vestiges of Russian democracy. Such external pressure would at least leave hope for the gradual growth of political and civil society in Russia over the long term. Unfortunately, the West has apparently decided that Russia is too important as an economic and strategic partner to risk confrontation over democratic values.

The Palestinian case differs significantly from the other cases in the study. Although separatism was on the agenda for the PKK, ETA, and the Chechen rebels, the creation of independent states was not an acceptable option for their respective ruling governments. In contrast, Israel and the Palestinians opted for a two-state solution, although the final borders of a Palestinian state are still disputed. As such, the Palestinian state is transitioning to democracy, while struggling to determine the final borders of the Palestinian entity. As part of the battle for liberation, radical groups, both secular and religious, implement violence and terrorism targeting Israelis in both Israel and in the occupied territories. To stem the violence, the Palestinian Authority ruled by the Fatah Party needed to address the grievances of their population, while constrained in their actions by a continuing occupation. Both Israeli actions and internal corruption in the Palestinian Authority stalled any real progress in the democratic transition. When elections occurred in January 2006, Hamas, a group on the EU and U.S. terrorist list, gained power.

Clearly, the outcome of the Palestinian election poses significant challenges for Israel and the international community. Yet our argument remains consistent. Under any party, the PA needs to develop the population's allegiance to the regime and ultimately to a democratic system. Therefore, there is a possibility that if Hamas strengthens the democratic process as they claimed they would, the Palestinian population, despite Hamas' public stand that it will not negotiate with Israel, might find the prospect of increased violence with Israel as detrimental to their interests. At the very least, the international community should convince Hamas to prolong its truce with Israel in the hope that future dialogue can be implemented. If Hamas fails to implement significant democratic restructuring, the result will be violence directed toward Israel.

This study also sheds light on how policymakers and academics ought to define and/or categorize terrorism. Again, qualifying the term requires analysts and policymakers to view it in a political and strategic context. At the heart of this context are the concepts of political community, political culture, and legitimacy. It is the fight for legitimacy that characterizes terrorism. States, therefore, must carefully diagnose the issues, acknowledge real grievances if they exist, and consider all political, economic, information, and security force tools available to address and combat terrorist threats. When the political system refuses to acknowledge real grievances and/or the government takes disproportionate and extreme action, then domestic and even international populations may view terrorists as legitimate. Policies of restraint and reconciliation in combination with prudent counterterrorist tactics toward terrorist groups seem most effective for the state's struggle for legitimacy. Spain and Macedonia's restraint gained them domestic and international support; Turkey and Russia's unrestrained response worked against their interests in both the international and domestic arenas. What this point suggests is that a keen knowledge of each terrorist group, grievances, and goals must be scrutinized carefully before prescribing policy. In other words, a "one-size-fits-all" approach toward terrorism results in too many blind spots; each terrorist group requires a unique political and counterterrorist policy.[6]

What does this mean for U.S. policymakers? We argue that the National Security Strategy rightly views democracy as a significant weapon against the efforts of terrorists to acquire legitimacy. However, the means to a democratic end matters, and democracy may take different forms, depending on numerous factors: culture, economy, geography, region, and history. In sum, the transitional process is not linear, and all types of scenarios must be analyzed to prepare for, at best, anticipated instabilities, and, at worst, unintended consequences. Policymakers who ignore unpleasant possibilities are frankly derelict in their duties.

Given the transnational nature of much of contemporary terrorism, policymakers must view issues from a regional perspective. What happens on one side of a border can have great impacts on the other side. Interestingly, the U.S. military rightly has regional commands, but the Department of State is still organized around embassies. Not only does this inhibit good coordination between State and Defense, but it also creates blind spots concerning those threats that cross borders and especially actions that can have unintended dangerous spillover effects. Moreover, societal grievances can also overlap state borders, putting pressures on more than one government. No wonder terrorists and other nonstate actors thrive where state borders present vulnerable seams to exploit.

For the United States, there is no option other than working with allies, IGOs, and NGOs. In truth, the United States should encourage other states to do the same. A key aspect of legitimacy is the state's ability to protect its citizens from political terror—one of Larry Diamond's criteria for a liberal democracy. In the context of globalization, such protection can only be attained through interstate and IGO cooperation because terrorism crosses boundaries. For example, in the Basque case, France and Spain cooperated to marginalize ETA, and as a consequence, Spain successfully continued its democratization. The collaboration led France, a mature democracy, to reassess its values and policies. While Serbia's democratization may have helped Macedonia's struggle with the NLA in 2001, it appears that Macedonia's 2002 elections muted Serbia and Kosovo's antidemocratic forces. Greece's actions on the Öcalan case forced it to reevaluate its standards and policies, while highlighting Turkey's justice system. The case of Turkey and Macedonia also highlighted the role of the IGO, namely the EU. EU pressure may bolster a state's ability to govern effectively by providing economic benefits and by demanding policy and value shifts of member countries. While 25 years ago, people may have scoffed at the idea of a Europeanized Spain, 25 years from now, a Europeanized Turkey may be taken for granted.

U.S. policymakers must also grasp how cooperation with other states influences foreign and domestic policies. In other words, there may be dangers with cooperating with political leaders who are not democratic minded. How states view torture, justice, and other key issues must be understood as states address the threat of terrorism. Martha Crenshaw in an astute article, "Why America? The Globalization of Civil War," ends with what she calls a "preposterous idea" concerning U.S. foreign policy:

> The United States has been susceptible to international terrorism primarily because of its engagement on the world scene and its choice of allies. . . . Future American foreign policy must consider the risk of terrorism as a central factor in calculating interests and strategies.[7]

This idea may seem disturbing and distasteful, but is also partly accurate. The inability of states to address real societal grievances risks ceding power to terrorist organizations who offer desperate people an alternative. As argued earlier, Hamas may have actually resonated with the population, not so much due to its stance on Israel, but more due to the disgraceful performance of Fatah. For the not-so-long term, we must address not only the act of terrorism but also its roots. Of course, when the United States is linked to illegitimate regimes, U.S.-professed values begin to come under scrutiny, both at home and abroad.

The problem is that not every state leader wants to address real grievances because that would require political reform. What leaders must realize, however, is that political reform at home is necessary for a peaceful and stable region and world. The UN report, "Towards a New Security Consensus," describes the changed nature of state sovereignty due to today's global security environment:

> In signing the Charter of the United Nations, States not only benefit from the privileges of sovereignty but also accept its responsibilities. Whatever perceptions may have prevailed when the Westphalian system first gave rise to the notion of State sovereignty, today it clearly carries with it the obligation of a State to protect the welfare of its own peoples and meet its obligations to the wider international community.[8]

The report acknowledges that not all states have been able or willing to meet those obligations, and when they cannot, the international community must respond.[9] Our cases that succeeded or show promise are those that had help from the international community, whether in the form of the EU or allies. Future success may depend upon how well the United States leads the international community in creative and focused effort. But to know what means to use, the United States must rethink its security paradigm.

As policymakers craft policy, they must acknowledge that the United States or any other state cannot ultimately decide the fate of other peoples, societies, or states. They must choose their own future and the way ahead for that future. Our cases demonstrate that culture, geography, and many other variables matter when states are in the process of reform. The path they choose will not be linear nor will it exactly replicate other paths. The best the United States and the international community can do is help create the conditions that will facilitate good choices. This is frustrating, especially for the United States, which likes to produce quick results in everything. However, patience, worldliness, empathy, intelligence, and hard work are the hallmarks of good policy . . . there is no short cut.

It is important to also recognize that given the transnational nature of threats, the line between domestic and foreign policies is blurred. As the United States examines its national security structures, it should not lose sight of the target of the terrorist group—the political legitimacy of its adversary. The United States must resist the temptation to weaken its liberal democratic values in the name of security. As a superpower, it must encourage other states to adhere to liberal democratic values as well. The United States can provide diplomatic, economic, informational and military assistance to states undergoing the democratization process. By cooperating against transnational threats and adhering to liberal democratic values, the United States will assure itself a leading role in the international community and better embark on a policy of engagement, not appeasement. In the past, the United States chose stability over democracy by supporting entrenched but illegitimate regimes. What the catastrophic events of September 11 demonstrated, however, is that stability comes with a price.

NOTES

PREFACE

1. Kenneth Waltz, *Man, State, and War* (New York: Columbia University Press, 1959).

INTRODUCTION

1. Donald J. Hanle, *Terrorism: The Newest Face of Warfare* (Washington, DC: Pergamon-Brassey's International Defense Publishers, 1989), p. 104.

2. Boaz Ganor, *The Counter-Terrorism Puzzle* (New Brunswick, NJ: Transaction Publishers, 2005), p. 1.

3. Ibid., p. 105.

4. Philip B. Heymann, *Terrorism and America: A Commonsense Strategy for a Democratic Society* (Cambridge, MA: The MIT Press, 1998), p. 3.

5. "A More Secure World: Our Shared Responsibility," Report of the High-Level Panel on Threats, Challenges, and Change, *United Nations 2004* 48. Accessed on January 4, 2005 at http://www.un.org/News/dh/infocus/terrorism/.

6. Heyman, p. 9. For further discussion on the questions proposed, see Heymann, pp. 7–9.

7. Paul Wilkinson, "Freedom and Terrorism." In *Terrorism: Roots, Impact, Responses*, ed. Lance Howard (New York: Praeger, 1992), p. 156. See also, Peter Chalk, *West European Terrorism and Counter-Terrorism: The Evolving Dynamic* (New York: St. Martin's Press, 1996), p. 95.

8. Chalk, p. 95.

9. Cindy Combs, *Terrorism in the 21st Century* (Upper Saddle River, NJ: Prentice Hall, 1997), p. 8.

10. Bruce Hoffman, "Defining Terrorism." In *Terrorism and Counterterrorism: Understanding the New Security Environment*, eds. Russell Howard and Reid Sawyer (Guilford, CT: McGraw-Hill/Dushkin, 2004), p. 23.

11. For a comprehensive analysis of terrorism in context see Martha Crenshaw, ed. *Terrorism in Context* (University Park, PA: The Pennsylvania State University Press, 1995).

12. For a full discussion on the forces of globalization and fragmentation, see James Rosenau, "The Complexities and Contradictions of Globalization." In *Understanding International Relations*, eds. Daniel J. Kaufman, Jay Parker, and Kimberly C. Field (New York: McGraw-Hill, 1999), pp. 756–762. Also, see Jessica Mathews, "Power Shift." In *Strategy and Force Planning*, 3rd edition, eds. Strategy and Force Planning Faculty (Newport, RI: Naval War College Press, 2000), pp. 93–106.

13. John Arquilla and David Ronfeldt, "The Advent of Netwar: Analytical Background," *Studies in Conflict and Terrorism* 22, no. 3 (July–September 1999): 194–195. David Ronfeldt concludes from two articles in a special issue of the journal that "networking is spreading among various terrorist and extremist groups—and that their leaders are doing a lot of thinking about how to gain advantages from the information revolution." In David Ronfeldt, "Netwar Across the Spectrum of Conflict: An Introductory Comment," *Studies in Conflict and Terrorism* 22, no. 3 (1999): 191.

14. Alan Cullison, "Inside Al-Qaeda's Hard Drive," *The Atlantic Monthly* 294, no. 2 (September 2004): 2. Accessed January 4, 2004, at http://proquest.umi.com.

15. The idea of global immediacy is found in Lorenzo Valeri and Michael Knights "Affecting Trust: Terrorism, Internet and Offensive Information Warfare." In *Terrorism and Political Violence* 12, no. 1 (Spring 2000): 16. The quotation is found in Ibid., p. 17.

16. The idea of vulnerabilities and the importance of cooperation is taken from Gregory D. Grove, Seymour E. Goodman, and Stephen J. Lukasik, "Cyber-Attacks and International Law," *Survival* 42, no. 3 (Autumn 2000): 89–90.

17. Chris Dishman, "Review Article: Trends in Modern Terrorism," *Studies in Conflict and Terrorism* 22, no. 4 (1999): 360–361.

18. Robert J. Bunker, "Weapons of Mass Disruption and Terrorism," *Terrorism and Political Violence* 12, no. 1 (Spring 2000): 44.

19. Cited from President Bush's speech at West Point, June 1, 2002, by the *National Security Strategy, 2002*.

20. Please see Mahmud Faksh, *The Future of Islam in the Middle East: Fundamentalism in Egypt, Algeria, and Saudi Arabia* (Westport, CT: Praeger, 1997), p. 24, as first discussed and referenced in Cindy R. Jebb, *Bridging the Gap: Ethnicity, Legitimacy, and State Alignment in the International System* (Lanham: Lexington, 2004), p. 244.

21. Although the question of whether democracy reduces or enhances the threat of terrorism is a timely and important one, relatively few studies exist on the subject. For a useful review of the literature, see Quan Li, "Does Democracy Promote or Reduce Transnational Terrorist Incidents?" *Journal of Conflict Studies* 49, no. 2 (April 2005): 278–297. Quan Li's own study finds that democracy both increases and decreases the threat of terrorism.

22. Gregory F. Gause, III, "Can Democracy Stop Terrorism?" *Foreign Affairs* 84, no. 5 (October 2005). For a useful counterargument, see Jennifer L. Windsor, "Promoting Democracy Can Combat Terrorism," *The Washington Quarterly*. 26, no. 3 (Summer 2004): 43–58.

23. Grant Wardlaw, "The Democratic Framework." In *The Deadly Sin of Terrorism: Its Effect on Democracy and Civil Liberty in Six Countries*, ed. David A. Charters (Westport, CT: Greenwood Press, 1994), p. 6.

24. David A. Charters, "Conclusion." In *The Deadly Sin of Terrorism: Its Effect on Democracy and Civil Liberty in Six Countries*, ed. David A. Charters (Westport, CT: Greenwood Press, 1994), p. 225.

25. Ralf Dahrendorf, "On the Governability of Democracies." In *Comparative Politics: Notes and Readings*, ed. Roy C. Macridis and Bernard Brown (Fort Worth, TX: Harcourt Brace College Publishers, 1996), p. 332. This section on legitimacy has been modified from Jebb, pp. 296–298.

26. Ibid., p. 333.

27. Ibid., p. 340.

28. Augustus Richard Norton, "The Security Legacy of the 1980s in the Third World." In *Third World Security in the Post-Cold War Era*, ed. Thomas G. Weiss and Meryl A. Kessler (Boulder, CO: Lynne Reinner Publishers, 1991), p. 20.

29. Norton, p. 20.

30. Pierre Manent observes that "Today's popular term 'identity' is a terribly impoverished substitute for the older term 'community,'" in Pierre Manent, "Democracy Without Nations?" *Journal of Democracy* 8, no. 2 (April 1997): 97.

31. David Easton, "The Analysis of Political Systems." In *Comparative Politics: Notes and Readings*, ed. Roy C. Macridis and Bernard Brown (Fort Worth, TX: Brooks/Cole Publishing Company, 1996), p. 52.

32. Michael C. Hudson, Arab Politics: *The Search for Legitimacy* (New Haven, CT: Yale University Press, 1977), pp. 389–390.

33. Philip Norton, *The British Polity*, 2nd edition (New York: Longman, 1991), pp. 32–35.

34. Gabriel A. Almond and Sidney Verba make the point that the sense of trust is extended to the political elite. In Almond and Verba, *The Civic Culture: Political Attitudes and Democracy in Five Nations* (Princeton, NJ: Princeton University Press, 1963), p. 490. See Almond and Verba, pp. 473–505 for their concluding thoughts on civic culture.

35. Juan J. Linz and Alfred Stepan, "Toward Consolidating Democracies," *Journal of Democracy* 7, no. 2 (1996): 15–16.

36. Francis Fukuyama, "The Primacy of Culture," *Journal of Democracy* 8, no. 1 (1995): 14.

37. Russell Bova, "Democracy and Liberty: The Cultural Connection," *Journal of Democracy* 8, no. 1 (January 1997): 112–113, 124.

38. Both quotes are from Larry Diamond. He describes the elements of liberal democracy as civil liberties, etc. In Larry Diamond, "The Global State of Democracy," *Current History* 99, no. 641 (December 2000): 414–415.

39. For theoretical discussions, see Seymour Martin Lipset, Kyoung-Ryung Seong, and John Charles Torres, "Social Requisites of Democracy," *International Social Science Journal* no. 136 (May 1993): 155–175; and Larry Diamond, "Rethinking Civil Society, toward Democratic Consolidation," *Journal of Democracy* 5, no. 3 (July 1994): 5–17.

40. See Arthur L. Stinchcombe, *Constructing Social Theories* (New York: Harcourt, Brace, and World, 1968), p. 161; Theda Skocpol, "Bringing the State Back In:

Strategies of Analysis in Current Research." In Peter Evans, Dietrich Rueschemeyer, and Theda Skocpol eds. *Bringing the State Back In* (New York: Cambridge University Press, 1985), pp. 6, 8, 9–20.

41. Robert Putnam with Robert Leonardi and Raffaella Y. Nanetti, *Making Democracy Work. Civic Traditions in Modern Italy* (Princeton, NJ: Princeton University Press, 1993), p. 176.

42. See the Congressional Research Service Report at http://italy.usembassy.gov/pdf/other/RL32845.pdf.

43. See Daniel Brumberg, "The Trap of Liberalized Autocracy," *Journal of Democracy* 13, no. 4 (October 2002): 56–68.

44. For a discussion of Arab support for democracy see Mark A. Tessler, "Gauging Arab Support For Democracy," *Journal of Democracy* 16, no 3 (July 2005).

45. Sam Zia Zarifi of Human Rights Watch, quoted in Rachel Morarjee, "Donors to Confront Tough Task in Kabul," *Financial Times* (January 30, 2006): 3.

46. Club de Madrid, "The International Summit on Democracy, Terrorism, and Security," Vol. III, *Toward a Democratic Response* (Madrid: Club de Madrid, 2005).

47. Ibid.

48. For a discussion on building comparative theories based on regional cases, specifically middle-range and grand theories, see Howard J. Wiarda, *Introduction to Comparative Politics: Concepts and Processes* (Belmont, CA: Wadsworth Publishing, 1993), pp. 171–172.

49. As cited in Jennifer L. Windsor, "Promoting Democratization Can Combat Terrorism," *The Washington Quarterly* 26, no. 2 (2003): 44.

Chapter 1

1. Samuel Huntington refers to the third wave of democratization, beginning in 1974 with Portugal. The first wave occurred at the turn of the nineteenth century; the second wave began after World War II; and, finally, the third wave including Portugal and Spain. "After Twenty Years: The Future of the Third Wave," *Journal of Democracy* 8, no. 1 (October 1997): 3–12.

2. Linz and Stepan, pp. 87–88.

3. Howard J. Wiarda, "Spain 2000: A Normal Country?" *Mediterranean Quarterly: A Journal of Global Issues* 11, no. 3 (Summer 2000): 39.

4. Goldie Shabad and Francisco Jose Llera Ramo, "Political Violence in a Democratic State: Basque Terrorism in Spain." In *Terrorism in Context*, ed. Martha Crenshaw (University Park, PA: The Pennsylvania State University Press, 1995), pp. 412–413.

5. "The Basques, origins and language," Center for Basque Studies, University of Nevada, Reno. Accessed at http://basque.unr.edu on January 16, 2006.

6. Shabad and Ramo, pp. 415–417.

7. Ibid., pp. 31–32. The information about the Basques and the Civil War is from Shabad and Ramo. The characterization of the regime is from Kenneth Maxwell and Steven Spiegel, *The New Spain: From Isolation to Influence* (New York: Council on Foreign Relations, 1994), p. 5.

8. Wiarda, 53–54.

9. Shabad and Ramo, p. 419. The quote is found on Shabad and Ramo, p. 419 and they cite Robert P. Clark, "Language and Politics in Spain's Basque Provinces." *Western European Politics* 4 (January1981): 93.

10. Shabad and Ramo, pp. 419–420.

11. Robert P. Clark, *The Basque Insurgents: ETA, 1952–1980* (Madison, WI: The University of Wisconsin Press, 1984), p. 18.

12. Ibid., pp. 410–411.

13. Chalk, p. 55.

14. Linz and Stepan, p. 107.

15. Ibid., pp. 112–113.

16. Shabad and Ramo, p. 446.

17. The effectiveness of the regime to deal with ETA in a restrained manner will be evident throughout the discussion of this case.

18. Ibid., pp. 448–451.

19. Ibid., p. 453.

20. Ibid., p. 460.

21. Ibid., p. 461.

22. Ibid., p. 466.

23. Ibid., p. 461.

24. Linz and Stepan, p. 95. See Linz and Stepan, pp. 91–96 for a fuller discussion on Suarez.

25. Robert Hislope, "Ethnic Conflict and the 'Generosity Moment'." *Journal of Democracy* 9, no. 1 (1998): 141–142.

26. Hislope, pp. 143–145.

27. Linz and Stepan, p. 99.

28. Ibid., pp. 101–102.

29. Ibid., pp. 105–106.

30. Francisco J. Llera, "Conflicto en Euskadi Revisited." In *Politics, Society, and Democracy: The Case of Spain*, ed. Richard Gunther (Boulder, CO: Westview Press, 1993), p. 191.

31. Llera, p. 191.

32. Linz and Stepan, pp. 108–109.

33. Howard J. Wiarda. *Iberia and Latin America: New Democracies, New Policies, and New Models* (Lanham, MD: Rowman and Littlefield, 1996), pp. 57–60.

34. Michael M. Harrison, "France International Terrorism: Problem and Response." In *The Deadly Sin of Terrorism: Its Effect on Democracy and Civil Liberty in Six Countries*, ed. David A. Charters (Westport, CT: Greenwood Press, 1994), pp. 103 and 113.

35. Ibid., p. 123.

36. Shabad and Ramo, p. 443.

37. Ibid., pp. 444–445.

38. Michel Wieviorka, "French Politics and Strategy on Terrorism." In *The Politics of Counter-Terrorism: The Ordeal of Democratic States*, ed. Barry Rubin (Washington DC: Johns Hopkins University, 1990), pp. 63–64. The discussion on the two events is from Harrison, p. 123. Michael Harrison claims that Ipparretarak was active as late as 1992 in Harrison, p. 104.

39. The discussion of the assassination is from Harrison, p. 123. The banishment of separatist groups is from Shabad and Ramo, p. 444.

40. Harrison, pp. 123–124 and Shabad and Ramo, p. 444.

41. Harrison, p. 124.

42. Wieviorka, pp. 72–73.

43. Harrison, pp. 124–125. The quotation is found in Harrison, p. 125.

44. Ibid., pp. 124–125.

45. Linz and Stepan, pp. 105–106.

46. Shabad and Ramo, pp. 443–444.

CHAPTER 2

1. Ergun Özbudin claims that Turkey is not just the only secular state in the Islamic world, but also the only democratic one. See Ergun Özbudin, *Contemporary Turkish Politics: Challenges to Democratic Consolidation* (Boulder, CO: Lynne Rienner, 2000), p. 1.

2. Svante E. Cornell, "The Land of Many Crossroads: The Kurdish Question in Turkish Politics," *Orbis* 45, no. 1 (Winter 2001): 31.

3. Doğu Ergil, "The Kurdish Question in Turkey," *Journal of Democracy* 11, no. 3 (2000): 123.

4. Ibid., p. 123.

5. Cornell, p. 32.

6. Kemal Kirişci, "Disaggregating Turkish Citizenship and Immigration Practices," *Middle Eastern Studies* 36, no. 3 (July 2000): 3.

7. Ergil, p. 124. Detailed statistics on Balkan migration to Turkey reveal that close to 840,000 people, mostly from the Balkans, migrated to Turkey. Close to 400,000 people came from Greece between 1923 and 1939. See Kirişci, pp. 7–8. The influx of Greeks from Turkey pushed the existing Slavic population north to current day Macedonia and Bulgaria, while the Greek refugees settled in what is commonly referred to as Aegean or Greek Macedonia. See P.H. Liotta and Cindy R. Jebb, "Cry, the Imagined Country: Legitimacy and Fate of Macedonia," *European Security* 11, no. 1 (Spring 2002): 54.

8. Ergil, p. 124.

9. Ibid., pp. 124–125.

10. Cornell, p. 33.

11. Ibid., p. 34

12. Ergil, p. 123.

13. Ibid., pp. 125–127.

14. Hugh Poulton, "The Turkish State and Democracy," *The International Spectator* XXXIV, no. 1 (January–March 1999): 4. Accessed on May 15, 2001, at https://www.cc.columbia.edu/sec/dlc/ciao.

15. Kemal Kirişci and Gareth M. Winrow, *The Kurdish Question and Turkey: An Example of a Trans-State Ethnic Conflict* (London: Frank Cass, 1997), p. 127.

16. Ibid., p. 128.

17. Ibid., p. 127.

18. Cornell, p. 31.

19. The Republican's Peoples Party is also referred to in the literature by the acronym CHP. We will use RPP in this study.

20. Michael M. Gunter, *The Kurds and the Future of Turkey* (New York: St Martin's Press, 1997), p. 7.

21. Ibid., pp. 7–8.

22. C. H. Dodd, *Democracy and Development in Turkey* (North Humberside, England: The Eothen Press, 1979), p. 135.

23. Some scholars consider the military's intervention in 1997 as a military coup. See Jeremy Salt, "Turkey's Military 'Democracy'," *Current History* 98, no. 625 (February 1999): 72–78.

24. Cengiz Çandar, "Redefining Turkey's Political Center," *Journal of Democracy* 10, no. 4 (1999): 129. Accessed on January 4, 2006 at http://muse.jhu.edu.

25. Özbudin, "Turkey: How Far from Consolidation," *Journal of Democracy* 7, no. 3 (1996). Accessed on January 15, 2006 at http://muse.jsu.edu.

26. Salt, p. 72.

27. Ozbudin, *Contemporary Turkish Politics*, p. 33.

28. Ibid., p. 34.

29. Gerassimos Karabelias, "The Evolution of Civil-Military Relations in Post-War Turkey, 1980–95," *Middle Eastern Studies* 35, no. 4 (October 1999): 134.

30. Cengiz Çandar, "Redefining Turkey's Political Center," *Journal of Democracy* 10, no. 4 (1999). Accessed on January 4, 2006 at http://muse.jhu.edu.

31. Özbudin, *Contemporary Turkish Politics*, pp. 57–59.

32. Robert D. Kaplan, *Eastward to Tartary* (New York: Random House, 2000), p. 107.

33. Çandar, pp. 130–131.

34. Ibid.

35. Salt, p. 72.

36. Ibid., p. 73.

37. Ibid., pp. 72–75.

38. Ibid., p. 76.

39. Umit Cizre and Menderes Çinar, "Turkey 2002: Kemalism, Islamism, and Politics in the Light of the February 28 Process," *South Atlantic Quarterly* 102 (Spring/Summer 2003): 312.

40. Ibid.

41. Salt, p. 72.

42. Cizre and Çinar, p. 312.

43. Henri J. Barkey and Graham E. Fuller, *Turkey's Kurdish Question* (Lanham, MD: Rowman and Littlefield Publishers, 1998), p. 133.

44. Ibid., p. 118.

45. Cornell, p. 38.

46. Gunter, p. 19.

47. Hugh Poulton, *Top Hat, Grey Wolf and Crescent: Turkish Nationalism and the Turkish Republic* (New York: New York University Press, 1997), pp. 234–235.

48. Cornell, p. 40.

49. Radu, p. 59.

50. Poulton, p. 243.

51. Douglas Frantz, "Where Misery Abounds, the Kurds Make Merry," *New York Times* (March 23, 2001): A4.

52. Ibid.

53. Ayse Betul Çelik, "Transnationalization of Human Rights Norms and Its Impact on Internally Displaced Kurds," *Human Rights Quarterly* 27, no. 3 (August 2005): 993–994.

54. Poulton, *Top Hat*, pp. 248–250.

55. Kirişci and Winrow, p. 131.

56. Radu cites an open letter from Danielle Mitterand, "An Open Letter to President Öcalan," September 1, 1998, posted by the American Kurdish Information Network at http://www.kurdistan.org/Articles/dmforpeace.html. See Radu, p. 54.

57. Ibid., pp. 54–56.

58. U.S. Department of State, "Country Reports on Human Rights Practices for 1991" (Washington, DC: 1992): 1247. As cited in Kirişci and Winrow, p. 128.

59. P. Robins, "The Overlord State: Turkish Policy and the Kurdish Issue," *International Affairs* 69, no. 4 (October 1993): 664. As cited in Kirisci and Winrow, p. 128.

60. Ibid., pp. 128–129.

61. Ibid.

62. Stephen Kinzer, "In Turkey, Press's Lot Includes Jail Time," *New York Times* (June 14, 1998): 1.

63. "Turkey to Amend Anti-Terror Laws to Enhance Struggle Against PKK," *Agence France Presse* (July 21, 2005). Accessed on January 15, 2006, at http://web.lexis-nexis.com.

64. Gunter, p. 19.

65. Ibid. State Security Courts handle cases of freedom of expression. Their duties are contained in Article 143 of the Constitution to "deal with offenses against the indivisible integrity of the State and its territory and nation, offenses against the Republic, which are contrary to the democratic order enunciated in the Constitution, and offenses which undermine the internal or external security of the State." See Hugh Poulton, "The Turkish State and Democracy," p. 9.

66. Barkey and Fuller, pp. 136–139.

67. Çandar, pp. 132–135.

68. Ibid., p. 135.

69. "Turkey Nervous," *The Economist* (March 3–9, 2001): 49.

70. "Turks Blame Government for Economic Crisis," *U.S. Department of State, Office of Research* (May 2, 2001).

71. Sultan Tepe, "Turkey's AKP: A Model 'Muslim-Democratic' Party?" *Journal of Democracy* 16, no. 3 (July 2005): 71.

72. Ibid., 74.

73. Ahmet Insel, "The AKP and Normalizing Democracy in Turkey," *South Atlantic Quarterly* 10, no. 2 (Spring/Summer 2003): 293. The September 12 regime refers to the 1982 constitution that was a result of the military coup of September 12, 1980. Constitutional changes were implemented and imposed on society implementing "an authoritarian and conservative statist conception of politics."

74. Ibid., p. 295.

75. Ibid., pp. 298–299.

76. Tepe, p. 72.

77. Özbudun, p. 144.

78. Susan Sachs, "Rebel Violence in Turkey Could Erode Kurds Gains," *New York Times* (October 1, 2004): A8.

79. Ilene R. Prusher, "Iraq Colors Kurdish Campaign in Turkey's National Election," *Christian Science Monitor* (November 1, 2002): 7.

80. Ibid.

81. Yigal Schleifer, "Turkey's Kurds Languish in Poverty," *Economist* (August 31, 2005): 6. Accessed on January 16, 2006 at http://proquest.umi.com.

82. Catherine Collins, "Kurdish Rebels Seek a Ceasefire; Turkish Leader's Visit Raised Hope for Peace," *New York Times* (August 20, 2005): 4.

83. For information on new PKK attacks see "Turkey to Amend Anti-Terror Law to Enhance Struggle against PKK," *Agence France Presse* (July 21, 2005).

84. Steve Wood and Wolfgang Quaisser, "Turkey's Road to the EU: Political Dynamics, Strategic Context and Implications for Europe," *European Foreign Affairs Review* 10 (2005): 149.

85. Ziya Onis and Suhnza Yilmaz, "The Turkey–EU–U.S. Triangle in Perspective: Transformation of Continuity?" *Middle East Journal* 59, no.2 (Spring 2005): 267.

86. Wood and Quaisser, p. 149.

87. Onis and Yilmaz, p. 267.

88. Ibid., p. 269.

89. Ergil, "The Kurdish Question," p. 122.

90. Aslan Gündüz, "Human Rights and Turkey's Future," *Orbis* 45, no. 1 (Winter 2001): 28.

91. Onis and Yilmaz, p. 269.

92. The 1648 Treaty of Westphalia is recognized as the establishment of the state-centric international system that delineates state sovereignty and nonintervention. See Barry Buzan and Thomas Dietz, "The European Union and Turkey," *Survival* 41, no. 1 (Spring 1999): 50–51.

93. Ibid.

94. Ilana Navaro, "Breaking Turkish Taboos," *The Jerusalem Report* (May 8, 2000): 2–3. Accessed on April 4, 2001 at http://web.lexis-nexis.com.

95. Ibid.

96. Ibid.

97. Fotios Moustakis, "An Expanded EU and Aegean Security," *Contemporary Review* (November 2000): 278.

98. Suzan Fraser, "Turkey's Kurdish Language Schools to Shut Down over Lack of Interest, Bureaucratic Hurdles," *Associate Press Worldstream* (August 1, 2005). Accessed on January 15, 2006 at http://web.lexis-nexis.com.

99. Çelik, pp. 992–993.

100. Ibid., p. 993.

101. Resat Kaşaba and Sibel Bozdoğan, "Turkey at a Crossroad," *Journal of International Affairs* 54, no. 1 (Fall 2000): 10.

102. Walker and Fromkin, p. 4.

103. Ibid.

104. Thomas Fuller, "Why Giscard Spoke Out on Turkey and the EU," *International Herald Tribune* (December 4, 2002). Accessed on December 30, 2002, at http://www.iht.com/frontpage.html.

105. Cengiz Çandar and Graham E. Fuller, "Grand Geopolitics for a New Turkey," *Mediterranean Quarterly: A Journal of Global Issues* 12, no. 1 (Winter 2001): 37.

106. Buzan and Dietz, p. 49.

107. As quoted in Fotios Moustakis, "An Expanded EU and Aegean Security, *Contemporary Review* (November 2000): 277.

108. Ibid.

109. Wood and Quaisser, p. 150.

110. Onis and Yilmaz, p. 271.

111. Ibid., p. 272. For a similar discussion, see Wood and Quaisser, p. 150.

112. Volker Perthes, "Points of Difference, Cases for Cooperation: European Critiques of U.S. Middle East Policy," *Middle East Report* (Fall 1988): 30.

113. Önis and Yilmaz, p. 270.

114. Ibid., p. 274.

115. Ibid., pp. 275–276.

116. Michael M. Gunter, "The Continuing Kurdish Problem in Turkey after Ocalan's Capture," *Third World Quarterly* 21 (October 2000): 850.

117. The PKK had implemented a ceasefire in 2000, but called it off in June 2004. See "Turkey to Amend Anti-Terror Law to Enhance Struggle Against PKK."

118. "Days of Terror: Turkey and the Kurds," *Economist* (July 23, 2005): 38.

119. Bruce Falconer, "One Border, Two Worlds," *National Journal* (September 10, 2005). Accessed on January 22, 2006, at http:proquest.umi.com.

120. Candar, p. 130.

121. Cizre and Çinar, p. 310.

122. Cornell, p. 35.

123. Thomas W. Smith, "Civic Nationalism and Ethnocultural Justice in Turkey," *Human Rights Quartely* 27, no 2 (May 2005): 437.

CHAPTER 3

1. John Brademas, "Promoting Democracy and Reconciliation in Southeastern Europe," *Mediterranean Quarterly: A Journal of Global Issues* 12, no. 1 (Winter 2001): 51–52.

2. Dr. Gjorge Ivanov, "The Albanian Question in Macedonia: The Macedonian Perspective." Lecture given in October 2000, at Ohrid, Macedonia.

3. See P. H. Liotta and Cindy R. Jebb, *Mapping Macedonia: Idea and Identity* (Westport, CT: Praeger, 2004), pp. 27–30 for discussion on the rise of the KLA or *Ushtria çlirimatare e kosovës*. Interestingly, this group seemed to transform from a terrorist group to a recognized force through the 1990s.

4. See Liotta and Jebb, pp. 163–179, which depicts the full document. This document is unique as it was signed by leaders of Macdeonia: President Trajkovski; four of the major parliamentary party leaders; and, representatives of the United States and the European Union. See also, Vasko Popetrevski, and Veton Latifi, "The Ohrid Framework Agreement Negotiations," *Conflict Studies Research Center* (June 2004).

5. The portion in quotation marks indicates how Richard Harteis paraphrased Kenneth Hill in P. H. Liotta, "The Future Republic of Macedonia," *European Security* 9, no. 1 (Spring 2000): 93.

6. Stoyan Pribichevich, *Macedonia: Its People and History* (University Park, PA and London: The Pennsylvania University Press, 1982), p. 95.

7. Janissaries were an elite military that included a "system of converting Christian boys to Islam and training them under the immediate supervision of the Sultan ..."

See Don Peretz, *The Middle East Today*, 5th edition (New York: Praeger, 1988), p. 55.

8. The point concerning Islamic conversion is from Ackerman, Alice, *Making Peace Prevail: Preventing Violent Conflict in Macedonia* (Syracuse, NY: Syracuse University Press, 1999), p. 54 and the discussion concerning religious toleration and lack of proselytizing is from Pribichevich, p. 99. Note that the Janissaries were recruited from the Ottoman non-Muslim population. See Pribichevich, pp. 96–97 for details.

9. Pribichevich, pp. 99–100. The quote is found on p. 100.

10. Ackerman, p. 54.

11. Ibid.

12. John Shea, *Macedonia and Greece: The Struggle to Define a New Balkan Nation* (Jefferson, NC: McFarland and Company, 1997), p. 166.

13. Shea, pp. 169 and 171.

14. Keith Brown. Interview at the Watson Institute for International Studies, Brown University, April 4, 2001.

15. Ackerman, p. 55.

16. Aydin Babuna, "The Albanians of Kosovo and Macedonia: Ethnic Identity Superceding Religion," *Nationalities Papers* 28, no. 1 (March 2000): 68.

17. Ibid., pp. 68–69.

18. Erich Frankland, "Struggling with Collective Security and Recognition in Europe: the Case of Macedonia," *European Security* 4, no. 2 (Summer 1995): 366.

19. Jeffrey Smith, "Birth of New Rebel Army: Macedonian Guerilla Group Forming in Kosovo Poses Threat of Expanded Conflict in Balkans," *The Washington Post* (March 30, 2001): a1. Accessed at http//infoweb5.newsbank.com on May 1, 2001.

20. "War in the Balkans Again?" *The Economist* (March 24–30, 2001): 57–58.

21. Ibid. Note that Tetovo has a population of 70,000 with 90 percent Albanian as reported in Steven Erlanger, "Wide Offensive by Macedonia Presses Rebels," *The New York Times* (March 26, 2001): a10.

22. Stephane Lefebvre, "The Former Yugoslav Republic of Macedonia," *European Security* 3, no. 4 (Winter 1994): 713–714.

23. Shea, p. 156.

24. Ibid., pp. 217–219.

25. Loring M. Danforth, *The Macedonian Conflict: Ethnic Nationalism in a Transnational World* (Princeton, NJ: Princeton University Press, 1995), pp. 142–143.

26. "Macedonia-Constitution." Accessed at http//www.uniwuerzburg.de/law/mk00000_.html on April 18, 2001.

27. Ivanov, p. 1.

28. Ibid., p. 3. Note that the terms, "ethnic Macedonians," "Slavs," and "Macedonians," are used interchangeably in the literature as well as throughout this case.

29. Shea, p. 242.

30. "Macedonia, the Former Yugoslav Republic of," *CIA World Fact Book 2000*. Accessesed at http://www.odci.gov/cia/publications/factbook/geos/mk.html on April 2, 2001. The ethnic Albanian estimate is found at Babuna, p. 81.

31. "1999 Country Reports on Human Rights Practices: Former Yugoslav Republic of Macedonia," U.S. Department of State, 1–16. Accessed at http://www.

state.gov/www/global/human_rights/1999_hrp_report/macedonia.html on April 2, 2001.

32. Ibid.

33. Babuna, pp. 80–81.

34. Ibid., p. 83.

35. Ibid., pp. 81–82.

36. Ibid., p. 82.

37. Liotta, p. 80. Notably, Xhaferi became far less conciliatory and far more divisive in his language following his election defeat in 2002.

38. Ibid., p. 80.

39. Ibid., p. 81.

40. Ackerman, p. 59.

41. Ibid., p. 57.

42. Ackerman, pp. 57–58.

43. Shea, p. 236.

44. Ackerman, p. 66.

45. Ibid., pp. 66–67.

46. Keith Brown. Interview at the Watson Institute for International Studies, Brown University, April 3, 2001.

47. Ackerman, p. 67.

48. Ibid., p. 94.

49. Ibid., p. 93.

50. According to the international observers of FYROM's elections, the elections were "marginally more transparent than previous ones" because a repeat vote occurred as a way to address inconsistencies. Still, more ethnic Macedonians (33–65 percent) believe that the elections were fair than ethnic Albanians (59–32 percent) who believe they were fair. See "Opposition SDSM Pulls Ahead in FYROM," *Opinion Analysis*, Office of Research, Department of State (April 21, 2000).

51. "Opposition SDSM Pulls Ahead in FYROM," *Opinion Analysis*, Office of Research, Department of State (April 21, 2000).

52. "Macedonian Albanians' Political Influence Gives Them Reason for Optimism: But May Feed Suspicion among Ethnic Macedonians," *Opinion Analysis*, Office of Research, Department of State (May 9, 2000).

53. "Public Says Ailing FYROM Economy Needs Trade and Investment for Growth," *Opinion Analysis*, Office of Research, Department of State (May 4, 2000).

54. "Opposition SDSM Pulls Ahead in FYROM," *Opinion Analysis*, Office of Research, Department of State (April 21, 2000).

55. "Europe: Oh No, Not War in Macedonia As Well," *The Economist* (March 10–16, 2001): 46–47.

56. Ibid., "Europe: Passing Clouds?" *The Economist* (March 3–9, 2001): 49.

57. Ibid., p. 49.

58. Steven Erlanger, "Use Words, Not Guns, Balkan Leader Tells Rebels," *The New York Times* (March 28, 2001): a4. The demand for the census and change in the preamble is from Steven Erlanger. "Wide Offensive by Macedonia Presses Rebels," *The New York Times* (March 26, 2001): a10.

59. Erlanger, "Use Words," p. a4.

60. Ibid.

61. Steven Erlanger, "Wide Offensive by Macedonia Presses Rebels," *The New York Times* (March 26, 2001): a1 and a10. The quotations are found on p. a10.

62. Ibid., p. a10.

63. Ibid.

64. Carl Bildt, "A Second Chance in the Balkans," *Foreign Affairs* 80, no. 1 (January–February 2001): 154.

65. Ibid., p. 155.

66. Ibid.

67. "The EU and Southeastern Europe: On the Road to Europe: First Stabilization and Association Agreement to be signed on April 9, 2001 with Former Republic of Yugoslavia," *Europa.* Accessed at http://europa.eu.int/comm/external_relations/see/news/memo01_127.htm on April 25, 2001. Note that Slovenia and Hungary are applicant EU countries and are sometimes considered Balkan countries. For a review of the applicant process, see "A Survey of EU Enlargement: Europe's Magnetic Attraction," *The Economist* (May 19–25, 2001): 3–4.

68. "Macedonia: Stability Pact Coordinator on Prospects for Peace," *BBC Worldwide Monitoring* (March 19, 2001). Accessed at http://infoweb5.newsbank.com on May 1, 2001.

69. "Macedonians Disillusioned by NATO Action in Kosovo: Albanians Still Support NATO and Feel Safer with Troops in FYROM," *Opinion Analysis,* Office of Research, Department of State (April 25, 2000).

70. Keith Brown. Interview at Watson Institute for International Studies, Brown University, April 3, 2001.

71. See concerning Rugova's rejection of violence. See footnote below, reference Chris Patten.

72. "Commissioner Patten to Visit Skopje," *External Relations: The EU and South Eastern Europe* (April 2, 2001). Accessed at http//europa.eu.int/comm./external_relations on May 1, 2001. The discussion on aid to Serbia and Kosovo is from Chris Patten, "Debate on Conflict Prevention/Crisis Management," *External Relations: The EU and South Eastern Europe* (March 14, 2001). Accessed at http//europa.eu.int/comm./external_relations on May 1, 2001.

73. "Europe: Passing Clouds?" p. 48.

74. Leonard J. Cohen, "Post-Milosevic Serbia," *Current History* 100, no. 644 (March 2001): 100.

75. Ibid., p. 105.

76. Ibid.

77. Ibid., p. 100.

78. The points about the police, contacts, currency, and wages are from Eric D. Gory, "Building a 'Normal, Boring' Country: Kostunica's Yugoslavia," *Current History* 100, no. 644 (March 2000): 113. The rest is from Cohen, pp. 106 and 108.

79. "UN Official Welcomes Kosovar Albanians Freed from Serbian Jails," *UN: Bringing Peace to Kosovo News Reports* (April 25, 2001). Accessed at http://www.un.org/peace/kosovo/news/kosovo2htm on May 1, 2001.

80. "Security Council Members Condemn Ambush in FYR of Macedonia," *UN: Bringing Peace to Kosovo News Reports* (April 25, 2001). Downloaded on May 1, 2001 from http://www.un.org/peace/kosovo/news/kosovo2htm.

81. "Kosovo: Serb Representative Rejoins Panel Drafting Legal Framework for Self Government," *UN: Bringing Peace to Kosovo News Reports* (April 25,

2001). Accessed at http://www.un.org/peace/kosovo/news/kosovo2htm on May 1, 2001.

82. "Albania: Getting Better," *The Economist* (February 24–March 2, 2001): 53.

83. "Europe: Passing Clouds?" p. 49.

84. "FYR of Macedonia: President Calls for Greater Control of Border Crossing with Kosovo," *UN: Bringing Peace to Kosovo News Reports* (April 10, 2001). Accessed at http://www.un.org/peace/kosovo/news/kosovo2.htm on May 1, 2001.

85. Peter Liotta, *Dismembering the State* (Lanham, MD: Rowman and Littlefield, 2000), pp. 324–325.

86. Biljana Vankovska, "Part II, The Elections and Their Aftermath: The Victory and Uncertainty of Formal Democracy in Macedonia," 9. Accessed at http://www.boell.de/downloads/konflikt/vankovska_pt2.pdf on January 3, 2003.

87. Ibid., p. 8.

88. Liotta and Jebb, p. 98.

89. *Background Note: Macedonia, Department of State*. Accessed at http://www. state.gov on January 16, 2006.

90. Robert Hislope, "Organized Crime in a Disorganized State: How Corruption Contributed to Macedonia's Mini War," *Problems of Post-Communism* 49, no. 3 (May–June 2002): 33.

91. Samuel P. Huntington, *Political Order in Changing Societies* (New Haven, CT: Yale University Press, 1968).

92. Quoted in Robert D. Kaplan, "Looking in the Eye," *Atlantic Monthly* (December 2001): 78.

93. Hislope, p. 34.

94. The preceding paragraphs in this section are taken directly from Liotta and Jebb, *Mapping Macedonia*, pp. 93–95.

95. Ali Ahmeti's role is from Vankovsky, p. 9.

96. Ibid., p. 11.

CHAPTER 4

1. For the *Freedom House* survey, see at http://www.freedomhouse.org/template. cfm?page=70&release=317.

2. A much higher estimate is offered by the respected scholar, S. Frederick Starr, who puts the number of Chechen deaths over the past decade at 200,000. "A Solution for Chechnya," *Washington Post* (September 17, 2004).

3. Theda Skocpol, *States and Social Revolutions* (Cambridge: Cambridge University Press, 1979), p. 29.

4. Max Weber, *Economy and Society*, eds. Guenther Roth and Claus Wittich, (Berkeley, CA: University of California Press, 1978), p. 56.

5. For an informed discussion of state capacity, see Merilee Grindle, *Challenging the State. Crisis and Innovation in Latin America and Africa* (Cambridge: Cambridge University Press, 1996).

6. See Arthur L. Stinchcombe, *Constructing Social Theories* (New York: Harcourt, Brace, and World, 1968), p. 161.

7. Theda Skocpol, "Bringing the State Back In: Strategies of Analysis in Current Research." In Peter Evans, Dietrich Rueschemeyer, and Theda Skocpol, eds. *Bringing the State Back In* (New York: Cambridge University Press, 1985), pp. 6, 8, 9–20.

8. Robert Putnam, Robert Leonardi, and Raffaella Y. Nanetti, *Making Democracy Work. Civic Traditions in Modern Italy* (Princeton, NJ: Princeton University Press, 1993, p. 176.

9. See Michael Burton, Richard Gunther, and John Higley, "Elites and Democratic Consolidation in Latin America and Southern Europe: An Overview." In John Higley and Richard Gunther, eds. *Elites and Democratic Consolidation in Latin America and Southern Europe* (New York: Cambridge University Press, 1992), p. 343.

10. Nancy Bermeo, "Sacrifice, Sequence, and Strength in Successful Dual Transitions: Lessons from Spain," *The Journal of Politics* 56 (August 1994): 601–627.

11. See Michael McFaul, "State Power, Institutional Change, and the Politics of Privatization in Russia," *World Politics* 47 (January 1995): 236; and Jerry Hough, Evelyn Davidheiser, and Susan Goodrich Lehmann, *The 1996 Russian Presidential Election* (Washington, DC: Brookings Institution Press, 1996): ch. 2.

12. Linz and Stepan, p. 397.

13. Jeffrey D. Sachs, "Life in the Economic Emergency Room." In John Williamson, ed. *The Political Economy of Policy Reform* (Washington, DC: Institute for International Economics, 1993), pp. 501–524; and Anders Aslund, *How Russia Became a Market Economy* (Washington, DC: Brookings, 1995).

14. See for example, Stephen Handelman, *Comrade Criminal: The Theft of the Second Russian Revolution* (New Haven, CT: Yale University Press, 1995); Richard Lotspeich, "Crime in Transitional Economies," *Europe-Asia Studies* 47 (1995): 555–589; Victor Sergeyev, *The Wild East: Crime and Lawlessness in Post-Communist Russia* (Armonk, NY: M.E. Sharpe, 1998); and Andrew L.A. Goodman, "Organized Crime and Corruption in Russia and the NIS: A Framework for Comparative Analysis," unpublished MS (April 1997).

15. Ibid., pp. 2, 26.

16. *New York Times*, January 6, 1992.

17. See Joseph R. Blasi, Maya Kroumova, and Douglas Kruse, *Kremlin Capitalism: Privatizing the Russian Economy* (Ithaca, NY: Cornell University Press, 1997), p. 28 and p. 173ff.

18. Ibid., ch. 1, especially pp. 38–39.

19. Cited in ibid., pp. 35, 228. See also Aslund, ch. 2.

20. See Michael Ellman and Vladimir Kontorovich, eds. *The Destruction of the Soviet Economic System: An Insider's History* (Armonk, NY: M.E. Sharpe, 1998), especially the contributions by Yevgenii Yasin; Andrei Shliefer, "Agenda for Russian reforms," *Economics of Transition* (May 5, 1997): 227–231; and Aslund, *How Russia Became a Market Economy*.

21. Putnam, p. 184.

22. Jacek Kolchanowicz, "Reforming Weak States and Deficient Bureaucracies." In Joan Nelson, Jacek Kolchanowicz, Kalman Mizsei, and Oscar Munoz, *Intricate Links: Democratization and Market Reforms in Latin America and Eastern Europe* (New Brunswick, NJ: Transaction Press, 1994).

23. Juliet Johnson, "Russia's Emerging Financial-Industrial Groups," *Post-Soviet Affairs* 13 (October–December, 1997).

24. Aslund, "Why the Doomsayers are Wrong about Russia," *The Weekly Standard* (December 29, 1997); Aslund, "The Myth of Oligarchy," *Moscow Times* (January 29, 1998); and *Forbes* (September 7, 1998).

25. See Vladimir Shlapentokh, "Early Feudalism—the Best Parallel for Contemporary Russia," *Europe-Asia Studies* 48 (1996): 393–411.

26. Mikhail Delyagin, *RIA Novosti* (April 24, 1998); and Chrystia Freeland, "A People on the Edge of a Precipice," *Financial Times* (April 9, 1997).

27. Yegor Gaidar, *Dni porazheniia i pobed* (Moscow: Vagrius, 1996), p. 353.

28. Aslund, *How Russia Became a Market Economy*, pp. 95–96, 294–295, 313.

29. See Linz and Stepan, p. 391.

30. Stanley G. Payne, *The Spanish Revolution* (New York: Norton, 1970); and Payne, *The Franco Regime: 1936–1975* (Madison, WI: University of Wisconsin Press, 1987).

31. John Hall, ed. *States in History* (London: Blackwell, 1987), p. 288.

32. Michael Burton, Richard Gunther, and John Higley, "Elites and Democratic Consolidation in Latin America and Southern Europe: An Overview." In Higley and Gunther, pp. 345–346.

33. John Lowenhardt, *The Reincarnation of Russia* (Durham, NC: Duke University Press, 1995), p. 161.

34. Yitzhak M. Brudny, "Neoliberal Economic Reforms and the Consolidation of Democracy in Russia. Or Why Institutions and Ideas Might Matter More than Economics." In Karen Dawisha, ed. *The International Dimension of Post-Communist Transitions in Russia and the New States of Eurasia* (Armonk, NY: M.E. Sharpe, 1997), pp. 297–321. On this issue, see also Timothy Colton, "Politics." In Timothy Colton and Robert Legvold, eds. *After the Soviet Union. From Empire to Nations* (New York: Norton, 1992); and Lowenhardt, chap. 4.

35. Gaidar, *Dni porazheniia i pobed*. See also the interview with Chubais in *Forbes* (February 23, 1998).

36. Yitzhak Brudny, "The Dynamics of 'Democratic Russia,' 1990–1993," *Post-Soviet Affairs* 9 (April–June 1993): 141–170; and McFaul, p. 226.

37. M. Steven Fish, *Democracy From Scratch. Opposition and Regime in the New Russian Revolution* (Princeton, NJ: Princeton University Press, 1995), pp. 60, 65.

38. Ibid., p. 93.

39. Ibid., p. 210.

40. Stephen Fish, "The Advent of Multipartism in Russia, 1993–1995," *Post-Soviet Affairs* 11 (October–December 1995): 340–383.

41. Yitzhak M. Brudny, "Neoliberal Economic Reforms and the Consolidation of Democracy in Russia." In Karen Dawisha, ed. *The International Dimension of Post-Communist Transitions in Russia and the New States of Eurasia* (Armonk, NY: M.E. Sharpe, 1997), pp. 297–321, and also p. 308.

42. Guillermo O'Donnell, "Delegative Democracy," *Journal of Democracy* 5 (January 1994): 55–69.

43. Stephen White, Richard Rose, and Ian McAllister, *How Russia Votes* (Chatham, NJ: Chatham House Publishers, 1997), p. 133.

44. Theodore Von Laue, *Why Lenin? Why Stalin?* (New York: Harper and Row, 1936), p. 196.

45. Vladimir Putin, Annual Address to the Federal Assembly on May 16, 2003, at President of Russia Official Web Portal, http://www.kremlin.ru.

46. Ibid.

47. On diversionary war, see Jack Levy, "The Diversionary Theory of War: A Critique." In Manus I. Midlarsky, *Handbook of War Studies* (Boston: Unwin Hyman, 1989), pp. 259–288.

48. Edward Mansfield and Jack Snyder, "Democratization and War," *Foreign Affairs* 74, no. 3 (May/June 1995).

49. For an informed alternative argument for the First Chechen War as a political diversion, see Peter Reddaway, "Desperation Time For Yeltsin's Clique," *New York Times* (January 13, 1995): 29.

50. See Robert Bruce Ware and Ira Straus, "Media Bias on Chechnya," *Christian Science Monitor* (March 15, 2000).

51. For a balanced assessment of conditions in Chechnya at that time, see Sergei Kovalev, "Putin's War," *The New York Review of Books* (February 10, 2000). On Stephasin's statement, see Andrew Jack and John Thornhill, "Chechnya Assault 'A Long-Term Plan,'" *Financial Times* (January 31, 2000). Stepashin elsewhere argued that planning for a limited invasion of Chechnya after the Russian general, Gennady Shpigun, was kidnapped by Chechen rebels. See Jamie Dettmer, "Stepahsin Joins Putin Bandwagon," *Insight* (February 25, 2000).

52. Matthew Evangelista, *The Chechen Wars: Will Russia Go the Way of the Soviet Union?* (Washington, DC: Brookings, 2003), pp. 62–64.

53. Yelena Skvortsova, "Blown Up Space," *Obshchaya Gazeta* (March 16, 2000). Translated and reproduced in *Johnson's Russia List*, no. 4189.

54. Fund of Public Opinion, *Bulletin* (May 26, 1999).

55. For Putin's decree, see *Johnson's Russia List* (January 8, 2000).

56. Alexander Lebed accused the then Prime Minister Putin and President Yeltsin of engineering the incursion into Russian Dagestan by Chechen militants. As for the apartment bombings, Alexander Korzhakov, Yeltsin's former bodyguard, accused oligarch Boris Berezovsky, who is closely connected to Yeltsin, of responsibility for the bombings. See Julie Corwin, "Lebed Posits Secret Agreement between Basaev and Russian Leadership." *RFE/RL Caucasus Report* (September 30, 1999); and Natalya Shuyakovskaya, "Korzhakov Says Bombings Were Berezovsky's Doing," *The Moscow Times* (October 28, 1999): 1. It should be recalled that the Russian press had accused Korzhakov of instigating the First Chechen War. For another account that blames the Kremlin for orchestrating the incursion into Dagestan and the urban bombings, see Igor Oleinuk, "Vlast Ostaiotsia v Rukakh 'Sem'i," *Novaya Gazeta* (January 10, 2000).

57. As quoted by Roy Medevedev in "Getting to Know Putin," *Rossiyskaya Gazeta* (March 11, 2000). Reproduced in *Johnson's Russia List*, no. 4188.

58. On the First Chechen War, see Stephen J. Blank and Earl H. Tilford, Jr., *Russia's Invasion of Chechnya: A Preliminary Assessment* (Carlisle Barracks: U.S. Army War College, 1995).

59. See Masha Gessen, "Lockstep to Putin's New Military Order," *New York Times* (February 29, 2000).

60. *Mosnews*, "Russian Parliament Approves NGO Bill in Final Reading despite Criticism" (December 23, 2005).

61. Vladimir Simonov, "Russia Devises Protection against Color Revolutions" *RIA Novosti* (November 24, 2005).

62. As recounted in Mark Kramer, "The Perils of Insurgency," *International Security* 29, no. 3 (Winter 2004–2005): 61.

63. *Mosnews.com* at http://www.mosnews.com/feature/2004/09/01/terror.shtml. For Orlov's account of Russia's inhumane prosecution of the First Chechen War, see O.P. Orlov and A.V. Cherkasov *Rossiia—Chechnya: Tsep' Oshibok i Prestuplenii* (Moscow: Zveni'ia, 1998).

64. Khassan Baiev, "A History Written in Chechen Blood," *Washington Post* (February 24, 2004): A21. Also see his *The Oath. Surgeon Under Fire* (New York: Walker and Co., 2004). Baiev's book provides a valuable account of growing up as a Soviet Chechen and of life in wartime Chechnya, where he treated scores of Chechen and Russian combatants, including Shamil Basayev.

65. "Putin Makes a Lightning Visit to Chechnya's Capital," *Chechnya Weekly* 6, no. 47 (December 15, 2005).

66. POLL: Validata.ru/e_e/Chechnya (August 2003); *Validata* "Public Opinion of the Chechen Population on the Actual Issues of the Republic" (March–August 2003). Accessed on September 1, 2003 at http://www.validata.ru/e_e/chechnya/eng/chechnya_details_21.html.

67. For Putin's comments, see Fiona Hill, "Stop Blaming Putin and Start Helping Him," *New York Times* (September 10, 2004): A25.

68. S. Frederick Starr, "A Solution for Chechnya," *Washington Post* (September 17, 2004).

69. C. J. Chivers, "Rebel's Death Stirs Debate on Strategy for Chechnya." *New York Times* (March 10, 2005): A9.

70. "Alkhanov: Poverty Helps Rebels," *Moscow Times* (November 2, 2004): 2.

71. "Chechnya Parliamentary Vote Goes as Planned," *Chechnya Weekly* 6, no. 45 (December 1, 2005).

72. For a similar proposal see Leon Aron, "Responding to Terrorism," *AEI Online* (September 1, 2004).

73. This paragraph draws on Fiona Hill, Anatol Lieven, and Thomas de Waal, "A Spreading Danger: Time for a New Policy toward Chechnya," *Carnegie Endowment for International Peace* (Policy Brief no. 35, March 2005).

CHAPTER 5

1. Joel Greenberg, "Hamas' Landslide Win a Political Earthquake; Israel Says It Won't Negotiate with Regime," *New York Times* (January 27, 2006): A1.

2. Alan Cowell, "Europeans Insist Hamas Must Disavow Terrorism," *New York Times* (January 27, 2006): 11.

3. In the period from 1882 to 1908, the number of Jews in Palestine increased from 24,000 to somewhere between 70,000 and 80,000. See Neville J. Mandel, *The Arabs and Zionism before World War I* (Berkeley, CA: University of California Press, 1976), p. 224. In addition, consult Mandel for a complete study on Arab reactions to Jewish immigration into Palestine from 1882 until World War I. He also discusses the growth of local Arab patriotism in Palestine.

4. In several pieces of correspondence between the British and Arabs, the British agreed to support the Arabs' request for independence after the war. The British left the boundaries of the areas promised to the Arabs deliberately ambiguous. In return for independence, the Arabs agreed to help the British defeat the Ottomans, who had

sided with Germany in World War I. These correspondences, which lasted from July 1915 to January 1916, became known as the Husayn–McMahon correspondence. Simultaneously, the British were negotiating with the French as to the areas in the Middle East that each country would control after the war. The agreement between the French diplomat, George Picot and the British, Mark Sykes (known as the Sykes–Picot agreement), was ratified in May, 1916. The agreement defined the areas of French and British control. The contradictions of these promises are examined in detail in Charles D Smith, *Palestine and the Arab-Israeli Conflict* (New York: St. Martin's Press, 1988), pp. 42–50 and in Howard M. Sachar, *A History of Israel: From the Rise of Zionism to Our Time* (New York: Alfred A. Knopf, 1979), pp. 92–96.

5. For an account of the specific riots and their causes see Smith, pp. 87–90 and Sachar, pp. 173–178.

6. For a detailed discussion of the background of both the 1929 and the 1936–1939 riots and the shaping of the Palestinian national movement as an active political force, see Yehoshua Porath, *The Palestinian Arab National Movement, 1929–1939: From Riots to Rebellion* (London: Frank Cass, 1977). For a comparison of the riots with the present day Intifada, see Aryeh Shalev, *The Intifada: Causes and Effects* (Boulder, CO: Westview Press, 1991), pp. 44–49. See also Mark Tessler, *A History of the Israeli-Palestinian Conflict* (Bloomington, IN: Indiana University Press, 1994), pp. 233–246.

7. For a very detailed study of the growth of the political, economic, and social infrastructure of the Jews in Palestine, refer to Sachar, pp. 65–85 and J.C. Hurwitz, *The Struggle for Palestine* (New York: Schocken Books, 1976), pp. 39–50.

8. Some scholars contend that some Palestinians, apprehensive that other Arab States would not allow the creation of an independent Palestinian state, supported the partition. Yet, the Palestine Arab Party and other Arab states opposed the creation of a Jewish state and wanted the entire mandate area to remain in Arab hands. See, Ian J. Bickerton and Carla L. Klausner, *A Concise History of the Arab-Israeli Conflict*, 2nd edition (Englewood Cliffs, NJ: Prentice Hall, 1995), p. 94.

9. An example of Arab pride in the results of the war of 1973 is indicated in many Arab countries by naming of areas after the war. In Egypt, for example, a bridge in Cairo is called the Tenth of October Bridge, commemorating the war.

10. The Israelis lost 2,552 men and over 3,000 were wounded. See Sachar, pp. 786–787.

11. Soon after the occupation, Israel recognized that the West Bank, dependent primarily on agriculture, would have suffered tremendous economic dislocation if farmers were deprived of access to markets in the East Bank. Therefore, on the suggestion of Lieutenant Colonel Israel Eytan, General Moshe Dayan approved and instituted the Open Bridge policy. Producers within the territories retained access to the Jordanian markets for their goods and gained admission to the Israeli market, thereby improving their general welfare. In addition, the Palestinians were able to acquire Jordanian products and visit family members in the East Bank, reducing the overall level of Palestinian frustration. Furthermore, it gave Israelis an opportunity to have some semblance of "peaceful" contact with Jordan. Many government officials in Israel anticipated an eventual dialogue or diplomatic channel opening between the two adversaries. See Sachar, p. 672 and Nadav Safran, *The Embattled Ally* (Cambridge: Harvard University Press, 1981), pp. 268–269.

12. Peter Riddell, "Bush Calls for End to Arab–Israeli Conflict," *Financial Times* (March 7, 1991): 1.

13. In late 1992, Israelis and officials from the PLO began meeting secretly to forge an agreement dealing with the West Bank and Gaza Strip. These negotiations took place in Oslo, Norway, and thus are referred to as the Oslo Accords. As a result of these mediations, on September 13, 1993, the Israelis and Palestinians signed an agreement at the White House called the Declaration of Principles on Interim Self-rule for Palestinians (DOP).

14. A day before Sharon's visit to the Temple Mount, Adnan Husseini, Chairman of the Islamic trust met with Jerusalem Police Chief, Yair Yitzhaki to convince him to have the visit canceled. See Lee Hockstader, "Street Army Spearheads Arab Riots," *Washington Post* (October 4, 2000): A1. This area, the site of the Dome of the Rock and Al Aqsa mosque and the location of the Second Jewish Temple, is sacred to both Muslims and Jews.

15. Neil King, Jr., and Jeanne Cummings, "Road Map Seeks Palestinian State within a Year," *Wall Street Journal* (February 28, 2003): A7. For a full discussion of the roadmap, see U.S. Department of State, "A Performance-Based Roadmap to a Permanent Two-State Solution to the Iraeli-Palestinian Conflict," April 30, 2003. Accessed on October 1, 2003 at http://www.state.gov/r/pa/prs/ps/2003/20062.htm.

16. For a discussion of the summit, see Robin Wright, "Mideast Summit: Sharon, Abbas Agree to Take Initial Steps toward Peace," *Los Angeles Times* (June 5, 2003): A1. Accessed on October 2, 2003 at http://proquest.umi.com.

17. Suzanne Goldenberg, "Bush Puts Peace Monitors in Place," *Guardian* (UK) (June 6, 2003): 17. Accessed on October 1, 2003 at http://proquest.umi.com.

18. Guy Chazan, "Militant is Killed, Further Clouding Truce in Mideast," *Wall Street Journal* (August 15, 2003): A6.

19. Nicole Gaouette, "Road Map in Peril as Cease-fire Ends," *Christian Science Monitor* (August 22, 2003). Accessed on October 1, 2003 at http://proquest.umi.com.

20. James Rosen, "Gaza Pullout has Risks, Rewards: Extremists on Both Sides Could Doom Gamble for Peace," *Sacramento Bee* (August 14, 2005): A1.

21. Parts of this section were modified from Ruth Margolies Beitler, *The Path to Mass Rebellion an Analysis of Two Intifadas* (Lanham, MD: Lexington Books, 2004), pp. 145–150.

22. Juan J. Linz and Alfred Stepan, "Toward Consolidated Democracies," *Journal of Democracy* 7, no. 2 (1996): 14.

23. See the Oslo II Accords and Gal Luft, "The Mirage of a Demilitarized Palestine," *Middle East Quarterly* 8 (June 2001). Accessed on August 31, at http://www.lexis.com. Gal explains that although Oslo II permitted the PA to have 30,000 police officers, they have more than 45,000 in the Palestinian security services. As for weapons, the number was limited to 15,240 firearms for police.

24. Declaration of Principles, Article VIII.

25. For the full text of the Cairo Agreement, see http://www.jewishvirtuallibrary .org/jsource/Peace/gazajer.html.

26. David Schenker, *Palestinian Democracy and Governance: An Appraisal of the Legislative Council* (Washington, DC: Washington Institute for Near East Policy, 2000), p. 4.

27. Amal Jamal, "State-Building, Institutionalization and Democracy: The Palestinian Experience," *Mediterranean Politics* 6, no. 3 (Autumn 2001): 2.

28. Jamal, p. 3.

29. Linz and Stepan, p. 14.

30. Jamal, p. 5.

31. As'ad Ghanem, "Founding Elections in a Transitional Period: The First Palestinian General Elections," *Middle East Journal* (Autumn 1996): 514.

32. Ziad Abu-Amr, "The Palestinian Legislative Council: A Critical Assessment," *Journal of Palestine Studies* 26, no. 4 (Summer 1997): 90–91.

33. Adir Waldman, "Negotiated Transitions to Democracy: Israel and the Palestinians as a Case Study," *Democratization* 7, no. 2 (Summer 2000): 115.

34. For a full explanation of the Palestinian electoral system, see Waldman, pp. 120–124.

35. Ibid., p. 121.

36. Hady Amr, "Electoral Systems and Democracy: Palestinian and South African Elections Compared, *Middle East Report* (October–December, 1996): 21.

37. Ibid., p. 21.

38. Ibid., p. 21.

39. Quan Li, "Does Democracy Promote or Reduce Transnational Terrorist Incidents?" *Journal of Conflict Resolution*, 49 no. 2 (April 2005): 284.

40. Ibid., p. 294.

41. Schenker, p. 31. Fifty-five seats of the eighty-eight-seat Parliament went to Arafat loyalists, while another twenty seats, although claiming to be independents, had some Fatah affiliation. See *San Francisco Examiner* (January 22, 1996): A10.

42. Waldman, pp. 125–126.

43. Glenn E. Robinson, "After Arafat," *Current History* (January 2005): 20.

44. Abu-Amr, p. 91.

45. Schenker, p.1.

46. Adrien Katerine Wing, "The Palestinian Basic Law: Embryonic Constitutionalism," *Case Western Reserve Journal of International Law* (Spring 1999): 385.

47. Schenker, p. 28.

48. Shu'aybi and Shikaki, p. 95. Prior to the Six-Day War in 1967, the West Bank was under Jordanian rule, while Gaza was administered by Egypt.

49. Jamal, p. 8.

50. Abu-Amr, pp. 91–92.

51. Azmi Shu'aybi and Khalil Shikaki, "A Window on the Workings of the PA: An Inside View," *Journal of Palestine Studies* 30, no.1 (Autumn 2000): 91–95.

52. Abu-Amr, p. 92.

53. Ghanem and Khayed, p. 44.

54. See poll no. 48 from the Center for Palestinian Research and Studies, at http://www.pcpsr.org/survey/cprspolls/2000/poll48a.html.

55. Deborah Horan, "Palestine: Journalist Jailed for Criticizing Lack of Freedom," *Inter Press Service* (May 21, 1997). Accessed May 24, 2002, at http://www.nexis.com.

56. Roy, "Palestinian Society and Economy," p. 7.

57. *AP Worldstream*, June 28, 1999.

58. *Los Angeles Times*, (September 9, 2000): A6.

59. Khalil Shikaki, "Palestinians Divided," *Foreign Affairs* (January–February 2002): 89.

60. Jamal, p. 14.

61. Abu-Amr, p. 93.

62. Ali Jarbawi, "Palestinian Politics at a Crossroads," *Journal of Palestine Studies* 25, no. 4 (Summer 1996): 29.

63. Shu'aybi and Shikaki, p. 96.

64. *Los Angeles Times*, (December 9, 1999). Accessed on May 30, 2002, at http://www.nexis.com.

65. Khalil Shikaki, "The Future of Palestine," *Foreign Affairs* 83 (November/December 2004). Accessed on October 27, 2005, at http://proquest.umi.com.

66. Ibid.

67. Ibid.

68. Rema Hammani and Salim Tamari, "The Second Uprising: End of New Beginning," *The Journal of Palestine Studies* 30, no. 2 (Winter 2001): 17.

69. Glenn E. Robinson, "After Arafat," *Current History* (January 2005): 20.

70. Ibid., p. 19.

71. As'ad Ghanem and Aziz Khayed, "In the Shadow of the Al Aqsa Intifada: The Palestinians and Political Reform," *Civil Wars* 6, no. 3 (Autumn 2003): 32–34.

72. For a full discussion of this argument see Ibid., pp. 34–39.

73. Ibid., p. 34.

74. Ibid., p. 35.

75. Abu-Amr, p. 7.

76. Ibid., p. 12. See also Mahmud Zahhar and Hussein Hijazi, "Hamas: Waiting for Secular Nationalism to Self-Destruct. An Interview with Mahmud Zahhar," *Journal of Palestine Studies* 24 no. 3 (Spring 1995): 81–88.

77. Mohammed Omar, "Hamas Scores Majorities in Gaza and Municipal Council Elections," *Washington Report on Middle East Affairs* (July 2005): 14.

78. Mark Tessler, "The Attitudes of West Bank and Gaza Palestinians towards Governance and the Relationship between Religion and Politics," *Palestine-Israel Journal of Politics, Economics and Culture* 11 (2004–2005): 50.

79. There is a clear debate whether or not Islam and democracy are compatible. This argument is beyond the scope of this chapter. The major contention here is that some of the Islamic groups are not seeking democracy, but a pure theocracy.

80. Aida Akl, "Can Democracy Stop Terrorism?" Accessed on November 15, 2005, at http://www.voanews.com/english/News/Analysis/2005-11-03-voa55.cfm.

81. This section is taken from polling data conducted by the Palestinian Center for Policy and Survey Research. See http://www.pcpsr.org/survey/polls/2005/p17e.pdf for complete results.

82. Steven Erlanger, "In a Stronghold, Fatah Fight to Beat Back a Rising Hamas, *New York Times* (January 23, 2006): A1.

83. William B. Quandt, "The Urge for Democracy," *Foreign Affairs* (July–August 1994): 3.

84. "Israel Retreats from Objection to Hamas Role in Elections," *New York Times* (October 24, 2005): A12.

85. Waldman, p. 119.

86. Quandt, p. 2.

87. Ibid.

88. Ibid.

89. Graham Usher, "The Politics of Internal Security: The PA's New Intelligence Services," *Journal of Palestine Studies* 25 no. 2 (Winter 1996): 32.

90. Beverly Milton-Edwards, "Palestinian Nation-Building: Police and Citizens as Test of Democracy," *British Journal of Middle Eastern Studies* 25 no. 1 (May 1998): 96.

91. Usher, p. 22.

92. Milton-Edwards, p. 110.

93. Clovis Maksoud, "Peace Process or Puppet Show," *Foreign Policy* 100 (Fall 1995): 116.

94. Milton-Edwards, p. 112.

95. *Jerusalem Post* (May 21, 2002): 4. For a perspective on "successes" of Operation Defensive Shield, see *Christian Science Monitor* (April 19, 2002): 6.

96. *Jerusalem Post* (May 21, 2002): 4.

97. According to the IDF, it seized 1,338 Kalashnikov assault rifles, 709 long rifles, 387 sniper rifles, 31 M-16s, 770 pistols, 49 anti-tank grenades and 5 launchers, 3 mortars, 30 machine guns, 97 bombs, and 65 pounds of explosives; and it also found 19 explosives laboratories. For additional statistics see *AP WorldStream* (April 10, 2002). Downloaded on June 13, 2002, from http://www.nexis.com.

98. *Christian Science Monitor* (April 19, 2002): 6.

99. Steven Gutkin, "Further West Bank Pullouts Will be Necessary," *Associated Press* (January 24, 2006). Accessed on January 27, 2006, at http://web.lexis-nexis.com.

100. Lally Weymouth, "A Very Fateful Step," *Newsweek* (September 19, 2005). Accessed on November 22, 2005, at http://ebscohost.com.

101. Hami Malka, "Forcing Choices: Testing the Transformation of Hamas," *The Washington Quarterly* (Autumn 2005): 39.

102. Jeroen Gunning, "Peace with Hamas? The Transforming Potential of Political Participation," *International Affairs* 80, no. 2 (2004): 234.

103. Ibid., p. 236.

104. Matthew A. Levitt, "Hamas Social Welfare: In the Service of Terror." In *The Making of a Terrorist: Recruitment, Training and Root Causes* ed. James J. F. Forest (Westport, CT: Praeger Security International, 2006), pp. 122–123.

105. Malka, p. 40.

106. Ibid., pp. 37–38.

107. Gunning, p. 238.

108. Ibid., p. 38.

109. Ibid., p. 42.

110. "Former President Carter says U.S. Should Find Ways around Banning Funding to Hamas-led PA," *Associated Press Worldstream* (January 27, 2006). Accessed on January 27, 2006, at http://web.lexis-nexis.com.

111. Ali Daraghment, "Hamas Wins Key Local Elections in Possible Harbinger of January Parliament Vote," *Associated Press* (December 16, 2005). Accessed on January 27, 2006 at http://web.lexis-nexis.com.

112. Ilene Prusher, "Why Hamas is Gaining in Palestinian Polls, *Christian Science Monitor* (January 25, 2006). Accessed on January 27, 2006 at http://web17.epnet.com.

113. Gunning, p. 249.

114. Joel Greenberg, "Hamas' Landslide."

CONCLUSION

1. For recent analyses on the Madrid train bombings see "An Election Bombshell," *The Economist* (March 20, 2004): 49, which also called these attacks the worst since Spain's civil war; also see, Elaine Sciolino, "In Spain's Vote, A Shock from Democracy (and the Past)," *New York Times*, (March 21, 2004): 3, Section 4; and "Bad Blood, Yes, But a Basis for a Bond," *New York Times* (March 21, 2004): 1–2, Section 4.

2. P. H. Liotta and James F. Miskel, "Dangerous Democracy? American Internationalism and the Greater Near East," *Orbis* (Summer 2004): 438.

3. Liotta and Miskel, p. 447.

4. Liotta and Miskel, 448.

5. "Voters Oust Ruling Party in Macedonia," *The New York Times*. Accessed on October 23, 2002 at http://www.nytimes.com/2002/09/16/international/europe/16MACE.html.

6. This point concurs with Grant Wardlaw's principle of counterterrorism, that is, "... terrorism must be countered in a discriminating, case-by-case manner." See Grant Wardlaw, "The Democratic Framework." In *The Deadly Sin of Terrorism: Its Effect on Democracy and Civil Liberty in Six Countries*, ed. David A. Charters (Westport, CT: Greenwood Press, 1994), p. 8.

7. Martha Crenshaw, "Why America? The Globalization of Civil War," *Current History* 100 (December 2001): 432.

8. "Part One: Towards a New Security Consensus," *Report of the High-Level Panel on Threats, Challenges, and Change to the Secretary General.* Accessed on January 23, 2006 at http://www.un.org/secureworld/report.pdf, pp. 21–22.

9. Ibid., p. 22.

SELECTED BIBLIOGRAPHY

BOOKS AND ARTICLES IN EDITED BOOKS

Ackerman, Alice. *Making Peace Prevail: Preventing Violent Conflict in Macedonia*. Syracuse, NY: Syracuse University Press, 1999.

Almond, Gabriel A. and Sidney Verba. *The Civic Culture: Political Attitudes and Democracy in Five Nations*. Princeton, NJ: Princeton University Press, 1963.

Barkey, Henri J. and Graham E. Fuller. *Turkey's Kurdish Question*. Lanham, MD: Rowman and Littlefield Publishers, 1998.

Beitler, Ruth Margolies. *The Path to Mass Rebellion: An Analysis of Two Intifadas*. Lanham, MD: Lexington Books, 2004.

Bickerton, Ian J. and Carla L. Klausner. *A Concise History of the Arab-Israeli Conflict*. 2nd ed. Englewood Cliffs, NJ: Prentice Hall, 1995.

Brown, Michael E. "Introduction." In *The International Dimensions of Internal Conflict*, ed. Michael E. Brown, 1–31. Cambridge, MA: The MIT Press, 1996.

Chalk, Peter. *West European Terrorism and Counter-Terrorism: The Evolving Dynamic*. New York: St. Martin's Press, 1996.

Charters, David A. "Conclusion." In *The Deadly Sin of Terrorism: Its Effect on Democracy and Civil Liberty in Six Countries*, ed. David A. Charters, 211–227. Westport, CT: Greenwood Press, 1994.

Clark, Robert P. *The Basque Insurgents: ETA, 1952–1980*. Madison, WI: The University of Wisconsin Press, 1984.

Combs, Cindy. *Terrorism in the 21st Century*. Upper Saddle River, NJ: Prentice Hall, 1997.

Crenshaw, Martha, ed. *Terrorism in Context*. University Park, PA: The Pennsylvania University Press, 1995.

Dahrendorf, Ralf. "On the Governability of Democracies." In *Comparative Politics: Notes and Readings*, ed. Roy C. Macridis and Bernard Brown, 283–293. Pacific Grove, CA: Brooks/Cole Publishing Company, 1990.

Danforth, Loring M. *The Macedonian Conflict: Ethnic Nationalism in a Transnational World*. Princeton, NJ: Princeton University Press, 1995.

Easton, David. "The Analysis of Political Systems." In *Comparative Politics: Notes and Readings*, ed. Roy C. Macridis and Bernard Brown, 48–57. Pacific Grove, CA: Brooks/Cole Publishing Company, 1990.

Gunter, Michael M. *The Kurds and the Future of Turkey*. New York: St. Martin's Press, 1997.

Gurr, Ted Robert and Muriel McClelland, "Political Performance: A Twelve Nation Study." In *Comparative Politics Series*, Vol. 2, nos. 1–18, ed. Harry Eckstein and Ted Robert Gurr, 395–413. Beverly Hills, CA: Sage Publications, 1971.

Hanle, Donald. *Terrorism: The Newest Face of Warfare*. Washington, DC: Pergamon-Brassey's International Defense Publishers, 1989.

Harrison, Michael M. "France and International Terrorism: Problem and Response." In *The Deadly Sin of Terrorism: Its Effect on Democracy and Civil Liberty in Six Countries*, ed. David A. Charters, 103–136. Westport, CT: Greenwood Press, 1994.

Heymann, Philip B. *Terrorism and America: A Commonsense Strategy for a Democratic Society*. Cambridge, MA: The MIT Press, 1998.

Hoffman, Bruce. "Low Intensity Conflict: Terrorism and Guerrilla Warfare in the Coming Decades." In *Terrorism: Roots, Impact, Responses*, ed. Lance Howard, 139–154. New York: Praeger, 1992.

Hudson, Michael C. *Arab Politics: The Search For Legitimacy*. New Haven, CT: Yale University Press, 1977.

Hurwitz, J. C. *The Struggle for Palestine*. New York: Schocken Books, 1976.

Jebb, Cindy R. *Bridging the Gap: Ethnicity, Legitimacy, and State Alignment in the International System*. Lanham, MD: Lexington, 2004.

Kaplan, Robert. *Eastward to Tartary*. New York: Random House, 2000.

Kirisci, Kemal and Gareth M. Winrow. *The Kurdish Question and Turkey: An Example of Trans-State Ethnic Conflict*. London: Frank Cass, 1997.

Levitt, Matthew A. "Hamas Social Welfare: In the Service of Terror." In *The Making of a Terrorist: Recruitment, Training and Root Causes*, ed. James J.F. Forest, 120–135. Westport, CT: Praeger Security International, 2006.

Linz, Juan J. and Alfred Stepan. *Problems of Democratic Transition and Consolidation: Southern Europe, South America, and Post-Communist Europe*. Baltimore, MD: The Johns Hopkins Press, 1996.

Liotta, P. H. *Dismembering the State*. Lanham, MD: Rowman and Littlefield Publishers, 2000.

Liotta, P. H. and Cindy R. Jebb. *Mapping Macedonia: Idea and Identity*. Westport, CT: Praeger, 2004.

Llera, Francisco J. "Conflicto en Euskadi Revisited." In *Politics, Society, and Democracy: The Case of Spain*, ed. Richard Gunther, 169–195. Boulder, CO: Westview Press, 1993.

Lloyd, Richmond. "Strategy and Force Planning." In *Strategy and Force Planning*, ed. Strategy and Force Planning Faculty, 1–17. Newport, RI: Naval War College Press, 2000.

Lomperis, Timothy J. *From People's War to People's Rule: Insurgency, Intervention, and the Lessons of Vietnam*. Chapel Hill, NC: The University of North Carolina Press, 1996.

Macridis, Roy C. and Steven L. Burg. *Introduction to Comparative Politics: Regimes and Change*. New York: HarperCollins, 1991.

Mandel, Neville J. *The Arabs and Zionism before World War I*. Berkeley, CA: University of California Press, 1976.

Mathews, Jessica T. "Power Shift." In *Strategy and Force Planning*, ed. Strategy and Force Planning Faculty, 93–106. Newport, RI: Naval War College Press, 2000.

Maxwell, Kenneth and Steven Spiegel. *The New Spain: From Isolation to Influence*. New York: Council on Foreign Relations, 1994.

Norton, Augustus Richard. "The Security Legacy of the 1980s in the Third World." In *Third World Security in the Post-Cold War Era*, ed. Thomas G. Weiss and Meryl A. Kessler, 19–33. Boulder, CO: Lynne Reinner Publishers, 1990.

Norton, Philip. *The British Polity*. New York: Longman, 1990.

Ozbudin, Ergun. *Contemporary Turkish Politics: Challenges to Democratic Consolidation*. Boulder, CO: Lynne Rienner, 2000.

Porath, Yehoshua. *The Palestinian Arab National Movement, 1929–1939: From Riots to Rebellion*. London: Frank Cass, 1977.

Poulton, Hugh. *Top Hat, Grey Wolf and Crescent: Turkish Nationalism in the Turkish Republic*. New York: New York University Press, 1997

Pribichevich, Stoyan. *Macedonia: Its People and History*. University Park, PA: Pennsylvania University Press, 1982.

Rosenau, James N. "The Complexities and Contradictions of Globalization." In *Understanding International Relations*, ed. Daniel J. Kaufman, Jay Parker, and Kimberly C. Field, 756–760. New York: McGraw-Hill, 1999.

Sachar, Howard M. *A History of Israel: From the Rise of Zionism to Our Time*. New York: Alfred A. Knopf, 1979.

Safran, Nadav. *The Embattled Ally*. Cambridge, MA: Harvard University Press, 1981.

Schenker, David. *Palestinian Democracy and Governance: An Appraisal of the Legislative Council*. Washington, DC: Washington Institute for Near East Policy, 2000.

Shabad, Goldie and Francisco Jose Llera Ramo. "Political Violence in a Democratic State: Basque Terrorism in Spain." In *Terrorism in Context*, ed. Martha Crenshaw, 410–469. University Park, PA: The Pennsylvania State University Press, 1995.

Shalev, Aryeh. *The Intifada: Causes and Effects*. Boulder, CO: Westview Press, 1991.

Shea, John. *Macedonia and Greece: The Struggle to Define a New Balkan Nation*. Jefferson, NC: McFarland and Company, 1997.

Singh, Baljit. "An Overview." In *Terrorism: An Interdisciplinary Perspective*, ed. Yonah Alexander and Seymour Maxwell Finger, 5–17. New York: John Jay Press, 1977.

Smith, Charles D. *Palestine and the Arab-Israeli Conflict*. New York: St. Martin's Press, 1988.

Tessler, Mark. *A History of the Israeli-Palestinian Conflict*. Bloomington, IN: Indiana University Press, 1994.

Wardlaw, Grant. "The Democratic Framework." In *The Deadly Sin of Terrorism: Its Effect on Democracy and Civil Liberty in Six Countries*, ed. David A. Charters, 5–11. Westport, CT: Greenwood Press, 1994.

Weber, Max. "Politics As A Vocation." In *From Max Weber: Essays in Sociology*, ed. H. H. Gerth and C. Wright Mills, 23–29. New York: Oxford University Press, 1946.

Wiarda, Howard J. *Iberia and Latin America: New Democracies, New Policies, and New Models*. Lanham, MD: Rowman and Littlefield, 1996.

Wiarda, Howard J. *Introduction to Comparative Politics: Concepts and Processes*. Belmont, CA: Wadsworth Publishing, 1993.

Wieviorka, Michel. "French Politics and Strategy on Terrorism." In *The Politics of Counter-Terrorism: The Ordeal of Democratic States*, ed. Barry Rubin, 61–90. Washington, DC: Johns Hopkins University, 1990.

Wilkinson Paul. "Observations on the Relationship of Freedom and Terrorism." In *Terrorism: Roots, Impact, Responses*, ed. Lance Howard, 155–166. New York: Praeger, 1992.

GOVERNMENT AND IGO DOCUMENTS, INTERVIEWS, AND LECTURES

Brown, Keith. Interviewed by the author on April 4, 2001 at the Watson Institute, Brown University.

Center for Palestinian Research and Studies. Poll no. 48 online at http://www.pcpsr.org/survey/cprspolls/2000/poll48a.html.

"The Constitution of the Republic of Turkey." Downloaded on April 18, 2001, http://www.turkey.org/politics/p_consti.htm.

Department of Social Sciences. "Briefing to Alumni." Lecture given in June 1999 at the United States Military Academy, West Point.

European Union. "Commissioner Patten to Visit Skopje." *External Relations: The EU and South Eastern Europe*, April 2, 2001. Downloaded on May 1, 2001, http://europa.eu.int/comm./external_relations.

European Union. "Debate on Conflict Prevention/Crisis Management." *External Relations: The EU and South Eastern Europe*, March 14, 2001. Downloaded on May 1, 2001, http://europa.eu.int/comm./external_relations.

European Union. "The EU and Southeastern Europe: On the Road to Europe: First Stabilisation and Association Agreement to be Signed on 9 April with Former Republic of Yugoslavia." *Europa*. Downloaded on April 25, 2001, http://europa.eu.int/comm/external_relations/see/news/memo01_127_htm.

Ivanov, Gjorge. "The Albanian Question in Macedonia: The Macedonian Perspective." Lecture given in October 2000 at Ohrid, Macedonia.

"Macedonia – Constitution." Downloaded on April 18, 2001, http://www.uni-wuerzburg.de/law/mk00000_.html.

United Nations. "FYR of Macedonia: President Calls for Greater Control of Border Crossing with Kosovo." *UN: Bringing Peace to Kosovo News Reports*, April 10, 2001. Downloaded on May 1, 2001, http://www.un.org/peace/kosovo/news/kosovo2htm.

United Nations. "Kosovo: Serb Representative Rejoins Panel Drafting Legal Framework for Self Government." *UN: Bringing Peace to Kosovo News Reports*, April 25, 2001. Downloaded on May 1, 2001, http://www.un.org/peace/kosovo/news/kosovo2htm.

United Nations. "Security Council Members Condemn Ambush in FYR of Macedonia." *UN: Bringing Peace to Kosovo News Reports*, April 25,

2001. Downloaded on May 1, 2001, http://www.un.org/peace/kosovo/news/kosovo2htm.

United Nations. "UN Official Welcomes Kosovar Albanians Freed From Serbian Jails." *UN: Bringing Peace to Kosovo News Reports*, April 25, 2001. Downloaded on May 1, 2001, http://www.un.org/peace/kosovo/news/kosovo2htm.

U.S. Central Intelligence Agency. "Macedonia – The Former Republic of." *CIA World Factbook 2000*. Downloaded on April 2, 2001 http://www.odci.gov/cia/publications/factbook/geos/mk.html.

U.S. Commission on National Security/21st Century. "Seeking a National Strategy: A Concert for Preserving Security and Promoting Freedom," April 15, 2000.

U.S. Department of State. "A Performance-Based Roadmap to a Permanent Two-State Solution to the Israeli-Palestinian Conflict," April 30, 2003. Downloaded on October 1, 2003, http://www.state.gov/r/pa/prs/ps/2003/20062.htm.

U.S. Department of State. "1999 Country Report on Human Rights Practices: Former Yugoslav Republic of Macedonia." Downloaded on April 2, 2001, http://www.state.gov/www/global/human_rights/1999_hrp_report/macedonia.html.

U.S. Department of State, Office of Research. "Economy Tops List of Concerns in Turkey," November 24, 1999.

U.S. Department of State, Office of Research. "Macedonian Albanians' Political Influence Gives Them Reason for Optimism: But May Feed Suspicion among Ethnic Macedonians." *Opinion Analysis*, May 9, 2000.

U.S. Department of State, Office of Research. "Macedonians Disillusioned by NATO Action in Kosovo: Albanians Still Support NATO and Feel Safer with Troops in FYROM." *Opinion Analysis*, April 25, 2000.

U.S. Department of State, Office of Research. "Opposition Pulls Ahead in FYROM." *Opinion Analysis*, April 21, 2000.

U.S. Department of State, Office of Research. "Public Says Ailing FYROM Economy Needs Trade and Investment for Growth." *Opinion Analysis*, May 4, 2000.

U.S. Department of State, Office of Research. "Turks Blame Government for Economic Crisis," May 2, 2001.

U.S. Information Agency, Office of Research and Media Reaction. "Ocalan Deserves Death Penalty, Many Turks Say," June 10, 1999.

The White House. "A National Security Strategy for a New Century," December 1999.

JOURNALS, MAGAZINES, AND NEWSPAPER ARTICLES

Abu-Amr, Ziad. "The Palestinian Legislative Council: A Critical Assessment." *Journal of Palestine Studies* 26, no. 4 (Summer 1997): 90–97.

Akl, Aida. "Can Democracy Stop Terrorism?" Downloaded on November 15, 2005, http://www.voanews.com/english/News/Analysis/2005-11-03-voa55.cfm.

"Albania Getting Better." *The Economist* (February 24–March 2, 2001): 53.

Amr, Hady. "Electoral Systems and Democracy: Palestinian and South African Elections Compared." *Middle East Report* (October–December 1996).

"Arben Xhaferi, Macedonia's Pivotal Albanian." *The Economist* (March 31–April 6, 2001): 50.

Arquilla, John and David Ronfeldt. "The Advent of Netwar: Analytical Background." *Studies in Conflict and Terrorism* 22, no. 3 (July–September 1999): 193–206.

Babuna, Aydin. "The Albanians of Kosovo and Macedonia: Ethnic Identity Superceding Religion." *Nationalities Papers* 28, no. 1 (March 2000): 67–92.

Bildt, Carl. "A Second Chance in the Balkans." *Foreign Affairs* 80, no. 1 (January/February 2001): 148–159.

Bova, Russell. "Democracy and Liberty: The Cultural Connection." *Journal of Democracy* 8, no. 1 (1997): 112–126.

Brademas, John. "Promoting Democracy and Reconciliation in Southeastern Europe." *Mediterranean Quarterly: A Journal of Global Issues* 12, no. 1 (Winter 2001): 51–56.

Bunker, Robert J. "Weapons of Mass Disruption and Terrorism." *Terrorism and Political Violence* 12, no. 1 (Spring 2000): 37–46.

Buzan, Barry and Thomas Dietz. "The European Union and Turkey." *Survival* 41, no. 1 (Spring 1999): 41–52.

Candar, Cengiz and Graham E. Fuller. "Grand Geopolitics for a New Turkey." *Mediterranean Quarterly: A Journal of Global Issues* 12, no. 1 (Winter 2001): 22–38.

Candar, Cengiz. "Redefining Turkey's Political Center." *Journal of Democracy* 10, no. 4 (1999): 129–141. Downloaded on December 15, 2000, http://muse.jhu.edu/journals/journal_of_democracy.

Carter, Ashton, John Deutch, and Philip Zelikow. "Catastrophic Terrorism: Tackling the New Danger." *Foreign Affairs* 77, no. 6 (November/December 1998): 80–94.

Çelik, Ayse Betul. "Transnationalization of Human Rights Norms and Its Impact on Internally Displaced Kurds." *Human Rights Quarterly* 27, no. 3 (August 2005): 969–997.

Chazan, Guy. "Militant is Killed, Further Clouding Truce in Mideast." *Wall Street Journal* (August 15, 2003): A6.

Cizre, Umit and Menderes Çinar. "Turkey 2002: Kemalism, Islamism, and Politics in the Light of the February 28 Process." *South Atlantic Quarterly* 102 (Spring/Summer 2003): 310–332.

Cohen, Leonard J. "Post-Milosevic Serbia." *Current History* 100, no. 644 (March 2001): 99–108.

Collins, Catherine. "Kurdish Rebels Seek a Ceasefire; Turkish Leader's Visit Raised Hope for Peace." *New York Times* (August 20, 2005): 4.

Cooper, Robert. "Integration and Disintegration." *Journal of Democracy* 10, no. 1 (1999): 1–9. Downloaded on December 15, 2000, http://muse.jhu.edu/journals/journal_of_democracy/v010/10.1cooper.html.

Cornell, Svante E. "The Land of Many Crossroads: The Kurdish Question in Turkish Politics." *Orbis* 45, no. 1 (Winter 2000): 31–46.

Cowell, Alan. "Europeans Insist Hamas Must Disavow Terrorism." *New York Times* (January 27, 2006): 11.

Daraghment, Ali. "Hamas Wins Key Local Elections in Possible Harbinger of January Parliament Vote." *Associated Press* (December 16, 2005). Downloaded on January 27, 2006, http://web.lexis-nexis.com.

Diamond, Larry. "The Global State of Democracy." *Current History* 99, no. 641 (December 2000): 413–418.

Dishman, Chris. "Review Article: Trends in Modern Terrorism." *Studies in Conflict and Terrorism* 22, no. 4 (1999): 357–362.

Ergil, Dogu. "The Kurdish Question in Turkey." *Journal of Democracy* 11, no. 3 (2000): 122–135. Downloaded on December 12, 2000, http://muse.jhu.edu/journals/journal_of_democracy.

Ergil, Dogu. "Identity Crisis and Political Instability in Turkey." *Journal of International Affairs* 54, no. 1 (Fall 2000): 43–62.

Erlanger, Steven. "In a Stronghold, Fatah Fight to Beat Back a Rising Hamas. *New York Times* (January 23, 2006): A1.

Erlanger, Steven. "Wider Offensive by Macedonia Presses Rebels." *The New York Times* (March 26, 2001): A1, A10.

Erlanger, Steven. "Use Word as, Not Guns, Balkan Leader Tells Rebels." *The New York Times* (March 28, 2001): A4.

"Europe: Oh No, Not War in Macedonia As Well." *The Economist* (March 10–16, 2001): 46–47.

Falconer, Bruce. "One Border, Two Worlds." *National Journal* (September 10, 2005). Downloaded on January 22, 2006, http://proquest.umi.com.

"Former President Carter says U.S. Should Find Ways Around Banning Funding to Hamas-led PA." *Associated Press Worldstream* (January 27, 2006). Downloaded on January 27, 2006, http://web.lexis-nexis.com.

Frankland, Erich. "Struggling With Collective Security and Recognition in Europe: The Case of Macedonia." *European Security* 4, no. 2 (Summer 1995): 354–379.

Fraser, Suzan. "Turkey's Kurdish Language Schools to Shut Down Over Lack of Interest, Bureaucratic Hurdles." *Associate Press Worldstream* (August 1, 2005). Downloaded on January 15, 2006, http://web.lexis-nexis.com.

Fukuyama, Francis. "The Primacy of Culture." *Journal of Democracy* 6, no. 1 (1995): 7–14.

Gaouette, Nicole. "Road Map in Peril as Cease-fire Ends." *Christian Science Monitor* (August 22, 2003). Downloaded on October 1, 2003, http://proquest.umi.com.

Ghanem, As'ad. "Founding Elections in a Transitional Period: The First Palestinian General Elections." *Middle East Journal* (Autumn 1996).

Ghanem, As'ad and Aziz Khayed. "In the Shadow of the Al Aqsa Intifada: The Palestinians and Political Reform." *Civil Wars* 6, no. 3 (Autumn 2003): 31–50.

Goldenberg, Suzanne. "Bush Puts Peace Monitors in Place." *Guardian (UK)* (June 6, 2003): 17. Downloaded on October 1, 2003, http://proquest.umi.com.

Gory, Eric D. "Kostunica's Yugoslavia." *Current History* 100, no. 644 (March 2000): 109–113.

Greenberg, Joel. "Hamas' Landslide Win a Political Earthquake; Israel Says It Won't Negotiate with Regime." *New York Times* (January 27, 2006): A1.

Grier, Peter. "A Terrorist Version of NATO?" *Christian Science Monitor* (February 16, 2001). Downloaded on February 16, 2001, http://ebird.dtic.mil/Feb2001/e20010216terrorist.htm.

Grove, Gregory D., Seymour E. Goodman, and Stephen J. Lukasik. "Cyber-attacks and International Law." *Survival* 42, no. 3 (Autumn 2000): 89–103.

Gundez, Aslan. "Human Rights and Turkey's Future in Europe." *Orbis* 45, no. 1 (Winter 2001): 15–30.

Gunning, Jeroen. "Peace with Hamas? The Transforming Potential of Political Participation." *International Affairs* 80, no. 2 (2004): 233–255.

Gunter, Michael M. "The Continuing Kurdish Problem in Turkey after Ocalan's Capture." *Third World Quarterly* 21 (October 2000): 849–869.

Gutkin, Steven. "Further West Bank Pullouts Will be Necessary." *Associated Press* (January 24, 2006). Downloaded on January 27, 2006, http://web.lexis-nexis.com.

Hammani, Rema and Salim Tamari. "The Second Uprising: End of New Beginning." *The Journal of Palestine Studies* 30, no. 2 (Winter 2001): 5–26.

Hislope, Robert. "Ethnic Conflict and the "Generosity Moment'." *Journal of Democracy* 9, no. 1 (1998): 140–153.

Hockstader, Lee. "Street Army Spearheads Arab Riots." *Washington Post*, (October 4, 2000): A.1.

Hoffman, Bruce. "Is Europe Soft on Terrorism." *Foreign Policy* (Summer 1999): 1–9. Downloaded on December 13, 2000, http://proquest.umi.com.

Horan, Deborah. "Palestine: Journalist Jailed for Criticizing Lack of Freedom." *Inter Press Service* (May 21, 1997). Downloaded on May 24, 2002, http://www.nexis.com.

Huntington, Samuel P. "After Twenty Years: The Future of the Third Wave." *Journal of Democracy* 8, no. 4 (October 1997): 3–12.

Insel, Ahmet. "The AKP and Normalizing Democracy in Turkey." *South Atlantic Quarterly* 10, no. 2 (Spring/Summer 2003): 293–308.

Jamal, Amal. "State-Building, Institutionalization and Democracy: The Palestinian Experience." *Mediterranean Politics* 6, no. 3 (Autumn 2001): 1–30.

Jarbawi, Ali. "Palestinian Politics at a Crossroads." *Journal of Palestine Studies* 25, no. 4 (Summer 1996): 29–39.

Jebb, Cindy R. "Liberal Democracy Versus Terrorism: The Fight For Legitimacy." Paper presented at the International Studies Association National Conference in Chicago, February 23, 2001.

Karabelias, Gerassimos. "The Evolution of Civil-Military Relations in Post-War Turkey, 1980–95." *Middle Eastern Studies* 35, no. 4 (October 1999).

Kasaba, Resat and Sibel Bozdogan. "Turkey at a Crossroad." *Journal of International Affairs* 54, no. 1 (Fall 2000): 1–20.

King, Neil Jr. and Jeanne Cummings. "Road Map Seeks Palestinian State Within a Year." *Wall Street Journal* (February 28, 2003): A7.

Kinzer, Stephen. "In Turkey, Press's Lot Includes Jail Time." *New York Times* (June 14, 1998).

Kirisci, Kemal. "Disaggregating Turkish Citizenship and Immigration Practices." *Middle Eastern Studies* 36, no. 3 (July 2000): 1–22.

Lefebvre, Stephane. "The Former Yugoslav Republic of Macedonia." *European Security* 3, no. 4 (Winter 1994): 711–733.

Li, Quan. "Does Democracy Promote or Reduce Transnational Terrorist Incidents?" *Journal of Conflict Resolution* 49, no. 2 (April 2005): 278–297.

Linz, Juan J. and Alfred Stepan. "Toward Consolidated Democracies." *Journal of Democracy* 7, no. 2 (1996): 14–33.

Liotta, P. H. "The Future Republic of Macedonia." *European Security* 9, no. 1 (Spring 2000): 68–97.

Luft, Gal. "The Mirage of a Demilitarized Palestine." *Middle East Quarterly* (June 8, 2001). Downloaded on August 31, http://www.lexis.com.

"Macedonia: Passing Clouds?" *The Economist* (March 3–9, 2001): 48.

"Macedonia: Stability Pact Coordinator on Prospects for Peace." *BBC Worldwide Monitoring* (March 19, 2001). Downloaded on May 1, 2001, http://infoweb5.newsbank.com.

Makovsky, Alan. "The New Activism in Turkish Foreign Policy." *SAIS Review* 19, no. 1 (1999): 92–113. Downloaded on December 15, 2000, http://muse.jhu.edu/journals/sais_review.

Maksoud, Clovis. "Peace Process or Puppet Show." *Foreign Policy* 100 (Fall 1995): 116–125.

Malka, Haim. "Forcing Choices: Testing the Transformation of Hamas." *The Washington Quarterly* (Autumn 2005): 37–54.

Manent, Pierre. "Democracy Without Nations." *Journal of Democracy* 8, no. 2 (April 1997): 92–102.

Milton-Edwards, Beverly. "Palestinian Nation-Building: Police and Citizens as Test of Democracy." *British Journal of Middle Eastern Studies* 25, no. 1 (May 1998): 95–119.

Moustakis, Fotios. "An Expanded EU and Aegean Security." *Contemporary Review* (November 2000): 277–280. Downloaded on December 15, 2000, http://proquest.umi.com/pdqweb.

Mufson, Steven. "Overhaul of National Security Apparatus Urged." *Washington Post* (February 1, 2001): 2.

Navaro, Llana. "Breaking Turkish Taboos." *The Jerusalem Report* (May 8, 2000). Downloaded on April 4, 2001, http://web.lexis-nexis.com/universe.

Omar, Mohammed. "Hamas Scores Majorities in Gaza and Municipal Council Elections." *Washington Report on Middle East Affairs* (July 2005).

Onis, Ziya and Suhnza Yilmaz. "The Turkey-EU–U.S. Triangle in Perspective: Transformation of Continuity?" *Middle East Journal* 59, no. 2 (Spring 2005).

Özbudin, Ergun. "Turkey: How Far from Consolidation." *Journal of Democracy* 7, no. 3 (1996): 123–138.

Perthes, Volker. "Points of Difference, Cases for Cooperation: European Critiques of U.S. Middle East Policy." *Middle East Report* (Fall 1988).

Poulton, Hugh. "The Turkish State and Democracy." *The International Spectator* XXXIV, no. 1 (January–March 1999): 1–14. Downloaded on April 4, 2001, http://www.cc.columbia.edu/sec/dlc/ciao.

Prusher, Ilene R. "Iraq Colors Kurdish Campaign in Turkey's National Election." *Christian Science Monitor* (November 1, 2002): 7.

Prusher, Ilene. "Why Hamas is Gaining in Palestinian Polls." *Christian Science Monitor* (January 25, 2006). Downloaded on January 27, 2006, http://web17.epnet.com.

Quandt, William B. "The Urge for Democracy." *Foreign Affairs* (July/August 1994): 2–7.

Radu, Michael. "The Rise and Fall of the PKK." *Orbis* 45, no. 1 (Winter 2001): 47–64.

Riddell, Peter. "Bush Calls for End to Arab-Israeli Conflict." *Financial Times* (March 7, 1991): 1.

Robinson, Glenn E. "After Arafat." *Current History* (January 2005): 19–24.

Ronfeldt, David. "Netwar Across the Spectrum of Conflict: An Introductory Comment." *Studies in Conflict and Terrorism* 33, no. 3 (July–September 1999): 189–192.

Rosen, James." Gaza Pullout has Risks, Rewards: Extremists on Both Sides Could Doom Gamble for Peace." *Sacramento Bee* (August 14, 2005): A1.

Sachs, Susan. "Rebel Violence in Turkey Could Erode Kurds Gains." *New York Times* (October 1, 2004): A8.

Salt, Jeremy. "Turkey's Military Democracy'." *Current History* 98, no. 625 (February 1999): 72–778.

Schleifer, Yigal. Turkey's Kurds Languish in Poverty." *The Economist* (August 31, 2005): 6.

Shikaki, Khalil. "Palestinians Divided." *Foreign Affairs* (January/February 2002).

Shikaki, Khalil. "The Future of Palestine." *Foreign Affairs* 83 (November/December 2004). Downloaded on October 27, http://proquest.umi.com.

Shu'aybi, Azmi and Khalil Shikaki. "A Window on the Workings of the PA: An Inside View." *Journal of Palestine Studies* 30, no. 1 (Autumn 2000): 88–97.

Smith, Jeffrey. "Birth of New Rebel Army: Macedonian Guerilla Group Forming in Kosovo Poses Threat of Expanded Conflict in Balkans." *The Washington Post* (March 30, 2001): A1. Downloaded on May 1, 2001, http://infoweb5.newsbank.com.

Smith, Thomas W. "Civic Nationalism and Ethnocultural Justice in Turkey." *Human Rights Quarterly* 27, no. 2 (May 2005): 436–470.

"A Survey of EU Enlargement: Europe's Magnetic Attraction." *The Economist* (May 19–25, 2001): 3–4.

Tepe, Sultan. "Turkey's AKP: A Model 'Muslim-Democratic' Party?" *Journal of Democracy* 16, no. 3 (July 2005): 69–82.

Tessler, Mark. "The Attitudes of West Bank and Gaza Palestinians Towards Governance and the Relationship between Religion and Politics." *Palestine–Israel Journal of Politics, Economics and Culture* 11 (2004/2005).

"Turkey Nervous." *The Economist* (March 3–9, 2001): 49.

Usher, Graham. "The Politics of Internal Security: The PA's New Intelligence Services." *Journal of Palestine Studies* 25, no. 2 (Winter 1996): 21–34.

Valeri, Lorenzo and Michael Knights. "Affecting Trust: Terrorism, Internet and Offensive." *Terrorism and Political Violence* 12, no. 1 (Spring 2000): 15–35.

Waldman, Adir. "Negotiated Transitions to Democracy: Israel and the Palestinians as a Case Study." *Democratization* 7, no. 2 (Summer 2000): 113–141.

Walker, Martin and David Fromkin. "The Turkish Miracle." *The Wilson Quarterly* 24, no. 4 (Autumn 2000): 72–87. Downloaded on December 15, 2000, http://proquest.umi.com/pdqweb.

"War in the Balkans Again?" *The Economist* (March 24–30, 2001): 57–58.

Weymouth, Lally. "A Very Fateful Step." *Newsweek* September 19, 2005. Downloaded on November 22, 2005, http://ebscohost.com.

Wiarda, Howard J. "Spain 2000: A Normal Country?" *Mediterranean Quarterly: A Journal of Global Issues* 11, no. 3 (Summer 2000): 30–61.

Wing, Adrien Katerine. "The Palestinian Basic Law: Embryonic Constitutionalism."
    Case Western Reserve Journal of International Law (Spring 1999): 383–426.
Wood, Steven and Wolfgang Quaisser. "Turkey's Road to the EU: Political Dy-
    namics, Strategic Context and Implications for Europe." *European Foreign
    Affairs Review* 10 (2005): 147–173.
Wright, Robin. "Mideast Summit: Sharon, Abbas Agree to Take Initial Steps Toward
    Peace." *Los Angeles Times* (June 5, 2003): A1.
Zahhar, Mahmud and Hussein Hijazi. "Hamas: Waiting for Secular Nationalism
    to Self-Destruct. An Interview with Mahmud Zahhar." *Journal of Palestine
    Studies* 24, no. 3 (Spring 1995): 81–88.

INDEX

About the Authors

Cindy R. Jebb, Colonel, U.S.A., is Professor and Deputy Head in the Department of Social Sciences at the United States Military Academy, West Point. A graduate of the United States Military Academy, she received her Ph.D. and MA in Political Science from Duke University and an MA in National Security and Strategic Studies from the Naval War College, where she also served as a West Point Fellow. Before reporting to West Point, she served in numerous command and staff positions in the United States and overseas. She coauthored *Mapping Macedonia, Idea and Identity* (Westport, CT: Praeger Publishers, 2004) with P.H. Liotta. She is also the author of *Bridging the Gap: Ethnicity, Legitimacy, and State Alignment in the International System* (Lanham, MD: Lexington Publishers, 2004).

P. H. Liotta is Professor of Humanities and Executive Director of the Pell Center for International Relations and Public Policy at Salve Regina. A former Fulbright Scholar to Yugoslavia during its breakup as a nation-state, he has traveled extensively throughout Africa, the former Soviet Union, Central and Southwest Asia, Europe, and the Balkan Peninsula. He has received a Pulitzer Prize nomination and National Endowment for the Arts Literature Fellowship, as well as the first International Quarterly Crossing Boundaries Award and the Robert H. Winner Award from the Poetry Society of America. His recent work includes *The Uncertain Certainty: Human Security, Environmental Change, and the Future Euro-Mediterranean*; *Mapping Macedonia: Idea and Identity*; and *The Exile's Return: Selected Poems* (published in Macedonian and translated by Bogomil Gjuzel.)

Thomas Sherlock received his doctorate in political science from Columbia University. He teaches comparative politics and international relations at the United States Military Academy at West Point where he is currently Head of Comparative Politics in the Department of Social Sciences. He is the author of numerous articles in journals and chapters in edited volumes. He is also the author of *Insurgent History and the Collapse of the Soviet Union* (Palgrave), which is forthcoming.

Ruth Margolies Beitler is an Associate Professor of International Relations and Comparative Politics in the Department of Social Sciences at the United States Military Academy, West Point. A graduate of Cornell University with a BA in Near Eastern Studies, she holds a Master of Arts of Law and Diplomacy from the Fletcher School of Law and Diplomacy, Tufts University, where she also received her Ph.D. in International Relations. She is author of *The Path to Mass Rebellion: An Analysis of Two Intifadas* (Lanham, MD: Lexington Books, 2004).